Ethnographic Refusals, Unruly Latinidades

School for Advanced Research
Advanced Seminar Series
Michael F. Brown
General Editor

Since 1970 the School for Advanced Research (formerly the School of American Research) and SAR Press have published over one hundred volumes in the Advanced Seminar series. These volumes arise from seminars held on SAR's Santa Fe campus that bring together small groups of experts to explore a single issue. Participants assess recent innovations in theory and methods, appraise ongoing research, and share data relevant to problems of significance in anthropology and related disciplines. The resulting volumes reflect SAR's commitment to the development of new ideas and to scholarship of the highest caliber. The complete Advanced Seminar series can be found at www.sarweb.org.

Also available in the School for Advanced Research Advanced Seminar Series:

The New Death: Mortality and Death Care in the Twenty-First Century edited
    by Shannon Lee Dawdy and Tamara Kneese
Designs and Anthropologies: Frictions and Affinities edited by Keith M. Murphy and Eitan Y. Wilf
Trumpism, Mexican America, and the Struggle for Latinx Citizenship edited by Phillip B. Gonzales,
    Renato Rosaldo, and Mary Louise Pratt
Archaeologies of Empire: Local Participants and Imperial Trajectories edited by Anna L. Boozer,
    Bleda S. Düring, and Bradley J. Parker
Walling In and Walling Out: Why Are We Building New Barriers to Divide Us? edited by
    Laura McAtackney and Randall H. McGuire
How Nature Works: Rethinking Labor on a Troubled Planet edited by Sarah Besky and
    Alex Blanchette
The Psychology of Women under Patriarchy edited by Holly F. Mathews and Adriana M. Manago
Governing Gifts: Faith, Charity, and the Security State edited by Erica Caple James
*Negotiating Structural Vulnerability in Cancer Control: Contemporary Challenges for Applied
    Anthropology* edited by Julie Armin, Nancy Burke, and Laura Eichelberger
Puebloan Societies: Homology and Heterogeneity in Time and Space edited by Peter Whiteley

For additional titles in the School for Advanced Research Advanced Seminar Series, please visit unmpress.com.

Ethnographic Refusals, Unruly Latinidades

Edited by Alex E. Chávez and Gina M. Pérez

Foreword by Arlene M. Dávila

SCHOOL FOR ADVANCED RESEARCH PRESS • SANTA FE

UNIVERSITY OF NEW MEXICO PRESS • ALBUQUERQUE

ISBN 978-0-8263-6356-5 (paper)
ISBN 978-0-8263-6357-2 (electronic)

Library of Congress Control Number:
2022930192

Founded in 1889, the University of New
Mexico sits on the traditional homelands
of the Pueblo of Sandia. The original
peoples of New Mexico—Pueblo, Navajo,
and Apache—since time immemorial have
deep connections to the land and have made
significant contributions to the broader
community statewide. We honor the land
itself and those who remain stewards of this
land throughout the generations and also
acknowledge our committed relationship
to Indigenous peoples. We gratefully
recognize our history.

Cover illustration: *Woman Talking with
Megaphone* © WeAre, Getty Images,
and David Flores

Composed in Minion Pro and Gill Sans

The seminar from which this book resulted
was made possible by the generous support
of the Andrew W. Mellon Foundation. This
research has been made possible in part by
support from the Institute for Scholarship in
the Liberal Arts, College of Arts and Letters,
University of Notre Dame. The writing was
facilitated in part by the generous support of
the Hulbert Center for Southwest Studies at
Colorado College.

Dedicated to all the people,
communities, friends, and loved ones
who have accompanied us in our lives and work,
showing us the hopeful power of refusal
along our journeys.

Foreword   ix
      Arlene M. Dávila

Introduction   xiii
      Ana Aparicio, Andrea Bolivar, Alex E. Chávez, Sherina Feliciano-
      Santos, Santiago Ivan Guerra, Gina M. Pérez, Jonathan Rosa, Gilberto
      Rosas, Aimee Villarreal, and Patricia Zavella

CHAPTER ONE. "While You Are Struggling, You Are Healing": Latinas Enact
      Poder through the Movement for Reproductive Justice   1
      Patricia Zavella

CHAPTER TWO. Taíno and Afro-Taíno Narrative, Performance,
      and *Resistencia* in Puerto Rico and the United States   25
      Sherina Feliciano-Santos

CHAPTER THREE. The Urban Sonorous and Collective Witness in the City
      of Neighborhoods   47
      Alex E. Chávez

CHAPTER FOUR. Diasporic Signs: Puerto Rican Place-Making, Latinx
      Artivism, and the Aesthetics of Resistance   69
      Jonathan Rosa and David Flores

CHAPTER FIVE. Race, Trash Talk, and Dissent in Contemporary
      Suburbia   93
      Ana Aparicio

CHAPTER SIX. Trans Latina *Fantasías*: Creating Trans Latina Selves, Families,
      and Futures   115
      Andrea Bolivar

CHAPTER SEVEN. The Drug War, Drug Reform, and the Latinx Community:
      An Ethnographic Perspective from the Texas-Mexico Border
      and Colorado   135
      Santiago Ivan Guerra

CHAPTER EIGHT. Becoming a Sanctuary People: Latina/o Practices
of Accompaniment in Northeast Ohio   153
Gina M. Pérez

CHAPTER NINE. Witnessing in Brown: On Making Dead to Let Live   175
Gilberto Rosas

CHAPTER TEN. *Anthropolocura* as Homeplace Ethnography   195
Aimee Villarreal

Afterword. Uncertain Future(s): Latinidad, Anthropology, Institutions   219
Vanessa Díaz, Sergio Lemus, and Ryan Mann-Hamilton

References   227
List of Contributors   253
Index   255

FOREWORD

ARLENE M. DÁVILA

The publication of this volume could not be timelier or more necessary. These brilliant scholars offer us rigorous theoretical and empirical essays on Latinx ethnography, centering critical race studies within anthropology at large. Together, they argue that unless we center BIPOC (Black, Indigenous, and People of Color), genderqueer, and nonbinary epistemologies, anthropology will forever remain trapped in its ugly colonial past. This past becomes visible when we consider that most anthropology departments continue to relegate African American, Indigenous, and Latinx anthropologists to the margins, not unlike in 1973, when the first study of anthropology and its minority practitioners was issued.[1] This study exposed the fact that "minority anthropologists" were not being hired in anthropology departments; instead, they were concentrated in interdisciplinary and ethnic studies programs, where they were unable to access and train anthropology students and, consequently, transform the discipline overall.

It is long past time for anthropology to stop centering whiteness and start listening carefully to the scholars it has bypassed. It is unacceptable that generations of anthropologists have been trained primarily by white scholars and that our increasingly diverse students must learn about critical race theory and Latinx scholarship on their own. Most of all, it is troubling that anthropology continues to reproduce a "peoples and cultures of the world" epistemology in our faculty searches and departments, marginalizing those who study race in our midst, especially nonwhite anthropologists who work with disenfranchised communities in the United States and draw from critical race theory, ethnic studies, and Latinx studies.

Ethnographic Refusals, Unruly Latinidades provides a bold refusal to this and other types of anthropological mythmaking. Its contributors offer not only an intervention that any anthropologists seeking to move past the discipline's legacy should heed but also a vision of what the anthropology of the twenty-first century should look like. First, they highlight how our own communities and personal experiences create productive and revolutionary spaces for our research, challenging anthropology's longtime fetish for the "other" and the uncritical penchant for travel and discovery that has limited anthropologists' ability to imagine what constitutes suitable sites for fieldwork. They engage in a politics of refusal—a refusal to work, theorize, and write according to dominant value expectations. They model a revolutionary ethics that all anthropologists can learn from.

Second, my colleagues call for a critically self-reflexive anthropology designed to promote "equality- and justice-inducing social transformation."[2] Their analyses carefully model an awareness of the relations of power and inequalities produced between scholars and those we work with. Their active questioning of the politics of scholarship privileges collaboration and recognizes and advocates for the people and communities who are central to our work. This alone is revolutionary and challenges us to stop appropriating other people's theorizations, words, histories, and experiences for the benefit of our careers without considering the politics of our research. These scholars call for research that is rigorously ethical and political and that foregrounds questions of purpose: What is our research for? Who benefits from it? And whom do we write for? More personally, it asks scholars to come to terms with the levels of privilege that should be at the heart of any reckoning with these questions.

Third, and unsurprisingly, the anthropologists in this volume draw inspiration, learn from, and cite African American, Latinx, Chicana feminist, ethnic studies, and interdisciplinary scholars, fully aware that scholars who have written critically about race, racialization, and structural inequalities in the United States can more deeply inform their own work. Additionally, the contributors exemplify a publicly engaged scholarship in which cultural advocacy and antiracism are central—their insights are closely informed by the injustices they have witnessed while advocating for the people they work with. In the same spirit, vernacular politics of representation, language, and popular culture also stand at the center of many of the chapters. While these domains are often misrecognized and downplayed as "apolitical," the authors in this volume recognize they are among the most fruitful spaces for examination because they are the most accessible to disenfranchised populations.

Finally, the contributors move the conversation around representation and identity away from the dominant visual realm and toward the sonic and aural realms by examining speech, language, music, and sound as key elements of racialization and identity-making, thus anchoring their work in the performative spaces that they use to analyze the everyday living components of expressive cultures.

Theirs are the kinds of intersectional analyses everyone talks about, yet few scholars actually produce. However, this type of work is increasingly standard practice in Latinx studies, a field that demands an accounting of the interplay of class, race, gender, sexuality, and citizenship status, among the many other variables affecting Latinx communities, which comprise highly diverse populations with multiple identities. The contributors teach us to theorize politics deeply by accounting for the structural conditions of power; the political economy of migration, state violence, and urban policies; and the forms of policing and welfare that impact people's daily lives and the choices they make to live, to organize, and to refuse.

In all, these daring voices are filled with emboldening possibility and hope. Imagine if all anthropologists followed the contributors' lead and began their research with a rigorous questioning of their own identities, backgrounds, and positionality. Imagine if, instead of choosing fieldwork sites based on access, familiarity, or their own imaginations, they chose sites based on their ability to mobilize their identities, access, and backgrounds in the service of antiracist scholarship. I estimate that we would have far more ethnographies that expose institutions of power and white privilege than we do now. Let me be clear that I am not advocating for a politics of authenticity in which our backgrounds dictate the types of research we undertake and the issues we study. Rather, I call on anthropologists to stop fetishizing research "outside" our communities, which has produced generations of lukewarm apolitical and sometimes overtly racist work, when we could be engaging in far more meaningful ethnographic explorations. In short, we must fully reckon with our identities and privileges and use this knowledge to engage in work that would lead us to a more just world.

This volume needs to be adopted in introductory and graduate-level anthropology classes alike as an exemplar of the type of collaborative, intergenerational, interdisciplinary, and antiracist anthropological futurity we should all strive for. The authors provide an antidote to the colonial doldrums of this discipline, and their work could not come at a better time to address the growing reckoning with racial justice and inclusion within our discipline, the academy, and broader society. The fact that this book joins a legacy of foundational Advanced Seminar volumes published by SAR Press that have marked and influenced trends in new research is especially significant.

This foreword communicates my admiration and gratitude toward these contributors and the revolutionary change they are committed to bringing into the discipline. Because of their efforts in publishing this volume, more anticolonial anthropological work will become possible and new generations of Latinx and

BIPOC anthropologists will finally be able to read and cite a foundational SAR volume that *sees them*. I hope that all readers are likewise inspired by these scholars and that we all learn from their daring and timely call to start engaging in ethnographic refusals—to become unruly anthropologists with pride. The future of an anticolonial anthropology, of a more just world, depends on it.

Note

1. "The Minority Experience in Anthropology," Report of the Committee on Minorities in Anthropology, August 1973. https://www.americananthro.org /ParticipateAndAdvocate/Content.aspx?ItemNumber=1514.

2. Harrison 1997, 2.

Introduction

ANA APARICIO, ANDREA BOLIVAR, ALEX E. CHÁVEZ,
SHERINA FELICIANO-SANTOS, SANTIAGO IVAN GUERRA,
GINA M. PÉREZ, JONATHAN ROSA, GILBERTO ROSAS,
AIMEE VILLARREAL, AND PATRICIA ZAVELLA

As activist-scholars writing in the summer of 2020, we composed this introduction in a moment of despair and hope. The United States was then at the epicenter of the global COVID-19 pandemic, with nearly two million confirmed cases and over one hundred and eighty thousand deaths. As of October 2021, these numbers have only increased—despite the subsequent development and distribution of vaccines to treat the disease—to over forty-three million confirmed cases and upward of seven hundred thousand deaths. Given pervasive structural inequities in access to health care, which are compounded by entrenched socioeconomic disparities, African American and Latinx communities have experienced the highest rates of spread, infection, and death in the country. The lack of adequate testing and treatment for people who work jobs and perform services considered essential has exposed them to the disease more than it has people who have been able to work from home, which has impacted them disproportionately and laid bare the fact that Black and Brown bodies are disposable within the American racial project. And in the midst of the wildfire of COVID-19 and calls to socially distance in order to mitigate its spread, thousands nevertheless took to the streets across the country to protest the murderous consequences of policing in Black communities. The police murders of George Floyd in Minneapolis and Breonna Taylor in Louisville and the shooting of Jacob Blake in Kenosha, Wisconsin, reveal, once again, the institutionalized violence of white supremacy—in the guise of law enforcement—that has historically brutalized and terrorized Black communities. Black activists, freedom workers, and allies from a multitude of communities joined together in defiance, in refusal, to demand policing and criminal justice reform, in many cases advocating for the complete abolition of this system. These issues have been paramount for activists denouncing the criminalization of migrants, the militarization of the United States-Mexico border, and the migrant carceral complex, linking anti-Black structural violences to policies, practices, and ideologies that demean and diminish the lives of immigrants and Latinx communities more broadly. As Keeanga-Yahmatta Taylor has observed, the bitter anger of multiracial protesters in Minneapolis and beyond runs deep and reflects "the sense that the state is either complicit or incapable of effecting substantive change."[1]

We had glimpses of this bitter anger in the wake of yet another act of violence in the summer of 2019, when a gunman, acting on the basis of hateful rhetoric proclaiming an alleged "Hispanic invasion," killed twenty-two people in a Walmart in El Paso, Texas, on August 3. This event not only reflected what journalist Jorge Ramos described as a "massacre foretold"—given then-president Trump's consistent xenophobic attacks on migrant and Latinx communities specifically—but was also a consequence of what anthropologist Leo Chavez has referred to as the Latino Threat Narrative, or the pervasive idea that Latinxs are an "invading force . . . bent on conquering land that was formerly theirs . . . and destroying the American way of life."[2] While the rhetoric of invasion and its insidious consequences are nothing new, Gilberto Rosas and Carlos Martínez-Cano argue that the Trump administration's immigration practices enacted "new layers of injustice and cruelty" that detained, punished, and killed migrants: "The El Paso, Texas–Ciudad Juárez, Mexico border is a site where . . . new zero-tolerance realities are indeed a palpable part of everyday life."[3] We witnessed these zero-tolerance realities at work in the implementation of the Remain in Mexico program, which has led to thousands of asylum seekers, largely from Central America and the Caribbean (most recently Haiti), living in tents along the US-Mexico border while more than sixty thousand were returned to Mexico to wait for asylum hearings, violating US and international law. The cruelty of "zero-tolerance" enforcement is seen in the separation of thousands of children from their parents while in detention, a practice considered "torture" by physicians.[4]

And we observed these practices once again four days following the tragedy in El Paso, as federal agents detained approximately 680 migrant workers from seven poultry plants across the state of Mississippi in the largest workplace raids in US history, ripping apart migrant communities, instilling fear, and sowing financial insecurity in households.[5] The timing and scope of the Mississippi raids provoked anger across the political spectrum. The Congressional Hispanic Caucus criticized the Department of Homeland Security (DHS), demanding answers about the raids' cost and source of funding. In a letter to the department, the caucus explicitly linked the events in Mississippi to those in El Paso, writing, "This raid, which is the largest ICE raid in our nation's history, is a continuation of the Trump Administration's politically driven immigration agenda and efforts to target Latino families. It is also not lost on us that this operation occurred just days after one of the most horrific mass shootings targeting Latinos in America . . . ICE raids of this scale are not conducted for the purpose of immigration enforcement; instead, their purpose is to instill fear in Latino and immigrant communities at a time when Latinos are already living in terror."[6]

This refusal to be silent and the mass mobilizations that are often criticized as unruly, excessive, and extreme connect the tragic events in El Paso and Mississippi in 2019 to the national loss and rage in 2020. What also binds up these moments is the hopeful power of collective action or what Michelle Alexander has described as "a politics of deep solidarity rooted in love."[7]

This politics of deep solidarity also characterized the nearly two weeks of protests by more than a million Puerto Ricans across the island in July 2019 that resulted in Governor Ricardo Rosselló's resignation, the first such event in the island's history. The unprecedented mobilization was a response to allegations of corruption and years of political scandals—all of which were put on display most notably through leaked homophobic, sexist, and misogynistic communications between the governor and his aides, deriding journalists and political opponents, as well as mocking the struggles of Puerto Ricans in the wake of Hurricane Maria.[8] As anthropologist and public intellectual Yarimar Bonilla notes, these protests were historic not only due to their size and efficacy but also because of their creativity. As Veronica Dávila and Marisol LeBrón documented, protesters drew on old and new forms of protest to mobilize a range of people, including protesters "on horses, motorcycles, jet skis, kayaks, yoga mats and . . . banging pots. Yet it was the young people dancing provocatively on the steps of the oldest cathedral in the New World to the boom-ch-boom-chick-boom-ch-boom-chick of reggaeton beats that may have finally forced Rosselló out of office."[9] Protests, however, did not end with Rosselló's resignation.[10] Ongoing mobilizations—including the use of social media hashtag #RenunciaWanda to challenge the current governor and the proliferation of *asambleas del pueblo* (autonomous groups organized at the municipal level throughout the island)— speak both to a longer history of Puerto Rican activism and political mobilization and to what Bonilla refers to as "a time of new possibilities."[11]

This spirit of defiance, hope, and solidarity animated the initial conversations that seeded this anthology. We wanted to disrupt the notion that the xenophobic rhetoric and support for white supremacy by the forty-fifth president was exceptional, a view that delinks contemporary tensions from colonial histories of power.[12] In November 2017 a small group of us participated in a Presidential Panel at the American Anthropological Association meeting, focusing on ethnographic work documenting multiple efforts to challenge the ethnonationalist, anti-Mexican, and anti-Muslim policies of the Trump administration. We were subsequently able to continue this discussion with a broader group of colleagues during a week-long seminar at the School of Advanced Research (SAR) in April 2019 titled "Ethnographies of Contestations and Resilience in Latinx America," which provided the necessary intellectual space for us to come together as Latinx anthropologists and resume our conversation, share our research, think together, and reflect on the value and future of Latinx ethnographic practice. In the pages that follow, our collectively authored introduction lays out some of the most salient frameworks, questions, and conundrums we grappled with throughout the seminar, providing a roadmap for tracing our ethnographic approach in this anthology.

Intellectual Ancestry

To begin, we are anthropologists who value the extraordinary possibilities offered by ethnography. Yet we question the practical, methodological, and epistemological constraints the discipline often imposes upon field research. To paraphrase Chicana feminist Cherríe Moraga, we come from a long line of *vendidas*; that is, we identify with those who refuse normative expectations.[13] We are part of an intellectual community that disturbs the classic ethnographic encounter where, in the tradition of Malinowski, the detached observer—aided by so-called key informants—observes the "ethnographic other" for an extended period of time with the aim of discovering their elusive cultural patterns. Elsewhere, Renato Rosaldo critiques this expectation wherein the "lone ethnographer" learns "a culture" through the process of ritualistic encounter, subsequently attaining enough insider knowledge to render his subjects intelligible to the Western gaze (a gaze always tinged with imperialist nostalgia for those groups supposedly untouched by modernity).[14] This tactic is remarkably silent about differential power dynamics between ethnographers and interlocutors—along the lines of class, gender, race, sexual identity, age, political or religious affiliation, etc.—and has little to say about broader geopolitical circumstances revelatory of ethnographers' implicit support of neocolonial regimes.[15]

This traditional approach has been roundly criticized for its stilted representation, which homogenizes and objectifies the people being studied while willfully ignoring their flexibility, creativity, contestation, and refusal.[16] Scholars working in interdisciplinary fields like ethnic studies—especially in Black studies, Chicanx/Latinx studies, and Native American studies, as well as feminist studies and Queer studies—have fashioned robust critiques of this institutionalized form of so-called classic ethnography, often by pointing out the locals' skill in representing their own norms, beliefs, and practices in creative ways that undermine ethnographers' expectations.[17] In doing so, these scholars have called for an anthropology designed to promote "equality- and justice-inducing social transformation."[18] Such a perspective encourages us to reassess the contributions of those with whom we work, including collaborators whose skills are critical for our success yet receive little recognition.[19] Relatedly, the contributions of "native anthropologists"—ranging from representatives of the Black radical tradition to Indigenous scholars—have generated debates regarding the politics and poetics of anthropological writing that raise vital questions around the relationship between objectivity and literary representation.[20] We consider ourselves and our work, therefore, as part of broader efforts to "refuse anthropology." This refusal includes dismantling the norms expected of field research and modes of anthropological knowledge production, as a way of generating necessary and alternative perspectives that value collaboration with our interlocutors. Increasingly, ethnographers train with community members to work as insider-scholars, collaborate on the design and implementation of research, and use a variety of techniques (including photovoice or participatory action research projects), all of which allows more nuanced analyses and may lead to significant policy changes.[21]

Repeatedly, our work calls for a critical self-reflexivity that moves from rhetoric to praxis and marshals the power of bearing witness.[22] Feminist ethnographers, in particular, have called for work that, as Ruth Behar puts it, "breaks our heart," that is, ethnographies written in a personal voice, expressing the vulnerabilities and feelings we experience, particularly when witnessing abuses of power and social suffering.[23] Yet, far from a perspective that dwells on what the suffering subject endures,[24] we support the feminist push for transparency and ongoing dialogue wherein anthropologists commit to the people with whom we work and engage with them on behalf of shared political goals.[25] David Quijada and his colleagues highlight the value of a research process that offers a type of "radical inclusion" that begins with "informed understanding of personal experiences by those being legislated upon," which can profoundly impact the "social analysis, critical inquiry, and reform" suggested by research findings.[26] With these insurgent threads of critical scholarly inquiry in mind, our collection of chapters explores how Latinx ethnographers and interlocutors engage in collaborative encounters in contexts of refusal, ever mindful of how power shapes those very encounters and the analyses that emerge from them and of how ethnographic research plays a role in social transformation.

Latinidades

We seek to engage carefully with complex local and global structures of oppression that shape how gender, race, class, and place are configured, reproduced, and mobilized. This contextually and historically critical lens figures centrally in the methodological and theoretical approaches to Latinx ethnography that take shape across the pages of this volume. Our use of the term "Latinx" rather than Latina/o or Hispanic is intended to signal our engagement with critical dialogues about the ways that historical and contemporary constructions of Latinidad have alternately contributed to the contestation and reproduction of various forms of exclusion and erasure associated with phenomena such as gender and sexuality, racial and class hierarchies, and settler colonialities. "Latinx" has emerged as a genderqueer, or nonbinary, term in recent years that circulates widely in some contexts, yet remains relatively illegible or disfavored altogether in others.[27] Thus, we view "Latinx" not as a simple solution to histories of colonialism, patriarchy, and misogyny through which gender binaries and racial hierarches have been imposed and reproduced but, rather, as a crucial opportunity for reflection on and continued reimagination of the contours of Latinidad, where the "x" may exist as a reminder of both refusal and exclusion.[28] We deploy this term strategically as part of ongoing dialogues with the understanding that our terminologies are inherently imprecise, contested, and — perhaps most crucially — constantly shifting.

It is also important to acknowledge particular critiques of Latinidad and how we are positioned within them as activist-researchers and ethnographers who work in our homeplaces or in collaboration and in solidarity with the communities who have welcomed us. Some of the central problems with conceptions of Latinidad are the dangers and pretenses of the amalgam, or the categorical flattening of diversities and differences, which lead to various kinds of exclusions and erasures that reflect past and present racialized subjection and settler colonial structures of violence.[29] Similar to the ways that gender normativities have been reproduced in prevailing approaches to the study of Latinidad, narrow framings of race and ethnicity or intermixing have often led to the conceptualization of Latinxs as a "Brown" population located in the middle of an imagined Black-white binary. Indeed, the case for Latinx studies has been advanced as a critique of this binary and its attendant exclusions. However, this framing erases not only countless AfroLatinx experiences that powerfully demonstrate that Blackness and Latinidad cannot and should not be separated but also Latinx Indigeneities, which are elided in accounts that naturalize Latinidad as a variety of mestizaje. Critiques of racist, anti-Black, and anti-Indigenous thinking that have informed conceptions of Latinidad as the embodiment of an amalgamated "raza cósmica" underscore the importance of unmooring biological constructions of race rooted in eugenicist imaginations of purity and contamination from markers of cultural or racial difference. Undeniably, mestizaje subsumes or abstracts the Indigenous subject in ways that mimic settler colonial logics of discovery and replacement.[30] It carries the baggage of colonial violence and genocide and the conceits of European cultural and racial superiority as a necessary "civilizing" force that devalues Indigenous humanity and posits territorial claims as illegitimate or illogical in order to appropriate land and resources. This logic of elimination subsumes and flattens Indigenous and African difference while valorizing a mestizaje that privileges whiteness (and proximity to whiteness), modernist notions of *indigenismo*, and European temporalities and cultural norms—all of which braces the colonial formations of anti-Blackness and white supremacy that have historically produced the endemic anti-Black racism in our communities.[31] Thus, Latinidad, like the settler colonial logics that informed its development as an amalgamated ethnic category, "obscures the conditions of its own production."[32] And while Chicana feminist philosophers such as Gloria Anzaldúa and Cherríe Moraga among others have attempted to reclaim mestizaje as a shape-shifting metaphorical space where cultural conflicts, intersecting identities, and painful historical and embodied traumas are worked on—if not entirely worked out—mestizaje is nevertheless tied to settler colonial statecraft and genocidal practices that romanticize, displace, or erase ancestral and living Indigenous communities.

The forms of difference that Latinx carries are transhistorical and move across multiple settler nation-states in the Americas. Diverse Indigenous and African peoples experienced localized systems of oppression and restrictions on their freedom that developed in particular cultural, national, and regional contexts. In the United States, Latinidad simultaneously signals perpetual foreignness, "undesirable exogenous others," and the ideology of the immigrant nation.[33] The latter idea braces the immigrant narrative of discovery—the notion that migration is a matter of free will (instead of a forced choice, displacement, or a means of survival), a search for a better life, and hope for belonging within a more viable settler nation-state.

The term "Latinx," we acknowledge, may be considered a radically conservative call to gender and racial inclusion because it depends upon belonging or claiming space within the US white settler state and makes use of its coercive categories of difference. Yet, we also hold on to our aspirations for a more just future and embrace plurality and possibility in current and forthcoming approaches to analyzing interrelations and imbrications among diverse Latinidades, Blacknesses, and Indigeneities (as well as Asianness, Middle Easterness, and whiteness) in various historical and emergent ethnoracial positionalities. We seek to honor the important role that calls for Black-Brown solidarity and reclamations of Indigeneity have served in the remaking of identity and in historical organizing efforts, as well as how "Brownness" continues to anchor the everyday experiences of millions of Latinxs, while also moving beyond the assumption that Latinidad can be reduced to a single, isolated position within existing racial schema. Yet, we are fully aware of the limitations of adjacent terms like "people of color" as well, which emerged as a strategic way of building interracial coalitions but also have the capacity of homogenizing histories and experiences of oppression among racialized populations. In this volume, we aim to make visible ethnographically the complexities and possibilities of Latinx difference, signaling toward Latinidad as always socially contingent, contextual, and framed by both erasures and violences from without and within, in a word, unruly.

Homework

We as Latinx ethnographers grapple with the complexities and possibilities of Latinx difference in a range of places, including those typically defined as distinct, namely "home" and "the field." What has often been regarded as the central practice that sets anthropology apart from other humanistic sciences—long-term ethnographic fieldwork conducted in places far from home with people who are culturally distant from the researcher—is something we, like others before us, constantly interrogate. As a rule, going to the field has been understood as a personal and professional rite of passage that transforms the anthropologist into a knowledge-producing subject, an interpreter of cross-cultural encounters, a translator of difference, a writer of culture. According to this logic, the researcher travels to the faraway field and—however ill-equipped or unprepared—collects objects and knowledge about an "other." The researcher then returns home to render this assemblage of anecdotes and artifacts into scholarly texts or exhibits largely intended for academicians and university students. Every stage of this ritual process (training and scholarly preparation, fieldwork and data analysis, and the "writing of culture") has been and continues to be thought about deeply and critiqued. However, "home" and "the field" are relational concepts. The importance of recognizing this complexity was a recurring theme during our week together in Santa Fe. We shared with each other the challenges and joys of recognizing the ways that the field can be multisited, transnational, conjectural, or even virtual. For many of us, the field is not necessarily a remote or distinct location with clear boundaries and is never entirely separable from home. Similarly, home is not a feminized, private, intimate domain or stable enclosure.[34] Home as a sanctuary or familiar place that endures in memory or materially as a resting place where one feels security and belonging may be something yearned for, but never realized. Feminist critiques of home as an insular or idealized representation of domesticity or comfort reveal the multiple tensions, unequal economic and gender relations, and violences that occur within the home or in association with the private domestic space. That is to say, the foundations of home can be uncertain and unstable.

We grapple with home as a conceptual space between movement and dwelling, a homescape at the edge of Indigenous epistemologies and settler colonial ideologies, a space composed of historical memory and capitalist modernity, one that is productive of changing social and material conditions.[35] Therefore, a place called home—a homeplace—is not a stable location per se, but a space, atmosphere, affect, and dialectical relation always in motion, a process of building and undoing. As such, home embodies multiple tensions, imaginaries, and dislocations. Homeplaces can be uprooted and remade elsewhere and home can be constitutive of multiple places. Rather than existing as a definable location or protective space, home is experienced as a structure of feeling, a state of being-at-home in the world.[36] When home is understood in this way, fieldwork seems more akin to homework, which calls for a different level of accountability with respect to our actions and obligations to research partners who have extended to us their trust and hospitality. Moreover, homework is an important concept for us because we are conducting research in the United States and its territories, that is, within a white-settler state as racialized people who are in turn marginalized within the discipline of anthropology.

While the distinctions between home and field, native and outsider, and self and other are often porous and tenuous, it seems that research done "abroad," far from "home," is accorded great value and importance in a world that demands a certain privileged mobility in anthropological circles. This particular fetishizing of research conducted far away reveals how travel, discovery, and translation — as pillars of the discipline — are in fact signatures of anthropology's colonial origins, historical complicity with imperialism, and the designs of settler states. In the end, the notion that the "other" can be laid bare as an object of knowledge is both a liberal conceit and a colonial fantasy. The movement to decolonize anthropology and its methodologies stems from Indigenous, postcolonial, and feminist critiques of Eurocentric epistemologies, imperial modes of knowledge production, and the patriarchal gaze, as well as of liberal strategies to contain difference and repackage it to serve capitalist designs or settler colonial desires. And while the crisis of representation during the 1980s brought about some changes in ethnographic practice, research ethics, and writing, the quick fix of reflexivity (as both a methodological and an ethical stance) never fully decolonized anthropology; nor did it resolve the problem of representation. In other words, purported heightened awareness of both the differential power dynamics between researchers and participants and the implicit biases stemming from researchers' subjective angle of vision proved to be a smoke screen, an ideological buffer, a move toward innocence that used theory as a proxy for responsibility, allowing business to proceed as usual.

The sticky colonial and patriarchal residues of history remain within anthropology, particularly evidenced in its systematic exclusion of Indigenous, Black, Latinx, and genderqueer or nonbinary epistemologies and in its willful privileging of officialized research methodologies and institutions that produce detached knowledge about marginalized communities for public consumption — that is, favoring fieldwork over homework. Given this, homework is not only a critical interrogation of home but also homebuilding, that is, doing the activist work of creating a more livable and equitable future within anthropology where we can thrive in solidarity with our research partners. We cannot escape the fact that, as Latinx ethnographers, home is also the neoliberal institutions where we make our living and produce and disseminate research often under conditions of duress and which rely on our unpaid labor in support of "diversity."[37] As our colleagues in the Association of Black Anthropologists stated in their "Statement against Police Violence and Anti-Black Racism" in addressing the murderous actions of "white vigilantes and police officers":

> We urge our non-Black anthropology colleagues, especially our White colleagues who tend to reproduce the toxic effects of whiteness in anthropology departments, think tanks, research groups, and other spaces where anthropology is practiced across the nation, to move beyond the soul searching, despondency, and white guilt that this moment (and similar other moments) has engendered. Instead, we want members of the discipline to start at "home," to accept the ways that anthropology has been and continues to be implicated in the project of white supremacy (both in its implicit and explicit manifestations) and to lay out a clear path for moving forward. We want members of the discipline of anthropology to see the ways that white supremacy is manifest in their curricula, syllabi, graduate student recruitment and mentoring, hiring, and promotion practices. We want them to see and correct their refusal or inability to teach race, racism, the pathology of whiteness, and the banality of white supremacy; their marginalization of Black scholars and their scholarship.[38]

In solidarity, we argue that homework is a transformative pedagogy that makes higher education more accessible and hospitable to students, staff, and faculty of color. Homework is a research methodology and political stance that demands mutuality and more enduring relationships and obligations with the communities who have welcomed us. Homework is rooted in communal notions of respect and obligation. Homework is an aspirational, future-oriented, and coalitional practice of ethnography that recognizes our research partners and interlocutors as collaborators and intellectuals in their own right and demands a deeper and more sustained personal and political commitment. Homework also precedes homebuilding in creating collaborative spaces of sanctuary for ourselves and our research partners. And as the authors of this volume illustrate, homework is also more challenging and complex because we identify with our research partners and the struggles they are facing—that is, we have personal stakes in their refusals.

Listening in Solidarity

For anthropologists, ethnographic encounters often center around the ritual of privileging the discipline's own intellectual context—an extractive process that devalues the words of "others" while simultaneously admitting to being enlightened by their insights. Generating "data" from "subjects" in this way requires placing ourselves in situations where we witness and/or coax modes of social interaction. However, in these contexts, typically the methodological tool we rely on most—the ethnographic interview—impedes us from fully apprehending repertoires of communication and sociability particular to the communities with which we work. We, however, are concerned with exploring how our present-tense social entanglement with our interlocuters contains the potential to challenge the authorial flows of textual representation, in other words, how the ethnographic self is dialogized—an understanding of which demands reflection on what it means to listen.

Listening is typically associated with the deliberate channeling of awareness toward sound. Yet, this mode of auditory attention is neither self-evident nor isolated; rather, it is shaped by culturally and context-specific sets of interpretive practices that extend beyond the sonic. Listening, we suggest, involves interplay with a broad range of nonauditory (and thus multisensory) aptitudes and dispositions that overlap with wider cognitive, embodied, and affective engagements in the course of ethnographic fieldwork, all of which implicates attention, experience, and subjectivity.[39] To listen, then, is to participate in a communicative exchange where we simultaneously interact with and construct our social surround, a process that draws attention to the construction of meaning alongside our interlocuters across interactional spaces of encounter. Elsewhere, Alex E. Chávez lends the research context an "ethnographic ear" as a way of understanding how interlocuters' own stories are broadcast through the perceptual field of voicing—a concept that collapses the Western epistemological binary between the material-sonorous aspects and the immaterial-political meanings of sound.[40] With this expanded understanding in mind and with respect to the ethnographic context, listening reveals itself as an inherently political act comprised of culturally and historically situated modes of attention that circulate within social fields of meaning and experience contoured by power and politics. Understood in this way, listening opens up the potential for animating a radical project attuned to states of solidarity—a project where voices matter, that is, resonate both materially (sensorially) and immaterially (socially).

The authors in this volume advocate for listening in solidarity as a transgressive act that (1) foregrounds modes of ethnographic attunement that extend beyond the aural and thus account for intersubjective behaviors, feelings, and sensings and (2) assembles these multimodal attunements as constitutive of an ethical interpretive practice. To clarify further, ours is a call to transform an objectifying practice into an intersubjective phenomenal and social attunement. At once haptic, affective, and reciprocal, listening in solidarity foregrounds ethical commitments that extend beyond the supposed bounds of the methodological science of anthropological fieldwork. This is to aspire toward a different narrative than that which the discipline expects—to refuse the emic-etic distinction and locate ourselves too as racialized, gendered, and otherized subjects in our work and, ultimately, in a discipline that was never meant for us to begin with. Here(hear), we arrive at a unique and relational sensing with others (with ourselves), a latching onto that carries us along—an act both agentive and accountable, wherein our embodied presence enters into an entanglement between others' stories and our storied selves. In this way, listening in solidarity offers a way into transforming practices of translation, transcription, and writing so central to anthropological methods, which previous lauded volumes purported to accomplish but in fact never fully did, leaving much to be desired in that regard.[41]

Ethics

Recognizing our entanglements with the people with whom we work consistently informed the conversations we had during our week together at SAR. We grappled with questions about how we understand these engagements, the ways they are mutually transformative, and how best to represent and theorize around their complexity. In other words, how do these forms of engagement relate to questions about what ethical research should look like in anthropology? How do we write about the refusals, silences, and tacit understandings inherent in the kind of fieldwork we engage in and advocate for? And what insights can we gain from discussions not only beyond anthropology but beyond the academy as well? Listening in solidarity, acts of accompaniment, and witnessing are all practices that require specific kinds of careful ethnographic engagement and ethical responsibilities. In reflecting on our research experiences, we consciously extend the dialogues on what ethical fieldwork might look like and invite the reader to consider the forms of ethics required and expected from their own communities. And while we extend this dialogue based on our conversations with each other and with the communities with which we work, we ask that readers engage in this dialogue with themselves and their own communities in order to more carefully direct the ethical responsibilities that guide their research. With this in mind, we propose the following concepts and questions.

Accompaniment. Both in scholarly writing and community practice, accompaniment has reemerged as a framework guiding people's actions and dispositions in the context of unequal power relations. For faith-based activists, organizers, and scholars living and working in Latin America since the 1980s, as well as those familiar with liberation theology, accompaniment is a familiar principle informing ways of being and knowing grounded in a post–Vatican II commitment to preferential option for the poor, as well as for people and communities politically and socially marginalized. Activists and scholars concerned with liberation struggles in the Americas have long been inspired by theologians like Father Gustavo Gutiérrez, with his emphasis on the centrality of "liberating praxis" as the basis for the kind of solidarity and fellowship that should define interpersonal relationships and struggles to remedy inequality, or Archbishop Oscar Romero, who flouted church practices on behalf of the poor in El Salvador, or educator Paulo Freire, who argued for and lived by the principle of making the road by walking with ordinary people as they take control over their lives in Brazil. These commitments inform practices of accompaniment, which according to human-rights activist-anthropologist and medical doctor Paul Farmer is a humbling process that not only involves being "present on a journey with a beginning and an end" but also requires discernment, careful listening, and physical and social proximity with others to challenge the asymmetries of power that lead to structural violence.[42] It is this intentional linking of the fates of differentially located people that guides an array of social justice efforts, including those of immigration rights activists, freedom workers combatting anti-Black racism, Central American solidarity activists, those involved in prison reentry programs, health-care providers, social workers, and ethnographers.[43] As Barbara Tomlinson and George Lipsitz observe, part of the power of accompaniment lies in its demand for cultivating the capacity of "making connections with others, identifying with them, and helping them . . . it recognizes the inescapably and quintessential *social* nature of living in the world. It focuses on making connections with others, finding common ground, and uniting around concerns, interests, and ideas of the people with the greatest need for profound social changes."[44] Our conversations at SAR about accompaniment raised questions, including: Is our work as Latinx activist-ethnographers a form of accompaniment? What would an anthropology of accompaniment look like and entail? And how might our engagements with scholars in Latinx, American, ethnic, African American/Africana/Black, Indigenous, and Queer studies offer us models of accompaniment in our scholarly work as well?

How are we positioned? Sometimes ethnographers come from the community they study or share in similar linguistic and or cultural backgrounds; in other cases they may not have much in common with their subjects of interest at all. Each anthropologist will thus be interpolated in complex and divergent culturally specific ways that entail different forms of positioning, different levels of trust, different expectations for behavior—all in ways that test both our already-held knowledge and the limits of our comprehension. Moreover, positionality can certainly shift over the course of research and impact the kinds of stories we are told and how we then go on to retell those stories.[45] Our responsibility in reckoning with all of this is one we need to account for—in terms of our limitations and possibilities—within the context of ethnographic fieldwork, which also involves taking stock of people's investments in our work, the potential risks they take when participating, and how to account for that in our positioning, a process that also has its own limitations, admittedly evidenced by the scholars we have assembled for this volume.

Who benefits from our research? This question is a call for ethnographers to consider what the goals of our research are and to what extent they overlap with those of the communities we work with. Admittedly, ethnographic projects may benefit the careers of those who produce publications and receive grants for their projects, as well as advancing disciplinary knowledge, but how do they also advance the projects, interests, or goals of the communities or persons we engage with? Moreover, to what extent do we seek the input of communities with respect to what they would like to see accomplished through our work?[46]

Who do we write for? Attention to the multiple audiences for and investments in our work ought to remind ethnographers of the care they must take in crafting their writing. Who are our intended audiences and, in the process of writing, how do we give credit to our research collaborators in the field? Furthermore, how do we write in ways that may reach them and benefit them? As the chapters in this volume evidence, part of this involves enacting different kinds of refusals, that is, working, writing, and theorizing in ways that escape anthropology's methodological expectations and conceptualizations of culture and pushing beyond prevailing theories about what ethnography looks and sounds like—in spite of the ways in which many in the discipline may reject our projects, or even reject us altogether.

Refusals

To critically adopt refusal revives "the flesh of theory" and the theory of flesh.[47] This analytic animates the myriad ways Latinx and similarly positioned populations actively construct identities and claim the right to cultural expressions about their lived experience while being mindful that migrants in particular often feel ambivalent and that culture is neither coherent or static.[48] Marginalized people may also refuse to be researched, refuse to speak or to understand the dominant language, or refuse to honor international borders and internal checkpoints, among a host of *Other* practices. As Audra Simpson reminds us, refusal operates on many different levels, such as Mohawk refusal of the authority of the colonial state as well as the "everyday encounters that enunciate repeatedly to ourselves and to outsiders that 'this is who we are, this is who you are, these are my rights.'"[49] Refusal can also operate through subterranean existence that confounds dominant sensibilities about what constitutes resistance, as in the movements and practices of the young people who called themselves Barrio Libre.[50] Thus, refusal opposes dominant orders; but it is also contestation in ways unthought, or better put, unrecognized—illegible practices and modes of being and living. Refusal includes modes of thought, ways of life. The concept speaks to residual ways of life, contemporary ways of being, and future projects of existence that desert, escape, and abandon power, underlining an always emergent, historically and materially produced constitutive outside. It helps revive what anthropologist Karen Mary Davalos refers to as a "dialogue that never was," a dialogue pushed beyond the tensive demands of the seemingly opposed disciplinary apparatus of ethnic studies and anthropology (in our case).

Refusal occurs in sites as varied and as complex as our classrooms, as well as among populations such as our kin, be they biological or chosen. It informs our research agendas and our commitments to the populations we work with over careerist concerns. Refusal—analytically—holds that certain populations never submit. They oppose in creative, resourceful, and often extraordinary or extraordinarily subtle ways.[51] They refuse the impositions of the working day, the establishment of territorialities and settler states, and other kinds of power and modes of being.

Refusals, too, push against the discipline in capturing how marginalized populations are never just objects of research but are engaging in their own analytics: they are intellectuals in their own right; they want to tell stories of love, pleasure, as well as — or perhaps beyond — struggle and pain. Our ethnographic refusal comes from a healthy brown — taken as a subject position, not an already essentialized, colorist, compromised stance — pessimism regarding narratives of liberation and resistance that hold much sway in the discipline, so emblematic of both its deeply compromised liberal impulses and its existence as the handmaiden of colonialism. Refusal, thus, involves a "no" to telling everything.

Embracing refusal, however, should not be confused with an apolitical nihilism. Instead, refusal demands an analytical push away from normative analysis of what counts as research in anthropology, allied disciplines, and other dominant knowledge formations. And to analyze refusal itself and its myriad complexities demands a vertiginous decolonial reorientation, if not wholesale rupture with the tools of the master. It demands a queer inclusion in post- or antidisciplinary formations such as Queer, Black, Ethnic or Latinx studies. To analyze refusal, as Latinx ethnographers, stresses a deep accounting of the demands of research for the communities we work with — a reckoning with their concerns and agendas, a coming to grips with the colonial formations of the discipline, a recognition that too much academic research on Latinx and other marginal communities has become ventriloquism: they are the overstudied. Refusal recognizes, in other words, that when it comes to Latinx and similarly positioned populations, they — or is it we? — talk back, undermine, and confound (traditional) ethnographers; we talk back in the vein of Américo Paredes and Zora Neal Hurston. We are intent not on protecting, but rather, refusing the nexus of power and knowledge so that we may continue to build alternative worlds that include us.

Futures

It is this imaging and documenting of alternative worlds that the contributions to this anthology seek to highlight. In doing so, we move beyond and extend conventional discussions of agency, dissent, and resilience — key concepts not just in critical ethnographic work but in the lives of our interlocutors — to better understand and analyze the contemporary conditions and experiences of living and of refusal in Latinx communities. This requires us to imagine new analyses that belie expected theorizing, be it through listening in solidarity or other ethical investments. Indeed, as our colleague Gilberto Rosas suggests (chapter 9), this is a call to a radical anthropology that centers what is politically, ethically, and morally just, without any clear instructions, outlines, or outcomes. This perspective is inspired by our interlocuters, who themselves are invested in an array of social projects that work to imagine new narratives and attempt to author new futures.

The chapters that follow trace how it is that Latinxs actively struggle for and creatively imagine more just and equitable worlds. This consideration opens up a broader temporal question regarding the future of Latinxs in the United States, Latinx anthropology, and Latinxs in anthropology. Yet, throughout, the approaches to futurities held both by scholars and interlocutors are open-ended—no predictions are offered, for there are no easy, simple, or readily available answers to these questions. To be frank, we do not know what lies ahead. This uncertainty, however, is where possibility lies: from Latinx youth in Massachusetts, Long Island, and Chicago who wield art and grassroots organizing as vehicles for social change; to how the question of bodily autonomy, gender, and sexual autonomy are at the center of struggles around reproductive justice in South Texas and sex work in Chicago among trans women; to how, in this same spirit, sanctuary movement activists in Ohio draw on hopeful histories of past social movements to develop strategies for political organizing in the present, while Indigenous groups in Puerto Rico and New Mexico chart new genealogies that unearth occluded pasts of violence, exploitation, and appropriation in order to better understand the current moment and what may come—all of this evinces how horizons of possibility can rely deeply on the past.

Yet, the authors of this volume no doubt disturb understandings of the temporality of the present. In his foundational work, José Esteban Muñoz disrupts binarized distinctions between "future" and "present" and describes glimpses of an actually existing queer future in the present.[52] While Muñoz focuses on performances, he also draws attention to the quotidian as a key site of future-making. Thus, the ethnographic method—with its careful attention to otherwise mundane, day-to-day happenings in people's lives—is key to understanding the complicated ways in which past, present, and future social, cultural, and political vernaculars meet. Andrea Bolivar's concept of *fantasía* (chapter 6) draws on Muñoz to demonstrate future-making in the present. As sex-working transgender Latinas cultivate more livable futures for those who defy gender and racial normativity, they also engage in refusal forms of being, working, caring, and space-making in the present. Similarly, Sherina Feliciano-Santos (chapter 2) reveals that for Indigenous Taíno activists, "the space of their resistance and struggle is marked by tensions and alternatives: alternative pasts, alternative presents, alternative futures." And Chávez (chapter 3) also listens to how Chicago youth challenge us to embrace what is not quite in view, to embrace the possibility of an "abstract future on the horizon, yet presently in process, that claims the here and now in time, in space, and through sound." The array of ethnographic work in this volume, however, exudes no mere and facile optimism. Rather, it exhibits what performance studies scholar Ramón Rivera-Servera calls an "educated hope."[53] He argues that Latinxs are "optimistic while maintaining a critical grounding in the materiality of historical and contemporary experience," which results in what Muñoz calls "an alternative political affect that embraces futurity without venturing into an uncritical escapism."[54] The social actors in this volume, too, are optimistic *and* realistic. And so, the desire to bridge the past, present, and future in ways that work toward more radical potentialities for Latinxs is perhaps, too, a defining characteristic of Latinx ethnography, as we came to realize through our shared conversations. At one point during our SAR seminar, Ana Aparicio asserted, "We wouldn't be here if we weren't working toward the future." This—our "future work"—is also homework, our collective *tarea* that speaks to an impossible intellectual and political activism in the present, one that is sustained by the past and imagines and works toward achieving just and alternative futures.

With these arguments and concepts in mind, the title of this volume reflects our ultimate purpose in writing. Refusal is our analytical stance; it ought not be read as an ethnographic rendering of our observations of the actions—of refusal, resistance, etc.—that people themselves are engaging in within their daily lives. Our ethnographic refusal is manifested in seeking "the beyond" of what is often imagined in relation to the anthropological practice of ethnography. "Unruly Latinidades" refers to the way the very notion of Latinidad can often be narrow and constraining and to how our work illustrates and invites a more capacious, and therefore unruly, conceptualization of the term. Thus, while on the surface the concerns and issues we explore might appear to be narrowly confined to Latinidad, our survey of the landscape of contemporary political struggles suggests a broader range of experiences that can be understood in relation to Latinidad. Finally, in pairing the two, we call for an anthropology on our own terms that has substantive political contributions that—in contemporary parlance—bear the potential to decolonize the discipline methodologically, theoretically, and ethnographically. This is our way of staking a claim—one that does not elide, hide, or silence our complexities and vulnerabilities in the guise of detached scientism but rather foregrounds, struggles with, and challenges our compromised personhood as marginalized peoples and our *compromisos* (obligations) to those with whom we work.

Notes

1. Keeanga-Yahmatta Taylor, "Of Course There Are Protests. The State Is Failing Black People," *New York Times*, May 29, 2020, https://www.nytimes.com/2020/05/29/opinion/george-floyd-minneapolis.html?action=click&module=RelatedLinks&pgtype=Article.

2. Chavez 2013, 3; Jorge Ramos, "El Paso Was a Massacre Foretold," *New York Times*, August 10, 2019, https://www.nytimes.com/2019/08/10/opinion/i-fear-the-deaths-in-el-paso-wont-change-anything.html.

3. "Witnessing 'Zero Tolerance' on the Border," *Anthropology News*, December 17, 2018, http://www.anthropology-news.org/index.php/2018/12/17/witnessing-zero-tolerance-at-the-border/.

4. Soboroff 2020.

5. Similar kinds of workplace raids on migrant communities had occurred in Ohio just one year earlier. Miriam Jordan, "ICE Arrests Hundreds in Mississippi Raids Targeting Immigrant Workers," *New York Times*, August 7, 2019, https://www.nytimes.com/2019/08/07/us/ice-raids-mississippi.html. See also "Sen. Sherrod Brown Says He's Working to Help Immigrant Families in Sandusky-Area Raid," June 6, 2018, https://www.cleveland.com/metro/2018/06/sen_sherrod_brown_says_hes_wor.html.

6. Juliegrace Brufke, "Congressional Hispanic Caucus Calls for Answers on Mississippi ICE Raids," *Hill*, July 12, 2019, https://thehill.com/homenews/house/457148-congressional-hispanic-caucus-calls-for-answers-on-mississippi-ice-raid. In addition, 150 writers, artists, and leaders also signed a letter in solidarity with Latinx communities published in the *New York Times*, *El Nuevo Herald*, *La Opinión*, and *El Diario*. "Latino Actors, Writers Pen 'Letter of Solidarity' amid Fears," *New York Times*, August 16, 2019, https://www.nytimes.com/aponline/2019/08/16/us/ap-us-open-letter-latinos.html.

7. Michelle Alexander, "America, This Is Your Chance," *New York Times*, June 8, 2020, https://www.nytimes.com/2020/06/08/opinion/george-floyd-protests-race.html.

8. "Ricardo Rosselló Resigns as Governor of Puerto Rico," *El Nuevo Día*, July 25, 2019, https://www.elnuevodia.com/english/english/nota/ricardorosselloresignsasgovernorofpuertorico-2507862/; Dennis Costa, "The Most Controversial

Remarks in the Rosselló Chat Scandal," *El Nuevo Día*, July 14, 2019, https://www.elnuevodia.com/english/english/nota/themostcontroversialremarksinthe rossellochatscandal-2505583/. See also Yarimar Bonilla, "Why Would Anyone in Puerto Rico Want a Hurricane? Because Someone Will Get Rich," *Washington Post*, September 22, 2017.

9. Veronica Dávila and Marisol LeBrón, "How Music Took Down Puerto Rico's Governor," *Washington Post*, August 1, 2019, https://www.washingtonpost.com /outlook/2019/08/01/how-music-took-down-puerto-ricos-governor/.

10. Protests continued as the Puerto Rico Supreme Court unanimously ruled the appointment of Pedro Pierluisi as unconstitutional, resulting in his stepping down on August 7, and even as the former secretary of justice, Wanda Vasquez, was sworn in as governor later that day. William Ramírez, "After the Power of Protest Ousts a Governor, Puerto Rico Has a New Leader. For Now," ACLU, August 8, 2019, https://www.aclu.org/blog/free-speech/rights-protesters/after -power-protest-ousts-governor-puerto-rico-has-new-leader-now. See also Alejandra Roja, Patricia Mazzei, and Frances Robles, "Puerto Rico Supreme Court Ousts New Governor, and Another Is Sworn In," *New York Times*, August 7, 2019, https://www.nytimes.com/2019/08/07/us/puerto-rico-governor-wanda -vazquez.html.

11. Yarimar Bonilla, "Puerto Rican Politics Will Never Be the Same," interview by Jonah Walters, *Jacobin*, August 2, 2019, https://jacobinmag.com/2019/08 /puerto-rico-ricardo-rossello-governor-unrest. For a discussion of the origins of the asambleas del pueblo, see the interview with Jocelyn Velázquez on the *La Jornada Se Acabaron las Promesas* program on Radio Independencia, episode 101, August 16, 2019, https://www.youtube.com/watch?v=4G73Y7YvdoQ.

12. Rosa and Bonilla 2017.

13. Moraga 1983.

14. Rosaldo 1989. We deliberately write "his," because the ethnographer at the center of this narrative was usually a male subject.

15. Harrison 1997.

16. Castañeda 1996; Clifford and Marcus 1986; Paredes 1978 (1973).

17. Arvizu et al. 1978; Paredes 1993; Sillitoe 2015; Smith 1999.

18. Harrison 1997, 2.

19. This polemic extends back to the origins of anthropology, in which Franz Boas (like many other anthropologists) formed important relationships with his Native American translators, which enabled him to gain insight into and exper- tise in Native peoples' language and culture (Boas 1982).

20. Jones 1970; Gregory 1998; Gwaltney 1980; Hurston 1990; 1999; Hurston and Wall 1995; Hurston and Kaplan 2001; Ortiz 1969.

21. Schenker, Castañeda, and Lainz 2014; Langhout 2014.

22. Speed 2006, 71; also see Hale 2001; 2008; Hale and Stephen 2013; Tomlinson and Lipsitz 2013.

23. Behar 1996; also see Behar and Gordon 1995; Craven and Davis 2013; Desai 2013; Lamphere 2018; Wolf 1996; Zavella 1996.

24. Robbins 2013.

25. Speed 2006, 74; Hale 2001; 2008; Fassin 2017.

26. Quijada, Cahill, and Bradley 2013, 216.

27. De Onís 2017; Trujillo-Pagán 2018; Vidal-Ortiz and Martínez 2018; Rodriguez 2017.

28. Alan Pelaez Lopez, "The X in Latinx Is a Wound, Not a Trend," *Color Bloq: The Story of Us*, September 2018, https://www.colorbloq.org/the-x-in-latinx-is-a-wound-not-a-trend.

29. See Blackwell, Boj Lopez, and Urrieta 2017 for a fuller discussion.

30. See Glenn 2015.

31. Wolfe 2006.

32. Veracini 2010, 14.

33. Glenn 2015, 60.

34. Chawla 2014, 24.

35. See Clark and Powell 2008; Góralska 2020.

36. Chawla 2014, 25.

37. Contingent faculty make up more than 70 percent of the workforce in higher education. Colleen Flaherty, "The Gig Academy," *Inside Higher Ed*, October 10, 2019, https://www.insidehighered.com/news/2019/10/10/you%E2%80%99ve-heard-gig-economy-what-about-gig-academy.

38. "ABA Statement against Police Violence and Anti-Black Racism," June 6, 2020, https://aba.americananthro.org/aba-statement-against-police-violence-and-anti-black-racism-3/.

39. Rice 2015.

40. Chávez 2017; also see Erlmann 2004.

41. Here, we specifically refer to Clifford and Marcus 1986.

42. In Griffin and Weiss Block 2013, 127.

43. For examples of organizations using accompaniment as a framework guiding their engagement, see Freedom for Immigrants, https://www.freedomforim migrants.org/alternatives-to-detention; NISGUA (Network in Solidarity with Guatemala) and their Guatemala Accompaniment Project, https://nisgua.org /gap/; the Interfaith Movement for Human Integrity, Post-Release Accompaniment Project, http://www.im4humanintegrity.org/northern-california -immigration/; and the work of organizations like Taller de San Jose, which "offers accompaniment in a Mexican neighborhood in Chicago, helping service participants navigate health, judicial, and social service systems" (Villarreal Sosa, Díaz, and Hernández 2019); and Wilkinson and D'Angelo 2019.

44. Tomlinson and Lipsitz 2019, 23, 24.

45. Ranco 2006.

46. Garcia 2000.

47. See Moraga 1983.

48. We build on the notion that citizenship, a product of modernity, should be seen as multifaceted and more than juridical. Through shared social and cultural expressions, Latinxs, particularly migrants, assert their rights to space, dignity, and a sense of belonging (Bloemraad and Trost 2008; Caldwell et al. 2009; Del Castillo 2007; Flores and Benmayor 1997; Rosaldo 1994; 1997). This vernacular perspective on citizenship emphasizes people's quotidian social and cultural practices as well as their negotiations with and contestation of power in historically specific locales (Gálvez 2013).

49. Simpson 2007, 73.

50. See Rosas 2012.

51. Chávez 2017.

52. "Queer" meaning nonnormative and liberated in ways beyond the sexual, which includes racial.

53. Rivera-Servera 2012, 98. Rivera-Servera argues that hope constitutes a theory in practice of queer Latinidad.

54. Duggan and Muñoz 2009, 287.

CHAPTER ONE

"While You Are Struggling, You Are Healing"

Latinas Enact *Poder* through the Movement for Reproductive Justice

PATRICIA ZAVELLA

"Consuelo," an undocumented migrant living in a *colonia* near the US-Mexico border, became an activist with the Latina Advocacy Network (LAN) sponsored by the National Latina Institute for Reproductive Health.[1] She came to identify with LAN's discourse promoting *poderosas* (powerful women). Through LAN she learned about her rights and found the courage to confront her spouse about his violence and demand his respect; her husband now attends LAN events with her. In reflecting on the meaning of her activism, Consuelo said, "For me being a poderosa is a means of connecting with my dignity. It doesn't matter what I have suffered or my family has suffered or in my community. It doesn't matter the attacks that this government does or what people say or what my circumstances are. Those are negative details that bad people use so you don't believe in yourself." In a focus group I organized to understand women's activism, she reflected further on the process of becoming an activist:

> The first time that I heard that activists are poderosas it lifted my soul. You could see the pride in their faces. It is a way of coming to terms with yourself; that is, to be a human being. I know I have rights. I am connected and we are in community and nobody can take that away. Being a poderosa is something that has given me light in my life and I am very grateful and pleased to be part of something so large and so agreeable and that has helped me get ahead so much.

Consuelo contextualizes her agency within structural inequalities and highlights her relationships with others in similar circumstances; furthermore, her activism includes spiritual expressions.

1

I problematize women's agency and how ethnographers engage with women by asking, what does empowerment mean for Latinas living in poverty? I explore the apparent contradiction wherein women like Consuelo live in poor conditions yet come to embrace a discourse claiming they are powerful. I discuss the organizing strategies and discourse promoted by activists in the movement for reproductive justice working with LAN, which organizes mainly low-income Latinas—many of whom are undocumented and live in colonias—and contests state and federal policies within the framework of "Health, Dignity, and Justice." I reflect upon the implications of this activism for the politics of dissent by structurally vulnerable women. Specifically, what are the implications of these Latinas contesting the Trump administration's policies related to immigration and reproductive health?

According to Ann Bookman and Sandra Morgen, women's empowerment begins when they "change their ideas about the causes of the powerlessness, when they recognize the systemic forces that oppress them, and when they act to change the conditions of their lives."[2] Bookman and Morgen see empowerment as "a spectrum of political activities that range from acts of individual resistance to mass political mobilization that aim to challenge the basic power relations in society."[3] Thus, "empowerment is a *process* aimed at consolidating, maintaining, or changing the nature and distribution of power in a particular cultural context."[4] Further, Ruth Wilson Gilmore draws attention to struggles for social justice that occur within "forgotten places" marginalized through racialized capitalist practices and neoliberal state interventions, within which migrants attempt to survive.[5] Barbara Tomlinson and George Lipsitz suggest that, through accompaniment and improvisation, these spaces become insubordinate when residents nurture "new ways of knowing and new ways of being" and "a collective capacity for social justice can be developed and deepened."[6] Building on these approaches, I suggest we analyze women's activism using the analytic of *poder* (power), which signals vulnerable people's ability to develop skills or capabilities and aspire to better lives or even wellness, engaging in activism that advances social justice. Drawing on activist-research conducted in 2015 and 2018 that included interviews with national and Texas staff, a focus group with LAN participants, and LAN's use of social media, I analyze reproductive justice praxis in colonias and suggest it leads to women's empowerment and refuses Trump's neoliberal agenda.[7]

Neoliberalism entails a "massive disinvestment in families and communities" by the state through privatization and encourages individual responses to social problems, a process characterized by an assumption that those who struggle, particularly people of color, are deficient and responsible for their own misfortunes.[8] The US conservative movement goes further and promotes the politics of "reproductive governance," in which various actors use "legislative controls, economic inducements, moral injunctions, direct coercion, and ethical incitements to produce, monitor, and control reproductive behaviours and practices."[9] Reproductive governance is particularly evident in states that restrict abortion by targeting abortion providers, mandating pre-abortion wait times and fetal ultrasounds, reducing gestational ages for legal abortion, and pushing legislation mandating fetal "personhood" and parental consent for minors seeking abortions.[10] Reproductive governance is compounded by "legal violence," a convergence and implementation of immigration and criminal law with discourses that create extraordinary vulnerability for migrants, with origins in the Clinton era of immigration and welfare reforms that led to massive deportations and restricted access to social welfare.[11] This legal violence was exacerbated by the Trump administration's xenophobic rhetoric and "zero tolerance" immigration enforcement policies, designed to deter migration by separating children from their parents in detention, "metering" asylum seekers' access to hearings, leaving them in precarious conditions in Mexico or Guatemala, and building a wall along the US-Mexico border.[12]

Reproductive justice activists are contesting neoliberal reproductive governance of women and legal violence against migrants across the country. Working within a holistic framework that melds intersectionality and human rights, the movement's mission is to promote women's right to bear children free from coercion or abuse, terminate their pregnancies without obstacles or judgment, and raise their children in healthy environments, as well as the right to bodily autonomy and gender self-identification.[13] This social movement engages in grassroots organizing, policy advocacy at the local, state, and federal levels, and culture shift work that contests symbolic violence perpetrated through dominant narratives about women of color by framing their advocacy through the discourse of empowerment. Reproductive justice proponents believe that reproductive justice is only possible in communities free from state violence expressed through colonialism, neoliberalism, criminalization, or restrictive policies related to poverty, child welfare, the environment, immigration, reproduction, or education. The movement has been active since the 1990s, working with racially specific groups—African Americans, Asian and Pacific Islanders, Chicanas/Latinas, Native Americans, and Muslims—while simultaneously forging multisector and cross-racial coalitions for specific issues, including strategically using the political identity "women of color." They have honed specific organizing strategies and discourse about inclusivity and secular spirituality about balancing mind-body-spirit and expressing women's full selves.[14] Moreover, reproductive justice advocates honor their communities' rights to spiritual expression in relation to historical trauma by engaging in "healing justice." Initially formulated at the 2010 US Social Forum by activists, healing justice is "a practice of attention and connection" that heals the sense of being fractured or disconnected "that may be a result of trauma or oppressive socio-cultural narratives and practices. . . . It is a practice that asks social practitioners of all kinds to cultivate the *conditions* that might allow them to feel more whole and connected to themselves, the world around them, and other human beings."[15] Often, healing justice practice takes the form of narratives that include individual self-care in addition to community healing.

The Latina Advocacy Network has a long history of activism in which they mobilize poder, multiple forms of capacity-building that engage women in policy advocacy and culture shift on behalf of low-income Latinas. LAN is realizing empowerment in relation to historically specific structural conditions at the US-Mexico border, policies instigated by the Trump administration, and engagement by Latina activists. In what follows, I argue that empowerment is a complex process in which women move from developing their political subjectivity and embracing their identities as poderosas to expressing their spiritual power and open resistance.

Reproductive Governance and Legal Violence at the Border

Like eighteen other states, Texas did not expand Medicaid after the passage of the Patient Protection and Affordable Care Act. Even though Texas has the highest uninsured rate in the country (an estimated six million people), the state led a challenge to the ACA's constitutionality, garnering a favorable federal district court ruling.[16] In 2011 the Texas legislature cut state family planning funding by 66 percent and authorized the "affiliate rule," which barred health centers from receiving state funding if they were affiliated with facilities that provide abortions, essentially targeting Planned Parenthood. In 2013 the legislature passed one of the most restrictive abortion laws in the United States, requiring physicians performing abortions to have admitting privileges at nearby hospitals, banning most abortions after twenty weeks of pregnancy, and requiring that all abortion facilities meet the standards of an ambulatory surgical center. Women seeking abortions are required to undergo an ultrasound and counseling (including detailed descriptions of the ultrasound images) and then wait twenty-four hours before receiving the procedure, for which minors must have parental consent.

This antiabortion legislation immediately restricted access to health services to women of reproductive age whose reproductive health examinations often identify other health issues as well.[17] In South Texas, nine out of thirty-two state-funded family planning clinics closed, largely because physicians were unable to obtain hospital privileges, and those that remained open served 54 percent fewer clients.[18] There was also an increase in unplanned pregnancies and second-trimester abortions because of limited abortion services.[19] All of this took place in a context in which the four counties that make up the Rio Grande Valley near the Mexican border are home to 275,000 women of reproductive age, about two-thirds of whom are estimated to be in need of subsidized contraceptive services. After reviewing the consequences of restricting access to abortion services, Grossman and his colleagues concluded the Texas antiabortion legislation constitutes a "public health threat."[20] This was the legislation struck down by the Supreme Court in *Whole Woman's Health v. Hellerstedt* in 2016, a suit filed by the Center for Reproductive Rights with an amicus brief by the National Latina Institute for Reproductive Health.[21]

These chilling effects on women's reproductive rights were particularly challenging in the Rio Grande Valley, where the population is overwhelmingly Latinx, and legal violence is intensifying. More specifically, the lives of the approximately two million undocumented migrants in Texas have become increasingly complicated, as the Trump regime's policies led to an increase in migrant deaths, abuse of migrants by the Border Patrol, and increased suffering by migrants confined in deplorable conditions.[22] Further, Immigration and Customs Enforcement (ICE) has the authority to conduct searches and to inquire about one's legal status at checkpoints within one hundred miles of the US-Mexico border. In the Rio Grande Valley, there is a multiagency checkpoint run in collaboration between local, state, and federal agencies.[23] Such inquiries into people's legal status may lead to eventual deportation.[24] Compounding matters, in 2018 Trump mobilized the National Guard (which has been stationed at the border since 2014) to help the Border Patrol with surveillance and intelligence, even though unauthorized entries were at historic lows.[25] While civil rights organizations are challenging this border enforcement regime and residents warn one another about new checkpoints and workplace raids, people are cautious when driving and carefully consider when they need to drive outside their neighborhoods. In this borderland, the undocumented often delay accessing health care except for emergency care, which affects US citizens living in mixed-status households. Thus, these policies have exacerbated what Díaz-Barriga and Dorsey call a "state of exception," in which militarization and objectification through racialized, gendered logics lead to necropower that subjects migrants to extraordinary suffering or death while infringing upon the rights of US citizens.[26]

Accompanying Women from the Colonias

The Center for Reproductive Rights and the National Latina Institute for Reproductive Health (in everyday use shortened to National Latina Institute) are based in New York City. Founded in 1994, the National Latina Institute is among the largest of a network of over thirty nonprofit organizations in the United States (with one in Canada) using the reproductive justice framework. Besides New York, they sponsor Latina Advocacy Networks in Florida, Virginia, and Texas, which work on civic engagement related to immigrant and refugee rights, reproductive health, human rights and civil liberties, and race and ethnicity. In the Texas LAN, the participants are predominantly Latinas.

The discourse of "*soy poderosa*" (I am a powerful woman) is part of the National Latina Institute's strategic culture shift work.[27] Specifically, the term came to the forefront when the institute conducted a survey on Latinxs' views on abortion, mindful that 55 percent of Latinxs are Catholics and that the church condemns abortion.[28] The bilingual survey, administered to six hundred Latinx registered voters in twenty-five states, resulted in unexpected findings: 68 percent of the survey participants agreed with the statement "Even though Church leaders take a position against abortion, when it comes to the law, I believe it should remain legal." Further, 67 percent would support a close a friend or family member who had an abortion.[29] Eighty-one percent agree that abortions should be covered by private or state-funded health insurance.[30] According to the institute's former executive director Jessica González-Rojas, as they were analyzing the survey data, the researchers began referring to respondents who were highly engaged politically as "las poderosas." On this basis, the institute developed a campaign with the slogan "Soy Poderosa and My Voice Matters," which is endorsed by multiple allies. Since then, the National Latina Institute deploys *poderosa* discourse in their reports and social media and at public demonstrations.

The Center for Reproductive Rights and the National Latina Institute began collaborating on the Nuestro Texas campaign in 2007. For this purpose, they conducted research about the US-Mexico border region, including 188 interviews, documenting the poverty and poor access to health care for all, particularly focusing on women. In the aftermath of Texas's restrictive legislation, their report concludes: "The long delays [for provider appointments] are tantamount to a denial of reproductive health care because the window of opportunity to treat serious conditions such as breast, cervical, or uterine cancer may close by the time a woman finally sees a doctor."[31] Lucy Ceballos-Félix, associate director of field and advocacy, testified about the report's findings in Geneva in front of the United Nations Human Rights Committee during its periodic review of US compliance with the International Covenant on Civil and Political Rights.[32] She told me the attendees were shocked to hear about the poverty and denial of health care in the United States.

In her early days organizing women, Ceballos-Félix had used "old school" communication methods, borrowing an ice cream truck and driving around distributing flyers announcing an upcoming LAN meeting. Later she canvassed door-to-door and recruited women to join their activities. The personalized outreach is critical since many participants live in colonias. Ceballos-Félix now coordinates thirty women's groups in four counties in South Texas with the help of a subcommittee of women who have completed LAN's leadership institute.[33] The participants' ages vary tremendously. The majority are in their thirties and forties, although some are older, up to the eighties. Women are bringing their children to LAN events, so their work is intergenerational.

As unincorporated enclaves, colonias are home to many undocumented residents escaping severe poverty or repression in their countries of origin. Approximately 80 percent of colonia residents are at or below the poverty level and many suffer higher levels of chronic health problems than the average US population.[34] A third of the residents do not have a high school education and there are high percentages of female-headed households.[35] Seventy-eight percent of colonia residents, especially those in migrant households, experience food insecurity, which is associated with negative health outcomes.[36] The Rio Grande Valley has high rates of nutrition-related health problems such as diabetes, obesity, cardiovascular disease, and neural tube defects, as well as the nation's highest rates of cervical cancer, an area in which Latinas' incidence and mortality rates are in general higher than those of other women.[37] Poor access to health care is endemic, as there is little public transportation and colonia residents must travel long distances to access clinics that provide care on the basis of sliding fees for those with low incomes.[38] Historically, the *promotora* model—using health outreach workers and mobile clinics—has been used successfully in South Texas, providing health information and limited checkups to marginalized residents.[39] Funding for those programs was cut, however, when Texas passed the restrictive legislation mentioned above.

While colonias are often disparaged in public discourse, residents have been mobilizing to counter these views and express pride in their communities.[40] Women in particular attend LAN's monthly meetings and receive training about a host of issues—for example, how the legislature works, how to renew one's Deferred Action for Childhood Arrivals status, obstetric violence, tax law changes for small businesses, etc.—as well as a range of public health issues, such as preventing and coping with diabetes, accessing contraceptives, and getting tested for cervical cancer or Zika (a mosquito-borne virus that causes birth defects). After the clinics closed, LAN modified their workshops to provide more health information and trained women to administer their own breast exams and cope with the instances when they found lumps in their breasts. Similar to other contexts, when women shared their *testimonios* (life-stories) during LAN meetings they developed strong affective bonds and trust in one another; throughout, there has been ongoing reflection about the importance of respecting different perspectives among women.[41]

In preparation for a daylong human rights hearing on March 9, 2015, LAN members wrote about their experiences accessing health care. The event, "Our Voice, Our Health, Our Texas: A Women's Human Rights Hearing," sponsored by the Center for Reproductive Rights and National Latina Institute, documented how Texas's antiabortion legislation created barriers to women accessing any type of reproductive health services and thus was a violation of their human rights. The hearing featured testimonies by seventeen Latinas—diverse by country of origin, language use, age, and legal status—about their experiences trying to access health care in South Texas. The dire consequences of the restrictions included women being intimidated or unable to see a physician for their annual examinations, which led to late diagnoses of breast or cervical cancers, and an abortion that required driving an extraordinary distance amid discouragement by the clinic staff. In an effort to protect the undocumented, the women used pseudonyms and some read others' stories. The meeting included responses by state legislators and fellow activists from women's rights and immigrant rights organizations, who expressed their shock at the women's experiences and reiterated their support for addressing the barriers to accessing health care.

I traveled to the Rio Grande Valley in 2018 to learn about changes since the 2015 human rights hearing from LAN members. During a focus group, women reflected on their experiences providing testimonies at the hearings. Several admitted they had been very nervous about public speaking. One woman with a minor speech impediment recalled, "I don't know how to read well and I have some difficulty expressing myself. I invited my niece to accompany me. Between the two of us we were able to do well, tell their stories. We were fearful, but I told her no one is going to say anything and we will be successful at this." One of the organizers recalled:

> Beforehand they were saying, "No, you do it; I can't do it." And yet they did a marvelous job! They knew how important it was because the hearings were unique, something that had never been done here in Texas, especially in the Valley. All of them were well focused, secure that being there sharing their stories was very motivating, very powerful. And that event brought a tremendous change to those leaders. They have continued the strong work in the community but they became stronger. They gave the message that they were overcoming many barriers because the stories were very different but at the same time, here we are united. We are organizing. We are moving forward and we are helping—that was the message they gave that day.

Another organizer pointed out, "Women truly embraced a new way of seeing their lives. Some of the women had believed that there was no hope. But those hearings broke that fear that prevented any hope."[42] Consuelo recalled her experience giving her testimonio:

> For me it felt a little strange to give my story because in the past I had advocated for others and never for myself. And when I was writing my story I realized, oh my goodness, I did my own breast examinations! And I have overcome so many barriers! I don't have medical insurance and the clinics charge so much and sometimes I don't have work. And I began to have so many feelings. I felt a lot of happiness and I felt a lot of power; anger because so many years of telling our stories over and over and they

don't pay attention to us until the extreme of bringing our stories to the United Nations. That was super important but it gives us anxiety because our government has not taken care of us. We have to go look for help from another place. And I felt a lot of sadness because we are a good group of women but how many more stories are there? And then I was feeling the power within myself because I knew that something good would come out of this. I knew that this was the final proof of what we were engaged in for a long time. I feel like thanks to this and the training that LAN has given me, now I am part of the LAN and it opened some doors and that's good and I continue struggling so that those who have not benefited will have their time. And we are here to help them with what they need and I want to return and help them.

This survivor of domestic violence, who had struggled to value her own worth, now identified as powerful and was prepared to lead other women to find their own *poder*. Clearly women were gaining a public voice and confidence in shaping the debate about access to health care for all.

During this same trip, I was invited to an LAN meeting held in a member's home in a colonia. Conducted entirely in Spanish, the meeting began with a presentation about reproductive justice (see fig. 1.1), using the definition provided by Asian Communities for Reproductive Justice and the SisterSong Women of Color Reproductive Justice Collective:[43] "Reproductive Justice is a vision and an approach for the work of a community-based organization with the goal of social justice and advocacy, created by women of color and characterized by intersectionality and inclusion. We will gain reproductive justice only when everyone has the economic, social and political power to make their own decisions regarding their bodies, health, sexuality, families, and reproduction." Reproductive justice actively supports women's right to terminate their pregnancies, which the women I am writing about here endorse even though most of them identify as Catholic, since abortion is a legal right. In this way they are similar to the thousands of believers, including nuns and priests, who have formed Catholics for Choice.

Following the presentation on reproductive rights, a representative of the Mexican consulate discussed the process of getting an identification card, whereby one could obtain a birth certificate either by contacting the Mexican state in which they were born or by obtaining certificates from elementary or high schools in Mexico. The women were highly engaged with the presentations,

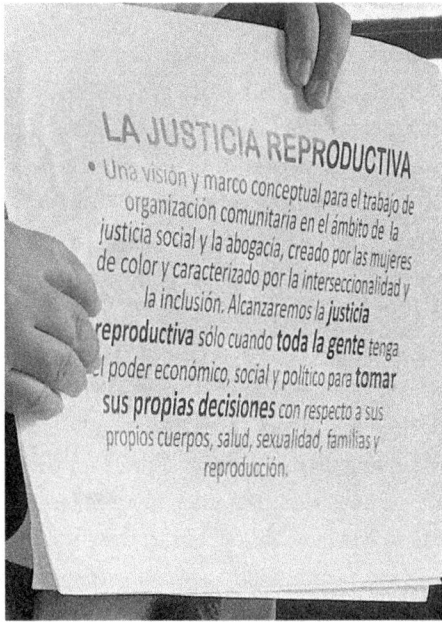

FIGURE 1.1 Definition
of reproductive justice.
Photo by Patricia Zavella.

posing lots of questions. Several confronted the consulate staff about their inability to secure identification cards in the past, opining, "The Mexican Consulate is no good for nothing!" The workshop organizers were impressed the women didn't let it go but instead insisted on describing their own experiences with the consulate to make their case.

Next, organizers from the National Latina Institute introduced their fall campaign. Specifically, they informed the attendees that the Trump administration had announced a proposed rule that would change "public charge" policies related to immigrants. Under long-standing policy, the federal government can deny an individual entry into the United States or adjustment to legal permanent resident status if the applicant is found likely to become a public charge. The proposed rule added the consideration of several government programs, including nonemergency Medicaid, Supplemental Nutrition Assistance Program, rental housing assistance programs, or Temporary Assistance to Needy Families, to public charge determinations. Critics predicted the change would lead to more uninsured individuals and negatively affect the health and financial stability of families, as well as the growth and healthy development of their children; further, they charged it would erode trust in public agencies and services, with a decline in crime reporting and use of programs that would affect immigrants and US citizens alike.[44] For example, the Department of Agriculture claims there are no consequences for authorized immigrants who participate in SNAP, yet many were avoiding accessing any benefits even before Trump's intended rule change.[45] By law the government must allow a period in which there is public commentary about such proposed policy changes; in this case, though the Trump administration formally adhered to this requirement, comments could only be submitted through an online portal that required an email address and comments in English.

After an explanation of the proposed policy changes and distribution of a Spanish fact sheet (that few actually read), the meeting organizers encouraged everyone to submit comments about how the proposed changes would affect them and their families. This entailed signing up for an email address for those who didn't have one, which worried women without documentation, so the organizers explained there was no way in which anyone could identify them if they had an email address. The women then wrote their comments in Spanish or dictated them to one of the organizers, who then translated them into English and helped the women submit them online, a slow, cumbersome process. After submitting their comments, the women played bingo and when winning would call out "¡Poderosa!" instead of "Bingo." Periodically throughout the day one of the LAN organizers would ask the entire group, "How are you feeling?" The women always responded, "¡Poderosa!"

It was instructive to participate in this form of civic engagement with women from the colonias. "Eveline," for example, an undocumented single parent whose husband had been deported to Mexico, had previously attended LAN's "Know Your Rights" workshops, as well as the leadership institute and monthly meetings. She advocates for herself in periodic meetings with ICE, which allows her to remain in the United States since her US-citizen son needs extraordinary health-care services. An entourage of LAN members accompanies Eveline during her periodic check-ins with ICE, holding signs and shouting chants demanding her release. She shared her comments about Trump's proposed public charge policy change: "This would affect my family because I do not have access to health care or healthy nutrition. This is personal to me because I have a son who has special needs for continuous medical care. I believe that this policy is not just for people who are looking to regularize their migratory status. I believe that assisted healthcare and healthy nutrition is a fundamental human right."

Eveline was proud that her knowledge of her rights has protected her. Like Consuelo, her experience circulates as a model of self-advocacy. LAN celebrated Eveline's one-year anniversary of being granted permission to remain in Texas with her citizen son. In her post on Facebook thanking people for their support, she said, "You poderosas are a light on the road. For whoever. Now we see how to move forward if there is a need."[46] Clearly Eveline and other women are internalizing the poderosa discourse and are vernacularizing it, critiquing how policies affect their own lives.[47]

I participated in LAN's three-day Leadership Development Institute held at the University of Texas Rio Grande Valley on October 26 to 28, 2018, which included colonia residents and undocumented participants. The purpose was to provide "a transforming weekend where visionary leaders are trained with tools and strategies ready to face and change the world!" Virtually all of the presentations were in Spanish, though translators were available. The institute began with a presentation I was asked to give about civic engagement, followed by presentations by state officials about voting rights and policies, within the context of Texas requiring identification to vote.

After my presentation, I invited questions and comments and there was a lively exchange. One of the themes was appreciation for my presentation, with several attendees expressing their gratitude in glowing terms. Afterward, several women introduced themselves and thanked me profusely. One even asked that we take a photograph together. I was touched by their effusive comments. The organizers explained that most of these women had completed very little schooling so the material was fresh to them. In discussing civic engagement that went beyond expected forms such as voting or attending city council meetings, I incorporated examples that pointed to their quotidian struggles and suggested that even if one cannot vote, helping others gain information and encouraging them to vote was important. I also introduced the notion of cultural citizenship, with examples such as their right to speak Spanish in public or display La Virgin de Guadalupe in their yards, and used photographs that resonated with their daily lives to illustrate my points. They felt validated by my suggestion that their quotidian practices of social and cultural citizenship were significant. It was a graphic reminder that women living in modest circumstances and who are unable to receive much schooling often internalize notions that their views do not matter. Leadership development that begins with women's experiences enables the process of *conocimiento* (consciousness), empowering them to recognize

FIGURE 1.2 Lucy Ceballos-Félix facilitating discussion at the Leadership Development Institute. Photo by Patricia Zavella.

their own struggles and rights, and encourages compassion for women in similar circumstances. According to Gloria Anzaldúa, also from the US-Mexico border region, conocimiento is a form of love that involves a multistage process of coming to awareness, and which begins with a jolt of understanding in relation to gender, family, and religion that leads to *nepantla*, a liminal space of openness to new perspectives.[48] As women commit to social activism, they move from conocimiento toward empowerment.

The institute training built on group agreements and definitions of key terms (capitalism, patriarchy, reproductive justice, etc.), and we were asked to engage with questions such as "What is transformational leadership?" "Who is a leader you admire and why?" and "What makes effective public speaking?" There were moments for reflection and discussion as well as collaboration in small groups about structural causes of health problems, represented visually by trees with deep roots. The twenty women who attended seemed very engaged, posing questions and offering observations based on their own experiences (see fig. 1.2). One lesson, which involved a mock demonstration, was about the ten roles related to staging an effective rally. Seven women disclosed they had never attended one before, and given their enthusiastic performances of the lesson's roles, I was surprised. For example, the "cheerleader," whose job was to promote active chanting, seemed to relish her role, and our march and chants—for example, "¡Aquí estamos y no nos vamos; abajo con ICE; somos poderosas!"— reverberated loudly through the campus halls.[49] On the final day, the participants graduated by having their photos taken while receiving certificates of completion and gifts. As an honorary LAN member, I was gifted a National Latina Institute T-shirt and graduated as well, a deeply meaningful gesture of inclusion. The women expressed their appreciation for the quality of the institute and how respectfully and warmly they were treated. María Bustamante, for example, was moved to share her written reflections with the group: "As we empower ourselves through consciousness, we prepare ourselves with value and without fear. We continue the struggle, opening pathways and transforming lives. In this great country that is formed by immigrants, we are part of this society. And we want the same rights to liberty and justice." Lucy Ceballos-Félix's final words were, "This is where the struggle receives breath. This is a commitment to yourselves." Afterward, we celebrated by taking a group photo, commemorating the transformation in which these women had participated, using the gender-neutral form of "we are powerful" (*somos poderosxs*). These women taught me a great deal about empowerment and the ways in which they attempt to change the structural inequalities and shaming discourses that shape their lives.

From Empowerment to Healing Justice and Open Resistance

These reproductive justice organizers and participants view their work as expressing deep spiritual meaning as well as political views. While some reproductive justice nonprofits incorporate spiritual practices directly into their organizational work, LAN does not.[50] However, the lead organizer identifies herself publicly as a Christian; many of the women are practicing Catholics, evident in the wearing of crosses or religious medals, and others are Protestants. During the focus group, an organizer mentioned that "the process of struggle is healing one's soul." When I asked her to clarify, another woman jumped in and stated, "Having a voice brings the power that carries women and transforms them. Gaining a voice is healing." Thus, expressing one's spiritual beliefs through social activism allows women to begin healing from the multiple traumas they have experienced as low-income racialized women who face life-threatening barriers to accessing health care and social equality.

These women also vernacularized their training by voicing their spiritual views about reproductive justice in their own ways. They informed me that prior to one of their meetings, the women decided to pray collectively for a member who was dying of cancer; generally speaking, they feel free to express their spiritual beliefs during meetings (see fig. 1.3). When using WhatsApp to communicate about upcoming events, many women send images of Christ or religious icons; they may also send blessings (e.g., "May God bless your day"). One of the organizers suggested they stop sending religious messages, even though she thought they were beautiful and she agreed with them, because the meetings are about politics. Nevertheless, the women continue to send religious greetings on WhatsApp. Overall, they are expressing nondenominal notions of spiritual poder—the power of collective prayer and blessings, good deeds, and mutual support, as well as the value of safe spaces—that gives them fortitude while respecting religious differences within the group. Thus, poder carries multiple meanings and is expressed in different registers. These women are fulfilling Loretta Pyles's notion of healing as "part of the path of individual and collective liberation from oppression, wherein liberation is a sense of feeling safe and at home in one's person."[51]

These women's sense of *empoderamiento* notwithstanding, reproductive governance continued during the Trump era. In 2017 the Republican-controlled Texas legislature furthered their antiabortion agenda through requirements that aborted or miscarried fetuses be cremated or interred and a "dismemberment ban" prohibiting dilation and evacuation abortions after fifteen weeks, which led to further lawsuits alleging the violation of the 2016 Supreme Court's ruling.[52] In 2018 the state of Texas directed eight million dollars (diverted from the Temporary Assistance for Needy Families program) to an organization that operates a network of clinics that dissuades people from seeking abortions and does not provide comprehensive health-care services.[53] In an *American Journal of Public Health* editorial, Gold and Hasstedt suggest that "Texas serves as a harbinger of what happens when family planning funding is slashed and the provider network dismantled. . . . These laws—enacted under the pretense of protecting women's health—actually threaten women's health and well-being."[54] Further, "increasingly this animus is extending beyond the provision of abortion services to women seeking contraceptive care, the family planning provider safety net, and now even to researchers looking to document the impact of policy changes. And all of that does not bode well for women and couples seeking to make the most basic decisions about childbearing."[55] In 2021 the Texas legislature passed SB8, which allows private citizens to sue anyone who helps a woman obtain an

FIGURE 1.3 Latina Advocacy Network speaker. Courtesy of the National Latina Institute for Reproductive Justice.

abortion after the detection of a fetal heartbeat; the plaintiffs may seek a penalty of $10,000, effectively barring most abortions. After the Supreme Court let the law stand, the Justice Department sued the State of Texas, arguing the law is unconstitutional because it deputizes individuals to enforce these new restrictions. While SB8 will likely come before the Supreme Court again, the cumulative effect of state-level legislative antiabortion activism is that in much of the South, the Southwest (except for Albuquerque and California), and the geographic center of the United States stretching from Texas to North Dakota, "abortion is becoming a much harder right for women to realize."[56]

Meanwhile, in addition to restricting abortion rights, Texas legislators passed a law that requires law enforcement officials in "sanctuary cities" to "comply with, honor and fulfill" ICE detainer practice and law, further entrenching legal violence toward migrants. The governor withheld state grant funds for Travis County programs (surrounding Austin) to ensure local compliance with the legislation. The Fifth Circuit appeals court supported key provisions of the bill, which made elected and appointed officials subject to a fine, jail time, and possible removal from office for violating all or parts of the legislation.[57] For its part, despite receiving more than a quarter of a million mostly critical comments, the Trump administration issued the above-discussed regulation denying legal permanent residence to those who have used government benefit programs, another policy designed to decrease immigration.[58] Around the same time, Trump also suggested that protesting should be illegal.[59] Clearly, enhanced reproductive governance and legal violence continue, especially in Texas with its 2021 attempt to bar abortion entirely.

In response to these developments, LAN has stepped up its activities as well. For example, they lobbied at the state capitol on behalf of expanding Medicaid in Texas, access to medical abortions, and "Rosie's Law," which would provide insurance coverage for low-income Texans seeking abortions who are enrolled in the Medicaid program.[60] They also support the federal Health Equity and Access under the Law Act, which would allow undocumented migrants to enroll in Medicaid, the Children's Health Insurance Program, or the ACA, and oppose the "gag rule" that makes it illegal for Title X providers (who provide other essential reproductive health care for those with low incomes) to refer patients for abortions.[61]

I asked LAN members what they thought of Trump's agenda and was told repeatedly a variant of one undocumented Mexicana's comment: "Things have changed a great deal, but we are not going to allow him to dominate us. We have rights here, and those are the ones that we are going to push for even though the president doesn't know our rights; he doesn't know that we are human beings. I don't know why he has such a twisted perception. So, we are showing him what it means to have rights!"

Las poderosas' contestation moved into open resistance during President Trump's visit to south Texas in 2019, when he rationalized the government shutdown by alleging there is a security crisis at the US-Mexico border. LAN members were out in full force, joining other demonstrators working on behalf of immigrant or labor rights. Their placards read, "Stand up against Trump's wall," "Our people do not need a wall at the border; they need health, dignity, and justice," and the gender-neutral "We are powerful!"[62] Across the street, the Trump supporters, mainly white people, wore MAGA hats and displayed anti-immigrant signs. Later, an "Emergency Rally" in Houston critiqued the "jailing" of migrant children and the Trump administration's practice of separating migrant children from their parents. With a history of brutal repression against Mexicans, protests in South Texas are often small and many undocumented residents feel intimidated about joining them, so these demonstrations were remarkable.[63]

During 2019 LAN's Facebook posts increasingly became more frequent and strident. There were numerous short film clips of women wearing blue and yellow National Latina Institute T-shirts and chanting, fists raised, "¡Somos poderosas!" LAN also posted articles on varied political issues on Facebook, including pieces discussing the range of gender identities, illuminating the needs of trans men for access to abortion, addressing white privilege and anti-Black racism in Latinx communities, protesting the shackling of women during childbirth, supporting paid family and medical leave, advocating the abolition of ICE, and instructing readers on how to make an effective argument that access to birth control is a human rights issue. Notably, LAN also posts images of events that include men.

LAN participants offer a vision of dynamic, ongoing social transformation. Responding to a question about the future, organizer Paula Saldaña said, "In my perfect valley there would be access to health services for everyone, including for immigrants. I would like immigration reform without barriers with a pathway to citizenship. Also, I would like that everyone has the opportunity to become well educated and that universities were not so expensive. I want the Valley to be prosperous and beautiful."[64] For her part, Lucy Ceballos-Félix stated, "I would like a future where there is real respect for human rights, where everyone has health, drivers' licenses, good jobs, and fair wages. I hope that someday we will have these in Texas. We have to continue struggling and educating our children and the coming generations so they continue our legacy. I truly believe that we will achieve this vision. Maybe it won't be during my generation but perhaps during my son's or my grandchildren's time. We will continue being united, continue the movement, and push forward the struggle."[65]

Conclusion

The combination of shifts in federal policy and enforcement practice with the goal of decreasing immigrant admissions, expanding deportations, and reproductive governance at the federal and state levels constitutes an extraordinary regime of power. However, we must historicize the contestation by Latinas in South Texas, who had already logged a decade of activism when Trump took office. Their activism, which ranges from acts of individual contestation to mass mobilization, is ongoing.[66]

The movement for reproductive justice mobilizes poder through grassroots organizing based in intersectionality that commits to the most vulnerable, engages in policy advocacy with a human rights frame expressing solidarity with transnational activism, and makes a claim on the state for the rights to health care and well-being that includes the undocumented. The Center for Reproductive Rights, with support by the National Latina Institute, won a key ruling by the Supreme Court that was directly informed by women's experiences of being denied access to health care. These activists aim to change the nature and distribution of power in Texas specifically and the United States more generally, moving the country toward social justice.

Moreover, these structurally vulnerable Latinas are engaging in a multigenerational process of empowerment that has been life-changing. Through trainings and self-reflexive workshops, women mobilize poder by expressing their compassion for others and gaining knowledge and skills—analyzing the causes of social problems and proposing remedies, writing and speaking publicly about their experiences, conducting their own breast examinations, finding and sharing resources in their communities, etc. This process of capacity-building leads them to embrace their right to publicly voice their critiques to those in power and find healing through struggle. They also mobilize multiple forms of power and inspire imaginaries in which everyone is afforded wellness and access to health care with dignity. LAN members suggest women's rights should be protected by the state and from the state and that men should support them as well. These women have vernacularized their training by incorporating their own notions of spirituality and claiming the power of collectivity and inclusion. The process of empoderamiento in places neglected by the state is built through accompaniment with reproductive justice advocates and making their communities places of possibility. As women enact this radicalized political subjectivity, they remind us that our work as ethnographers accompanying those living with structural vulnerabilities is to honor their expressions of poder on their own terms. Their model of working in coalitions with others for the rights of women and migrants may well have long-term consequences for the health and well-being of everyone.

Notes

1. In 2020 the Latina Advocacy Network changed its name to the Latina Institute for Reproductive Justice Texas and the national organization became the National Latina Institute for Reproductive Justice. I use the organizational names as they were when I conducted my research.

2. Bookman and Morgen 1988, 4.

3. Ibid.

4. Ibid. Emphasis in the original.

5. Gilmore 2008.

6. Tomlinson and Lipsitz 2019, 7, 155.

7. Craven and Davis 2013; Hale 2001; 2008.

8. Briggs 2017, 13.

9. Morgan and Roberts 2012, 243.

10. Guttmacher Institute 2014.

11. Menjívar and Abrego 2012.

12. A federal judge issued a national injunction in American Civil Liberties Union's 2019 class-action lawsuit, ordering the reunification of thousands of parents and children; yet, as of this writing, many have not been reunited ("Trump's Family Separation Crisis," ACLU, accessed August 10, 2019, aclu.org/families).

13. An intersectional approach includes epistemological practices that elicit alternative sources of knowledge about women's experiences; an ontological project that accounts for multiple identities and complex subjectivity and reconceptualizes agency while acknowledging the simultaneity of privilege and oppression; a form of coalitional politics grounded in solidarity rather than sameness; and a resistant imaginary that disrupts dominant social discourses about people of color and intervenes in historical memory, often using artwork or narratives (Crenshaw 1991; Hill Collins and Bilge 2016; May 2015).

14. Luna and Luker 2013; Price 2010; 2017; Ross and Solinger 2017; Silliman et al. 2004; Zavella 2017; 2020.

15. Pyles 2018, xix; my emphasis.

16. Abby Goodnough and Robert Pear, "Health Care Act Is Struck Down by Federal Judge," *New York Times*, December 15, 2018; Sarah Kliff, "Texas Is Waging a Battle to Overturn Obamacare," *New York Times*, June 27, 2020. On June 17, 2021, the Supreme Court ruled that the states and individuals who brought the lawsuit challenging the ACA's individual mandate do not have standing to challenge the law.

17. Bearak et al. 2020.

18. White et al. 2016.

19. Ibid.

20. Grossman et al. 2014, 73–74.

21. Adam Liptak, "Supreme Court Strikes Down Texas Abortion Restrictions," *New York Times*, June 27, 2016.

22. Passel, Cohn, and Rohal 2014; Manny Fernandez and Mitchell Ferman, "Migrant Centers Overflow, Deluging Shelters," *New York Times*, March 21,

2019; Miriam Jordan and Caitlin Dickerson, "End of a Policy Wasn't: The End of Migrant Family Separations," *New York Times*, March 9, 2019.

23. The 1996 Illegal Immigration Reform and Immigrant Responsibility Act gives local law enforcement agencies the power to enforce immigration law through Agreements of Cooperation in Communities to Enhance Safety and Security (Alvord, Menjívar, and Gómez Cervantes 2018).

24. Human Impact Partners and La Unión del Pueblo Entero 2018, 1; Esther Yu-hsi Lee, "Spate of South Texas Police Checkpoints Incite Fear among Immigrants," *ThinkProgress*, September 27, 2013.

25. Manny Fernandez, "Guardsmen, Seen and Unseen, Watch the Border," *New York Times*, April 12, 2018; Dara Lind, "Trump Is Mobilizing the National Guard to the US-Mexico Border for Literally No Good Reason," *Vox*, April 4, 2018.

26. Díaz-Barriga and Dorsey 2020.

27. Culture shift includes: (1) cultivating Latina leaders and spokespersons who can articulate the reproductive justice approach to issues; (2) conducting primary and secondary research to help them tailor their policy advocacy and messaging; (3) collaborating with artists and storytellers to create "culturally relevant and dynamic vehicles" for their core reproductive justice messages; and (4) cultivating relationships with traditional media and having a presence in social media in English and in other languages so as to reach broad and diverse audiences and influence opinion leaders (NLIRH 2013a, 6).

28. Pew Research Center 2014, 14.

29. Lake Research Partners 2011.

30. National Latina Institute for Reproductive Health, "Cabildeando Por Justicia Reproductiva en Texas," Latina Institute, April 10, 2019, https://medium.com /@latinainstitutecabildeando-por-justicia-reproductiva-en-texas-84ee9f0d6b3b..

31. Ibid., 7.

32. Center for Reproductive Rights, National Latina Institute for Reproductive Health, and SisterSong Women of Color Reproductive Justice Collective 2014.

33. Additional staff include a field coordinator, education manager, and senior trainer from New York City.

34. Center for Reproductive Health and National Latina Institute for Reproductive Health 2013, 2015a, 2015b; Mier et al. 2008; Sharkey, Dean, and Johnson 2011.

35. Day 2004. Nationally, of the 6.2 million women of reproductive age who are low-income and not US citizens, 46 percent are uninsured (Dawson and Sonfield 2020, 20).

36. Chilton et al. 2009; Tarasuk et al. 2015; Carney and Krause 2020.

37. NLIRH 2013b.

38. Núñez-Mchiri 2012, 115.

39. Balcázar et al. 2005; Forster-Cox et al. 2007; Philis-Tsimikas et al. 2011.

40. Hill 2003.

41. Latina Feminist Group 2001.

42. The hearing demonstrates the movement's use of cross-sector coalition building, storytelling as methodology, and strengths-based messaging (Zavella 2020).

43. Asian Communities for Reproductive Action and SisterSong 2005, 4.

44. National Latina Institute for Reproductive Health, National Asian Pacific American Women's Forum, and In Our Own Voice 2018. Twenty-five percent of children (over nineteen million) live in a family with an immigrant parent and 86 percent of these children were US citizens in 2018 (Henry K. Kaiser Foundation 2018, 1).

45. Caitlin Dewey, "Immigrants Are Going Hungry So Trump Won't Deport Them," *Washington Post*, March 16, 2017.

46. Facebook post, February 14, 2019.

47. Merry 2006; Gálvez 2013.

48. Anzaldúa 2015, 40.

49. Translation: We're here and we're not leaving; Down with ICE; We are powerful women.

50. Zavella 2020.

51. Pyles 2018, 134.

52. Mark Joseph Stern, "Texas' New Fetal Cremation Law Comes Close to Defying a Federal Court Order," *Slate*, June 8, 2017. Texas temporarily suspended abortions as "nonessential services" during the coronavirus pandemic (Sabrina Tavernise, "Texas Allows Abortions to Resume During Coronavirus Pandemic," *New York Times*, April 23, 2020).

53. Teddy Wilson, "Texas Takes Millions from Low-Income Families to Give to Anti-Choice 'Virtual' Clinic," *Rewire.News*, August 14, 2018, https://rewirenews group.com/article/2018/08/14/texas-takes-millions-from-low-income-families-to-give-to-anti-choice-virtual-clinic/. During the 2020 COVID-19 pandemic, abortion was ruled nonessential health services but was restored by the Fifth Circuit Court (Bearak et al. 2020; Tavernise 2020).

54. Gold and Hasstedt 2016, 970.

55. A Texas Health and Human Services Commission senior official who analyzed the effects of removing Planned Parenthood from the state's provider network was pressured to resign from his position (Gold and Hasstedt 2016, 971).

56. Wilson 2016, 89. Reproductive justice activists defeated an attempted municipal ban on abortion in Albuquerque (Zavella 2017).

57. Julián Aguilar, "Appeals Court Allows More of Texas' 'Sanctuary Cities' Law to Go into Effect," *Texas Tribune*, September 25, 2017, https:// www.texastribune.org/2017/09/25appeals-court-allows-more-texas-sanctuary -cities-law-go-effect/.

58. Michael D. Shear and Eileen Sullivan, "Policy Lets U.S. Reject the Poor for Green Cards," *New York Times*, August 13, 2019; Batalova, Fix, and Greenberg 2019.

59. Felicia Sonmez, "Trump Suggests That Protesting Should Be Illegal," *Washington Post*, September 5, 2018.

60. The proposed legislation is named after Rosaura Jiménez, who died in 1977 after an abortion administered by an unlicensed midwife in which she contracted a bacterial infection.

61. The gag rule imposes cost-prohibitive and unnecessary physical separation requirements on health centers that also provide abortions, requiring them to build separate entrances-exits, construct new centers, or hire a second staff; further, it clearly targets Planned Parenthood. Approximately 4 million patients rely on Title X health centers for reproductive health care (Gold and Sonfield 2019; Nia Martin-Robinson, "Black Women Deserve the Truth from Their Doctors. Trump Is Trying to Keep Us in the Dark," *Root*, March 8, 2019). As of this writing, the Ninth Circuit Court overturned a block on the gag rule (Helen Christophi, "'Devastating': Ninth Circuit Court Greenlights Trump's 'Gag Rule,'" *Rewire.News*, February 24, 2020.

62. Facebook post, February 18, 2019.

63. Paredes 1978; Montejano 1987.

64. NLIRH 2019, 5.

65. Ibid.

66. Alexander 2005.

CHAPTER TWO

Taíno and Afro-Taíno Narrative, Performance, and Resistencia in Puerto Rico and the United States

SHERINA FELICIANO-SANTOS

To identify as Taíno or Afro-Taíno is to resist a narrative that has already extinguished you. When your very subjectivity is posed as an impossibility, an unfeasible and, to some, ridiculous assertion, you become adept at representing yourself, caught between the stereotypes attached to who people think you should or shouldn't be and the practical experiences that have formed you as you are. How do you narrate yourself when the very possibility of your existence has been erased? How do you refuse a historical narrative that assumes your extinction while relying on the very institutions that produced such histories to increase your visibility and circulate your own version of history? Taíno and Afro-Taíno forms of resistance and refusal are entangled in their goals of creating community and obtaining visibility within their projects of cultural reclamation. Puerto Rico's consecutive colonialisms have shaped Taíno and Afro-Taíno strategies of community formation and of making visible their continued and contemporary presence. By listening to Taíno and Afro-Taíno narratives and performances, I engage with modes of knowing and making sense that may be neither canonical nor agreed upon by either the general public or scholarship, as well as with the critiques they engender of Puerto Rican national discourses of identity and belonging and broader concerns about sovereignty, crisis, and Puerto Rican futures.

Taíno and Afro-Taíno politics of identity and its related forms of refusal and resistance make visible the multiple subjectivities and positionalities produced through the successive colonialities of the Spanish and US empires. Claiming to be descendants of the Caribbean population who first encountered European colonizers, Taíno and Afro-Taíno are also claiming to be descendants of the first Indigenous group narrated to have become extinct as a result of colonization in the Americas. The Taíno struggle is telling of the mechanisms of empire and the national projects it enables. As nationals of an often-erased colony of the United States, Puerto Ricans as a whole are positioned as subaltern political subjects within the United States. However, the production of a national Puerto Ricanness in opposition to the United States has produced its own entanglements and hierarchies embedded in a hispanocentric rhetoric of racial blending. In Puerto Rico, claims to be Taíno, Afro-Taíno, or Afro-descended are rejections of national projects based on erasures of rights, trivializations of identity, and denials of lived inequalities.

For the Indigenous Taíno and Afro-Taíno activists among whom I have conducted research in Puerto Rico since 2006, the space of their resistance and struggle is marked by tensions and alternatives: alternative pasts, presents, and futures through which they highlight their different ways of doing and being and knowing. I trace their resistances and refusals, and the forms of struggle and protest they engender, in both the context of their development and continuity and the context of their challenge to the colonial discourses of racial blending that became hegemonic in twentieth- and twenty-first-century Puerto Rico. The recent surge in the number of people who publicly claim their Afro-Taíno and Taíno heritage is a rejection of the hierarchy implicit in the Puerto Rican racial triad and the orientations toward Spanishness, Americanness, and whiteness that it has encouraged. For example, Boricua musician Princess Nokia stated in an interview with *Teen Vogue* in 2017:

> Being an afro-Indigenous woman is a large part of me, to the core. I celebrate it more than anything. We are trying to heal from that colonization, that slavery that our country suffered from. How does one heal 500 years of whitewashing, and rape, genocide, disease, suffering? One claims the beauty of their ancestors. Young people are the fearless voices of our ancestors. We have the luxury to say, "I am African, I am Native American, I am Indigenous, I am all of these things that my grandparents were too misinformed, too ashamed, too uneducated to claim." Afro-Indigenous identity has been swept under the rug for a long time.[1]

The alternative historical threads and discursive spaces offered by the Taíno speak to the *resistencia* and transformative potential of Taíno political, economic, and narrative refusals and political resistances. Resistencia, as used by Taíno social actors, refers to the forms of ancestral resistance that have allowed them to persist in the face of historical genocide and colonial erasures.

Identifications with Taíno and Afro-Taíno narratives, subjectivities, and agencies frame the forms of decolonizing action and activism that inform many of their environmental, economic, and political projects. Here, I draw on anthropologist Audra Simpson's definition of the term "refusal" to indicate both the awareness and ongoing repudiation of the social discourses and structures that attempt to constrain Indigenous sovereignty and epistemologies in favor of white forms of governance and recognition. "Resistencia," on the other hand, is a term I use to describe the ways in which people navigate within these forms of governance and recognition to transform social discourses and structures that would attempt to constrain them.

Taíno and Afro-Taíno in Puerto Rico have long been resistant to historical narratives erasing their survival from Caribbean history. Through their alternative historical narrations, decolonizing epistemologies, and revitalization of Indigenous practices and spaces, many Taíno activists have been actively engaged in different scales and domains of agricultural, economic, and political advocacy for decades. After Hurricane Maria hit Puerto Rico in September of 2017, many Taíno activists on the island and in the diaspora coalesced in a call for a return to Taíno knowledge to protect Puerto Rico, some seeing the hurricane as a foretold sign that the island was on the wrong track to development. Coupled with the economic crisis, the post-Maria, Trump-era federal and state governmental response made explicit that for Taíno activists their revitalization was not only a matter of acknowledgment but also of the island's survival.

This chapter examines "Taíno: A Symposium in Conversation with the Movement," which took place on September 8, 2018. The symposium was related to a larger museum exhibition at the Smithsonian's National Museum of the American Indian, titled *Taíno: Native Heritage and Identity in the Caribbean* and held from July 2018 to October 2019. I analyze the symposium as a kind of event that encourages the public performance of dialogue among key figures around contemporary issues and concerns. Within this site of performative dialogue, I am interested in the stances taken, positions put forward, and narratives claimed by different Taíno and Afro-Taíno leaders and how they reflect broader patterns of refusal and resistance.

Performing Taínoness, Interrupting Figures of Puerto Ricanness

During the event, some of the Taíno panelists and audience members were dressed in their finer event regalia. The younger and middle-aged women often wore *naguas*, skirts with two panels of fabric (usually made of cotton, or *sarobei*) held together by a cord that surrounds the lower waist. Many of the older women wore loose and simple shift-style dresses with short sleeves. The fabric was often painted with Taíno symbols, and Caribbean shells and feathers adorned both the fabric on the dresses and the cotton bands in their hair. They wore jewelry made of autochthonous Caribbean seeds and shells and simple leather sandals. The men generally wore plainer clothes, including T-shirts proclaiming their Taíno identity, and sported jewelry made from seeds and shells that indicated their affiliation. Some Taíno women also chose to dress in plain clothes, wearing jewelry or T-shirts that indicated their Taíno identity.

A respected elder from a well-known Taíno organization with whom I had spent a lot of time since early in my research, Abuela Shashira, was adamant about Taíno people wearing their Taíno event regalia. Her visibility was an important articulation of her survival and presence as a Boricua Taíno person. She wanted to center Taíno aesthetics and visually represent her resistance to the logic of Caribbean Indigenous erasure. But the resistance was not only visual — it was also aural. Her feet were adorned with shell anklets that resonated with each step. Similarly, people in the audience would often employ maracas, fotutos, and long, handheld rattles made of shells to mark their excitement over the panelists' statements with Taíno sound. In the same aural vein, some Taíno spoke in English while others did so in Spanish. Taíno words were strewn throughout to mark the discursive space as a Taíno one. And thus, while the event was held in a generic museum auditorium, the space that day was decidedly Taíno.

These performances of Taínoness were key in highlighting both the visibility and cultural continuity of Taíno Indigeneity in Puerto Rico. They served as a rejection of narratives of romanticized mixture that erased the multiple histories of different Puerto Rican populations and discursively obscured differences in the understandings and privileges accorded to different experiences of Puerto Ricanness. The image of Taíno and Afro-Taíno participants dressed in a variety of ways and speaking a number of languages also had the effect of interrupting an anthropological epistemology of cultural cohesion and continuity. The appearance of the participants stood in contrast to more typical notions of belonging and identification, which are often circumscribed by discourses that attempt to define the permissible bounds of the nation and the identity of its population. In Puerto Rico, two figurations of identity have been especially significant in this delimitation.

The first, the racial triad, is a racial discourse that delineates the racial inheritance of each and every Puerto Rican as one premised on the mixture of African, Taíno, and Spanish culture and populations. In practice the politics of racialization and racism in Puerto Rico was much more complicated. It articulated a ranked hierarchy of race that either promoted, trivialized, or erased the extent and type of contribution each race was understood to make to the triad, in opposition to its claims of racial and cultural equality and harmony. While in formerly Spanish colonized Latin American countries in South and Central America the process of mestizaje "was oriented toward the exploitation of native people," and in North America, settler colonialism was oriented "toward the removal of native people to make way for English settlers and other imported and forced laborers from the Old World,"[2] the process in Puerto Rico arguably reflected aspects of both processes. Unlike other Spanish colonies on the continental mainland, Indigenous genocide in the Caribbean was widespread and the Native was discursively disappeared during the sixteenth century. The justification for the forced migration of African and Indigenous enslaved labor was the lack of a native population to exploit for the economic gain of Spanish colonizers. The early stages of the Spanish conquest and colonization in the Hispanic Caribbean, at least as historically narrated, resembled the processes involved in settler colonialism elsewhere. Anthropologists Lourdes Gutiérrez Najera and Korinta Maldonado describe settler colonialism's role as "a structuring force that in coproduction with the transatlantic slave trade, indentured labor, and other forms of racial ordering [enables] particular racial logics and forms of exclusions integral to global capital and empire."[3] Thus, the Caribbean's layers of colonialism encompass both racial blending rhetoric and settler colonial policies, making each, in turn, productive analytical lenses for understanding the ways in which the racial triad contained race and the histories of conquest, genocide, colonialism, and enslavement upon which it was premised. Additionally, the process of disappearing the island's Natives and banalizing the African experience of enslavement, making them both the generic heritage of all Puerto Ricans but the exclusive heritage of none, distanced any current European-descended Puerto Ricans from explicitly acknowledging or being held accountable for their racial and inherited privileges. In the context of Puerto Ricans in the diaspora, this racial framing is further complicated by Taíno and Afro-Taíno encounters with US racial structures and projections.[4]

The second figuration of Puerto Ricanness, anchored by the archetypal figure of the Jíbaro, centers Spanish heritage and moral values. Often figured as a hard-working, rural, white (perhaps tanned by work in the sun), heterosexual,

Catholic, and Spanish-speaking male peasant and family man, the archetypal Jíbaro has discursively delimited the bounds of acceptable and respectable Puerto Ricanness for the majority of the nation. Racial, sexual, religious, linguistic, and gendered ideologies are moored by the archetype all the while also underscoring the majority of the population's value and role as laborers and family builders in their position of reproducing the nation. In practice, however, this idealized and celebrated archetype was often removed from the reality of the island's actual rural peasant population, which was often neither white, Catholic, nor part of a nuclear family structure. The actual rural peasant population was often associated with its limited school education, dialect, lack of modernity, and need for elite interventions.

These two figurations of Puerto Ricanness have both overdetermined discourses of national cultural identity and interstitially left spaces for yet undetermined or underdetermined identifications on the ground. They have also been contested by both Black and Indigenous Puerto Ricans who refuse the multiracial narrative and its eclipsing of the inequities it encompasses. Instead, they claim and identify with the histories that have produced them as racialized subjects and critique the institutions that reproduce their exclusion and marginalization. Race scholar Jared Sexton critiques discourses of multiracialism in the context of the United States insofar as they conceal racial slavery and genocidal conquest by dehistoricizing race and erasing the fields of power involved in racialization and instead making race and racialization a matter of the "dubious phenomenology of perception."[5] By refusing and challenging the forms of multiracialism and racialization prevalent within Puerto Rico, Taíno join Afro–Puerto Ricans and Puerto Ricans in the US diaspora, among other marginalized groups, who have long publicly criticized ideologies and discourses of Puerto Ricanness that exclude those who speak English, are Black, are LGBTQIA+, non-Christian, and so on. For many of the Taíno and Afro-Taíno Puerto Ricans with whom I have spoken and whom I have observed, this refusal is about recognizing both the histories of violence, silence, and power that have produced them and their identification as Taíno or Afro-Taíno.

Rather than resist, most Taíno and Afro-Taíno refuse the legitimacy of histories that exclude them and discourses that erase them. In the context of refusal, they imagine political futures otherwise and outside of the hegemonic confines of the colonial and colonized nation. However, in the pursuit of political rights and visibility on the ground they often engage in a politics of resistance that subjects them to institutional, governmental, and academic scrutiny.[6] Their refusal of versions of Puerto Ricanness that erase them is premised upon their figuring of an alternative narrative of their survival and future continuity. Like anthropologist Michel-Rolph Trouillot, historian Manning Marable argues "that *history itself* is a central site of collective experience for the articulation of power relations and social hierarchies within any society. Historical narratives—the stories we teach about past events—become frameworks for understanding the past and for interpreting its meaning for our own time and in our individual lives. . . . These elements of our shared history thus help to influence public policy and the future direction of subsequent events and decisions that have not yet occurred."[7] Thus, the suppression of history is a technology of power that preserves power and domination. Anthropologist Amy Den Ouden has shown how settler colonial processes have both trivialized Indigenous reckonings of their own histories and detached them from their lands in order to justify colonial intrusions and claims to those very lands.[8] Thus, in refusing the dominant narrative, many Taíno activists argue that they embrace a decolonial stance by upholding family histories and practices as anchors of their identity as well as calling out the oppressive histories that have produced their racial subjectivities: the genocide and erasure of Taíno peoples and the consecutive enslavement and forced migration of African peoples.

By making explicit the racial positionalities that have informed their ancestral histories and their own experiences, the Taíno and Afro-Taíno decry attempts to silence and reorient them toward Latinx and Caribbean forms of whiteness as the measure of value, worthiness, and access. As argued by anthropologist Christopher Loperena, "white socio-spatial epistemologies" produced through mestizaje discourses materially and politically render invisible contemporary Indigenous people and negate "Indigenous and black territorial claims."[9] Given how these racialized national projects have operated throughout the Americas, Taíno and Afro-Taíno have sought transnational forms of coalition with other Native, Black, and Afro-Native peoples who have similarly experienced white settler violence and erasure. This politics and the dialogues that ensue, in turn, make possible and viable the envisioning of other kinds of possibilities and futures.

Afro-Taíno, in particular, upset racial ordering projects by being critical of the goal and orientation of racial blending rhetorics and rejecting the idea that Black and Indigenous are necessarily separate categories. Pointing to the entangled histories of marronage and Taíno hiding from colonizing forces, they see themselves as the resilient and enduring descendants of those who refused the

Spanish colony and enslavement and found alternative ways of creating solidarity and survivals. Their own visibility is often doubly questioned insofar as their
claims are measured against an optics of Taíno invisibility and Black hypervisi-
bility. This positionality resonates with historian and ethnographer Paul López
Oro's discussion of Garínagu, in which he describes the limitations of engaging
in an Afro-Latin@ movement that has trouble incorporating "their afroindigenous culture."[10] Similarly, groups with Afro-Native ancestry in the United States
have struggled with federal recognition mechanisms that assume and produce
racial categories as biologically distinct from and exclusive of each other, rather
than as vectors of political struggle and disenfranchisement.[11] Settler claims of
Indigenous extinction became the measure of Indigenous illegitimacy or authenticity. The concept of sincerity, instead, focuses on the never completely
knowable interiority of what people do as they navigate their worlds.[12]

In what follows I discuss Taíno narrative practices in order to establish how
Taíno build community and circulate their histories and forms of knowing. Engaging with these narratives requires also acknowledging Taíno epistemologies
and cosmologies. In my broader research with the Taíno, this meant understanding the role of abuelas in remembering and telling familial stories, teaching
Taíno practices and ethics, and socializing the younger generations into appropriate behaviors; being aware of the role of nonhuman entities and ancestral
spirits in circulating knowledge; and remaining cognizant of the forms of seeing,
hearing, and meaning-making that allow living people to communicate beyond
that which is explicit and more obviously visible.[13] These narratives are embodied
in the movements, sounds, and story-telling styles among the Taíno presenters
at the Smithsonian symposium and in the audience's responses, both of which
in their performance served as testament to Taíno survival and a living display
of their cultural commons.

Resisting and Visibility at the Museum

The Smithsonian National Museum of the American Indian (NMAI) in New
York City could be considered a contentious site at which to give a platform
to Taíno refusals and resistencias, given its role in representing, othering, and
crystallizing Indigenous and minoritized groups and their cultural heritage
in the past. Anthropologists have argued that representation in government
museum sites comes with a cost for those being represented and recognized,
namely, dependence on the recognition and authorization of the colonial state

apparatus.[14] However, given the disjunctures inherent to the Taíno experience of narrative and discursive erasures, the museum exhibit was also understood to serve as a site of negotiation and reassembling their legibility and legitimacy to a broader audience. Excited for the exhibit's potential citational trajectories, Taíno present at the event were largely enthusiastic about what the Smithsonian exhibit signified, while also being critical of the display of Indigenous cultural heritage as museum artifacts for public visual consumption at a site many Taíno and Boricuas generally would not be able to access. Primarily, for Taíno attendees the greatest focus was on how the exhibit's temporal representation of the Taíno in terms of their immediate past, present, and future empowered them in the rewriting of the historical attempts to erase their presence. Their awareness of the potential of this exhibit at a high-prestige museum to set new paradigms of knowing about the Taíno was understood as also securing their future engagements and potentials, by intervening in how they are remembered, known, and projected into the future, thus transforming the terms of how they are recognized by dominant colonial institutions. They saw their participation in this project as having two representational impacts: (1) interrupting their chronotopic representation as past to instead be understood as present and continuing into the future and (2) as a heightened moment in the project of building a new semiotic register through which their presence, actions, and beliefs could become indexical of and socially recognizable as legitimately Taíno. For the Taíno, their resistencia and vision of a future otherwise are grounded in alternative trajectories, logics, and ways of knowing, which though valued among themselves have often been couched within and illegible to more widespread discourses of the Puerto Rican nation. Indeed, these latter position experiences and filial trajectories claimed by the Taíno as banal, ignorant, and confused.

The symposium examined here was part of a larger exhibition event years in the making. Since at least 2015, the NMAI had planned, curated, and implemented an exhibit with the goal of documenting and representing Taíno survival and perseverance into the contemporary era. The symposium itself was organized as a complement to the exhibition and was a daylong event with three panels, each temporally organized. In preparation, the organizer arranged for the speakers from each panel to conduct a conference call in late July to decide upon key questions the moderator might draw on to guide the conversation as well as to get a sense of everyone's introductory remarks.

On September 7, I visited the NYC exhibit with members of my panel, including the Cacica Anaca and Abuela Shashira, the leader and elder of the

Puerto Rico–based Consejo General de Taínos Borincanos. I had met them and researched with them and their group since 2007 and was interested in their reactions to a museum exhibit at the Smithsonian. The exhibit itself presented a cogent narrative of Taíno perseverance. The rooms comprising it were filled with Taíno material culture, including ceremonial objects—such as *cemíes* and musical instruments—and everyday objects such as clay pots and eating utensils, enclosed in plexiglass. Some of the pieces had been found in pre-Columbian sites, others were made by contemporary artisans. On the walls, there were posters of newspaper articles, pictures, and Taíno art that presented a loose timeline of Taíno survival and activity. During our tour, the abuela commented several times that it was a bit contradictory for the exhibit to display Taíno artifacts that should be in Puerto Rico. Indeed, her comments highlighted the contrasting spatiotemporalities of an exhibit meant to highlight Taíno continuities with reference to pre-Columbian artifacts staged in an air-conditioned museum in New York. She spoke to the tensions inherent to staging inclusion at a federal government–funded museum, the same government that would never be able to officially recognize the Taíno and which had recently tightened its wallets vis-à-vis Puerto Rico in the wake of the economic crisis and Hurricane Maria. Looking at how these sacred objects, transformed by the museum setting into archaeological artifacts, were presented to the audience for their visual consumption and future conservation, I understood the abuela's concern and critique of the anthropological and museum enterprise, asking us to consider "Who is this for?" and to what ends. Committed to her politics of resistance, the abuela temporarily accepted this compromise with the anthropological museum in the interests of greater Taíno visibility and narrative repair. Upon leaving the exhibit, a few European tourists asked the abuela and Anaca if they were "real Indians" and proceeded to ask for a picture—they too were treated as an extension of the exhibit. Indeed, museums such as the NMAI have a fraught relationship with Indigenous representation and political projects. Historian Amy Lonetree explains how the initial NMAI exhibits in Washington, DC, catered to the comfort of an imagined white audience, sanitizing Indigenous histories in a postmodern appeal to the questioning of academic histories rather than centering Native histories and ways of knowing.[15] This resonates with the abuela's criticism of the exhibit, as she gazed at these sacred objects, wondering who the intended audiences were, if not her and her people.

Tensions among different Taíno groups were common during my research, often the result of misunderstandings and competition among groups over the

Taíno narrative and future directions. On the day of the symposium itself, I could sense the tension among Taíno from different organizations, yet I also sensed a shared commitment to the event and the importance of a performance, and perhaps an attainment, of unity. The first and last panels were largely composed of Boricua Taíno telling their own stories as testimony of resistencia and survival. The narrative *testimonios* that follow often start with each person's authenticating narrative of being Taíno and organizational affiliation.[16] Many considered the impact of Hurricane Maria in marking their personal and organizational time, as well as highlighting its significance as a site of trauma and potential unification. While the symposium was planned well ahead of Maria, its timing almost a year after the hurricane was understood as significant in maintaining bonds among oftentimes contentious groups. During the symposium, Taíno activists used their narratives to explain past misunderstandings among different organizations. However, many of these narratives revealed tensions among the different strategies, sites of resistance, and visions for Taíno futures. For example, not all groups are equally invested in, and in fact some refuse, government and international recognition through the United Nations or the US or Puerto Rican governments.[17] Rather, they seek interactional and felt acknowledgment, the right to Taíno ceremonial sites, as well as a voice in protecting Puerto Rico's environmental futures. Lastly, most, if not all, Taíno present at the exhibit called upon all Taíno to get involved in mobilized action on behalf of environmental, social, and political causes. Throughout, the narrative style often relied on affect and personal experience as a way of telling a larger political story and calling for action.

Narrating Resistencias: Abuelas and Refusing Extinction

I also [for] at one time or another thought that I was the only Taíno left, as the only person that identified as Taíno, I think a lot of people here can relate to that. One summer I had come back from a pow wow, and there was an event at Central Park and that day a friend of mine was Cherokee, says hello to me and then I tell him "Yeah man, here I am again, the last Taíno" and he goes, "No, no, no, no, there's more." I was like "What do you mean?" and he goes like "That guy right there is a Taíno."

In the above excerpt, Quisqueyan Taíno leader Jorge Estevez explains in English how he used to think he was the only Taíno left. In his opening statement at the

Smithsonian symposium, he narratively positioned how he experienced being Taíno, as feeling that he was the last in his line of Taíno people, often seeking out members of North American Native Nations at events and pow wows in order to connect with his Indigenous roots. It wasn't until he was an adult that he connected with a nascent Taíno organization full of people who like him were also Taíno. Jorge's speech continued and described the birth and growth of Taíno organizations as more people sought to politically, spiritually, and culturally organize around their shared ancestry and identification.

What are the conditions under which all of these people could be simultaneously individually aware of their Indigenous heritage while *not* being aware that there were other Taíno? With a focus on Guyana, English professor Shona Jackson sheds some insight on this issue. She argues that the relationship into which Blacks and Indigenous peoples "are placed under colonialism . . . is definitive for Caribbean modernity."[18] By rendering unimaginable the complex and contemporaneous colonial relationships of Blackness and Indigeneity, settler colonial narratives that assume that Indigenous genocide was complete and that the Native population was replaced by enslaved Africans have shaped the subjectivities available to non-European populations. The risk of enslavement impacted the decision of many Indigenous people to make themselves less visible to the invaders. American studies professor Alyosha Goldstein argues in reference to the Puerto Rican Taíno that "there are those who prefer not to be known or to be illegible to colonial epistemologies."[19] These acts of what anthropologist Elizabeth Povinelli calls "camouflage" were, according to political scientist Anthony Castanha, strategies of survival chosen by Taíno as they fled away from the eye of the Empire and established Indigenous communities in the mountains where they could practice their way of life.[20] In my interviews with some Taíno, they explained how these communities were in effect Afro-Indigenous, as many who were escaping enslavement came to these communities as well, blending practices, livelihoods, and beliefs throughout the Spanish colonial period. Some Taíno explained that the language shift from Taíno language to Spanish was a result of generations of camouflage and linguistic adaptation, where a rural variety of Caribbean Spanish eventually came to be the language of the Taíno even while they maintained their identity and cultural practices.

This pattern, they argue, held for a long time—until the American invasion of Puerto Rico and the eventual declaration of Puerto Rico as a commonwealth of the United States alongside the industrialization and modernization projects of a then-nascent governmental structure. Operation Bootstrap, for example, encouraged the labor migration of people from rural areas of Puerto Rico to cities in both Puerto Rico and the United States. Many families moved to cities such as Philadelphia, Chicago, and New York in the United States, encouraged by the availability of work in factories. The cultural counterpart of Operation Bootstrap, called Operation Serenity, was operationalized through a series of efforts, including the Institute of Puerto Rican Culture (ICP).[21] ICP's efforts were aimed at consolidating a Puerto Rican national shared culture by creating national parks, promoting the myth of racial blending, and holding festivals highlighting specific aspect of Puerto Rican culture.[22] Within these efforts, national parks were often created around Taíno ceremonial centers and the Taíno were made into symbols of the nation, claimable by all Puerto Ricans as a heritage, yet undeclarable as an identity.[23] For people who identified as *Indio*, this had two notable effects: (1) a loss of de facto rights to their ceremonial heritage and (2) the moving of families from their long-standing lands and ways of living to cities, including the education of new generations of United States citizens in the Puerto Rican public education system where they would be explicitly taught that all Taíno has been made extinct in the sixteenth century. These events are in line with many of the narratives of Taíno survival shared with me, where a clear pattern emerges in terms of the timeline along which Taíno traditional practices and Indian self-awareness were lost. In fact, the historical resistencia of the Taíno is often attributed to abuelas, who maintained their traditional practices and sought to teach them to their children and grandchildren, with different levels of success. For example, during the third panel on Taíno futures, Tai Pelli, a Boricua Indigenous leader affiliated with the United Confederation of Taíno People (UCTP) based in New York City, explained how her claiming of her Taíno identity was only possible due to the resistencia of many women before her: "If we are here it is due to the survival of those women, especially those women who had to carry the children that resulted from rape, just imagine the resistencia that woman would have had to have to raise the child of those people."[24]

Considering that family connections to different ethnoracialized ancestries in Puerto Rican families are relatively common, some cases reflect not just a Taíno Indigenous heritage, but also an African diasporic one. Peggy Alvarado, who was also on the third panel, is a published Dominican–Puerto Rican poet and educator based in the Bronx who claims both her Taíno and African heritage, in line with an increasing list of people in their thirties and younger who explicitly claim their African and Indigenous heritage while rejecting the European root that was historically foregrounded in Puerto Rican and Dominican discourses of racial blending. In describing her own heritage and practice, she mentions (in English) both Taíno and African ancestral practices: "The way I have been taught by my elders, the way I've been taught by elders in Lucumí, Palo, and Taíno . . ."

As the only person on the panel to explicitly to lay claim to both her African and Taíno heritage, Peggy Alvarado spoke to an emerging and growing audience of young people with similar backgrounds who actively challenge settler-colonial and mestizaje myths in the Spanish Caribbean by claiming two heritages often posed in contradiction to each other. Balanani, another Taíno leader based in Puerto Rico and affiliated with another organization, Concilio Taíno Guatu-Ma-Cu a Boriken, described her own experience of recognizing her Taíno roots after moving to Puerto Rico to live with her grandparents and great-grandparents several decades ago. Like other panelists, she acknowledges the role of her abuela in grounding her Indigenous identity:

> Mamá teaches me about plants, she would tell me, "We come from the Indians, always remember that, we come from Toro Negro," and I was living at the skirts of El Yunque, and she would tell me some things like what we heard this morning, many times we say, "Grandma is crazy, I am not going to listen to abuelita," but I listened to my great-grandmother out of respect, all of this makes sense to me.

In Balanani's narrative, she explained how after migrating to Puerto Rico at age eleven after being born in New York City, she was able to spend time with her great-grandmother, who was born in the early 1890s. Balanani related how she took seriously her great-grandmother's identification as an India from Toro Negro, thus leading her to claim her Indigenous heritage herself. Balanani's history illustrated some of the transitions that were precipitated by the island's industrialization efforts: her family's move to the United States, the younger and more educated members of the family dismissing the great-grandmother's family story, and Balanani's eventual move to Puerto Rico with her family as manufacturing jobs in the United States urban centers started diminishing. Balanani explained that Taíno resistencia depends on people talking to their elders and "continuing the knowledge, sitting down with our abuelas, and us continuing with our daughters, granddaughters, nieces." The future abuelas will maintain Taíno histories through their continuation of Taíno knowledge. Taking the abuelas' narratives seriously is a theme in narratives that aim to offer an alternative historical thread and timeline that showcase survival. Within these narratives, it is the rejection of the abuela's narrative in a modernizing Puerto Rico that leads to the widespread acceptance of Taíno extinction.

Taíno Futures: Responding to Economic and Natural Crises

Puerto Rican economic crises have been tied to a number of US economic policies on the island, including the expiration in 2005 of tax breaks initially meant to encourage the presence of US industries in Puerto Rico. Exacerbating this situation was the impact of the Great Recession in 2007–2008, the tariffs that affect the Puerto Rican ability to import and export goods independently, and a lack of autonomy in determining Puerto Rican economic debt repayments.[25] Eventually, the debt crises led the federal government to name a highly unpopular federal oversight board for Puerto Rico and to implement a debt repayment program that prioritized organizing the budget by making payments to banks over local education, infrastructure, and social welfare investments.[26]

When Hurricane Maria touched ground in Puerto Rico in September 2017, it only exacerbated and brought to light deep-seated problems in the local economy and in the limited autonomy built into the island's colonial framework.[27] Anthropologist Yarimar Bonilla has described how the hurricane "laid bare the forms of structural violence and racio-colonial governance that had been operating in Puerto Rico for centuries," revealing the "coloniality of disaster."[28] Several panelists at the symposium made clear that Hurricane Maria had a great impact on them and on their sense that a mobilization of Taíno traditional knowledge was imperative. Importantly, they saw the crisis precipitated by the hurricane as a manifestation of the deity Jurakán, which plays the role of cleansing and bringing things to light. Abuela Shashira of the General Council of Taíno explained in her speech at the symposium how the hurricane not only came to cleanse but also to call Taíno in the diaspora to return to the island, lifting the top layer of her dress to reveal a painted image of a petroglyph of the Taíno deity of fertility and land:

This Caguana you see here, this is your mother earth who wanted to come with me, she is waiting for the children of my Boriken, Puerto Rico needs you, not so much because of María, because I say that María went to clean up, María went to clean up lots of putrefaction that was in my land. My land needs you to continue fighting to save her.

Abuela Shashira physically laminated the Caguana on her own body and clamored, cried, and claimed the audience as Taíno, imploring them to return to the island. The hurricane is thus positioned as an event in an ongoing crisis in Puerto Rico that needs the diasporic Taíno to intervene and join the fight on the island's behalf. Later on, the theme of Hurricane Maria was brought up again by the panel moderator, Cuban Taíno leader, and scholar affiliated with the Taíno Nation of the Antilles, Dr. Jose Barreiro. He posed the following question to the panelists:

> What about the consciousness of Taíno, of community and of caring for each other contributed to the efforts after Maria? . . . How did the Taíno community in Puerto Rico respond to the issues of devastation of Maria?

Dr. Barreiro connected the Taíno diaspora's mobilization after María to their conceptions of community and the land. Among the three panelists, two were based in the diaspora and one was based in Puerto Rico, where she personally experienced Hurricane Maria and its devastating aftereffects. The panelists all converged on a narrative of mobilization and support among the diaspora and those on the island in the wake of the hurricane. They also agreed that many of the issues that led to the hurricane's scale of devastation preceded María. The first panelist to answer Barreiro's question, Tai Pelli, described what she saw as a beautiful form of unity that emerged:

> The second we had an opportunity to be able to send things to the island, we were doing it. . . . I saw unity from all the organizations and individuals that identify as Taíno and that for me is a beautiful thing. The other part is that I think that the traditional knowledge, that is a thing that we can help with and contribute.

In making an argument for the role of Taíno traditional knowledge as a contribution to be made in the wake of Maria's disaster, Tai Pelli stressed the importance of teaching Indigenous knowledge of medicinal plants, of agriculture, and of communal sharing as tangible, yet less material, contributions ahead of a future disaster, in addition to the material objects of food, clothing, lamps, and batteries that were sent immediately after Maria. The next panelist, Balanani, explained how after Maria, she relied on her ancestors' example to live on the island when she encountered herself without electricity for six months, without access to groceries, fresh water, and in the midst of losing several of her loved ones.

My ancestors didn't have electricity, I was without electricity in my house for six months . . . that maybe the plant was taken but underneath in the ground is the batata, under there is the yuca . . . but in the same way that it destroyed it also provided, because the waters were contaminated, but waterholes were revealed so that people could drink and people could bathe and we learned to return again to that community style. . . . The government did not help us. Many of the things that organizations sent, many things ended up decaying in shipping containers at the ports. . . . I suffered the shock of not only going from seeing my mother-in-law lose it all, that my father-in-law died, but two months later my husband died because he needed electricity for his CPAP, he wasn't able, he couldn't handle that blow and at fifty-four he died of a massive heart attack. María not only, María made me strong, because now I can confront many more things.

Balanani described her experience of loss and abandonment during María as a transformational experience, where self-reliance and reliance on community came to provide the services the government no longer could be counted on for. As she continued, she described how she relied on her diasporic connections, Indigenous knowledge, and local community for survival. However, she later explained how her own survival occurred alongside the death of her father-in-law and husband, whose health could not survive the lack of electricity. These deaths were among many that were not included in official governmental counts of deaths caused by Hurricane Maria.

The reflections on the experience of María also led to discussion of the future of the Taíno movement, which revealed concerns with the future of Puerto Rico and its land. Abuela Shashira explained how her own great aunt told her to beware of the sale of her land to the colonizer, drawing on a trope of not selling or gifting land often found in pro-independence literature. "But there, that elderly woman told me, 'No no no mamita, don't cry, because they are selling your land, they are in the beginnings of giving your land.' She lowered herself, put one knee on the ground and gave three slaps, 'look this land is neither gifted nor sold.'" Like Abuela Shashira, Tai Pelli asked the audience to do the work on the ground to ensure a future world for Taíno and all people. She discussed the environment and the role of Indigenous knowledge and dissent in the fight for the Earth:

It's important that you are also aware of the struggles with our environment, because there is a direct relationship between environmental violence [and] the reproductive health of our people . . . if I motivate you, to not only learn our family histories and our past, but that you are also aware of how you can protect and care for those future generations.

Tai Pelli's speech reminded the audience of the kinds of practical actions needed contemporaneously to ensure Taíno futures. Her call was also a call for organizational work, as Taíno organizations have been long dedicated to environmental and social protest in Puerto Rico, as well as land stewardship. Taíno involvement in social protest often aligns with calls for broader Puerto Rican sustainability and sovereignty. In fact, several Taíno have been visibly involved in large Puerto Rican protests that have criticized the Financial Board, in solidarity with University of Puerto Rico students, and in the summer 2019 protests that ousted the then-governor of Puerto Rico, Ricardo Roselló.

Conclusion

Contemporary Taíno movements have emerged at the fringes of discourses of the Puerto Rican nation that valued Indigeneity as a historical and cultural symbolic relic but not as a current identification. As a symbol, the Taíno were enmeshed with the goals of the state; as a group of people, their futures were not acknowledged as valuable to the Puerto Rican political project. Disavowed by the Puerto Rican colonial state, they continued to be rendered illegible, both interactionally and institutionally. Yet here they were, in a federal cultural institution, at the Smithsonian's National Museum of the American Indian in New York City, discussing their past, present, and future. The act of bracketed recognition became a platform for the Taíno to be acknowledged as Taíno while presenting their social project, a project implicitly endorsed, though not necessarily fully supported, by a federal governmental entity—the same government whose legal mechanisms for recognition would never apply to the Taíno.

While many groups at the symposium called for the need for greater unity, underlying the call is decades of struggles among groups with different visions for Taíno futures grounded in different visions of what acknowledgment and recognition (interactional, institutional, governmental?) look like and whether they needed it. Yet in New York City, over fifteen hundred miles from Puerto Rico, in the seat of the largest population of diasporicans, within the brackets of institutional recognition, there was a moment of hope that unity could be attained through a spontaneous and effervescent *areíto* (ceremonial dance) in the large hall of the National Museum of the American Indian after the symposium was over. While we ate a feast of Caribbean delights, while leaders and members of different groups held hands and embraced, there was a spark of hope for unity and further political action. The stakes were high: the right to produce and de-colonize Taíno and Afro-Taíno knowledge and knowledge about the Taíno and Afro-Taíno and the call for a return to and protection of the land had been woven throughout the panelists' talks. But, as the Taíno and Afro-Taíno explained, some of these issues were going to be resolved not through talk but rather through the affective connections that could emerge within Taíno practices of ceremonial music and dance. During this moment, what mattered is that they could rec-ognize each other, that they understood their shared group membership, their relations, their histories—that they felt their "citizenship," regardless of the insti-tutions that would pose citizenship as an impossibility for them.[29]

The stories shared throughout the symposium and reflected in my own field-work often described elders and ancestors who identified as Indio to describe their family, their practices, and identities but who did not yet articulate them-selves as political subjects mobilizing on the behalf of Taíno and Afro-Taíno identifications. The very *possibility* of their articulation as Taíno political subjects resulted from a series of political and economic events precipitated by Puerto Rico's changing relationship to the United States in the twentieth century and the coming together of several people who rejected the narrative of extinction, listening to their abuelas to say, "I am Taíno." The social project of Taíno and Afro-Taíno narrative refusal, political resistance, and social protest was made possible by these acts of resistencia and survival, which may not have had the same goals. In turn, the acts of solidarity in the wake of disaster and activism to prevent worsening environmental and political conditions are the grounds upon which Taíno and Afro-Taíno put forward political projects to imagine and work on behalf of a (yet unknowable) future otherwise. As expressed by Tai Pelli, but true for many Taíno and Afro-Taíno: "So that twenty-five years from now . . . any of my grandchildren, that they don't have to apologize nor ever feel that they have to give a long explanation because they say they're Taíno . . . that we can have and embrace all the elements that compose us genetically but that you have a right to your identity and no one can decide it for you." Tai Pelli's vision for the future is one in which Taíno are no longer rendered unintelligible to history and racial discourse in Puerto Rico, but where claims to Taíno and Afro-Taíno Indigenous heritage are legitimated and where Taíno and Afro-Taíno people are understood to have a right to make a claim to their Indigenous identity and to work on behalf of their vision of a community-based and sustainable future.

Notes

1. Eva Lewis, "Princess Nokia Is Melding Gothic Punk with Her Afro-Indigenous Identity," *Teen Vogue*, September 8, 2017, https://www.teenvogue.com/story/princess-nokia-fresh-finds. Since this 2017 *Teen Vogue* publication, Princess Nokia has been accused of misrepresenting her racial ancestry and identity. This points to the generally contested nature of auto-identification in claims to racialized ancestries in Puerto Rico, particularly Taíno.

2. Pineda 2017, 824.

3. Gutiérrez Nájera and Maldonado 2017, 809.

4. Blackwell, Boj-Lopez, and Urrieta 2017.

5. Sexton 2008, 4.

6. Simpson 2014.

7. Trouillot 1995; Marable 2006, 19–20.

8. Ouden 2005, 183.

9. Loperena 2017, 802.

10. López Oro 2016, 71.

11. Klopotek 2011; Miles 2015; Arndt 2014.

12. Jackson Jr. 2005, 42.

13. Feliciano-Santos 2017; 2019; 2021.

14. Coulthard 2014; Povinelli 2002.

15. Lonetree 2012.

16. Moraga and Anzaldúa 1981.

17. Simpson 2007.

18. Jackson 2012, 5.

19. Goldstein 2017.

20. Castanha 2011; Povinelli 2011.

21. Dávila 1997.

22. Martínez-San Miguel 2011.

23. Dávila 2001.

24. Unless otherwise noted, all excerpts have been translated from Spanish by the author.

25. Feliciano and Green 2017.

26. Yarimar Bonilla, "Why Would Anyone in Puerto Rico Want a Hurricane? Because Someone Will Get Rich," *Washington Post*, September 22, 2017, https://www.washingtonpost.com/outlook/how-puerto-rican-hurricanes-devastate-many-and-enrich-a-few/2017/09/22/78e7500c-9e66-11e7-9083-fbfddf6804c2_story.html.

27. Ficek 2018.

28. Bonilla 2020, 3.

29. Ong 1999, 2006; Simpson 2008, 2014.

CHAPTER THREE

The Urban Sonorous and Collective Witness in the City of Neighborhoods

ALEX E. CHÁVEZ

In May 2018 an exhibition titled *Peeling Off the Grey* opened at the National Museum of Mexican Art in the Pilsen neighborhood on Chicago's Southwest Side. The installation sought to figuratively peel "off the layers of gentrification in Pilsen. To expose, let breathe, and share with others what the turmoil and dismantling of a community's heart looks and feels like." Largely centered around the aesthetics of direct action and protest, the exhibition also included a sound installation featuring recorded voices of Pilsen residents speaking about displacement.[1] And so, as visitors entered the gallery, the soft, muted tones of people recounting their attachments to the neighborhood and to its history echoed through the space, sweeping over you as your eyes focused on a slideshow of hand-drawn black-and-white pictures depicting scenes of gentrification. One voice was that of a young woman who testified to her haptic sensing of the neighborhood:

> It's all the noise, it's all the families walking down the street . . . that sense
> of community where I feel like you walk down Pilsen now and I don't see
> as many families anymore. I don't see the señoras where they used to be—
> those little things that make that difference. It reminds me of when my
> mom had to move out of Pilsen because the rent was getting too high. We
> were there for fifteen years, so us having to leave was like, all our childhood
> is here on this block and you're making us leave? . . . It's the physical, it's
> the wood that you're walking by when you're heading up the stairs to my
> mom's house. . . . It was the walls that I painted five billion times. It was all
> those things. It was all those memories.

Participating artists included Diana Solís, Clandestino, Sarita García, Jaime Mendoza, the Chicago ACT Collective, Sebastian Hidalgo, Barrio Resistance, William Estrada, Juan-Carlos Perez, Amara Betty Martin, Joseph Mora, Luis Tubens, and Sam Kirk. The exhibition ran from May 11, 2018, through February 3, 2019, and was curated by Teresa Magaña—a teaching artist with the National Museum of Mexican Art, member of the all-female artist collective Mujeres Mutantes, and co-owner of the independent art gallery and artist co-op Pilsen Outpost. Just prior to its opening, however, the museum removed portions of the exhibition that openly criticized Chicago's Twenty-Fifth Ward alderman Danny Solis and his support of the Resurrection Project, an urban development organization criticized by the participating artists for promoting urban development projects that, in their eyes, exacerbated residential displacement in Pilsen. While the act of removing these portions of the installation was initially carried out without direct consultation with the artists or Teresa Magaña, she and the museum's staff curators eventually reached a compromise. The controversial components were reinstalled, but in a modified manner; black bars were now placed over the disputed images and messages. And while the artists ultimately made the decision to comply with the museum's request to censor portions of the exhibit deemed controversial, they issued a collective statement to clarify their position:

> When we originally chose to participate in the show, we saw it as an opportunity to bring attention to the systems of power that gentrify our neighborhoods. Instead of withdrawing from the show, we challenge all artists not to be complicit in the museum's choice to censor our message. We ask that artists "co-sign" this statement against censorship and exploitation of poor people. We also ask that artists unite by critically examining the role they play in gentrification when they paint murals for developers, receive DCASE [Department of Cultural Affairs and Special Events] grants, and seek out only resume building or financially lucrative opportunities. This is not the time to be silent nor divided.[2]

The artists' simultaneous acknowledgment and critique of the National Museum of Mexican' Art's influence in the neighborhood reveals the complex relationship between art, the contemporary politics of urban renewal, protest, and place-making in Chicago. Each of these elements forms part of a complicated web of cultural and material relations that constitute the social aesthetic of the neighborhood, or the intimate and dialectical significations (or mappings) of urban space amid ongoing displacements. These artists are not alone in voicing their critique within this tense context. Persistent activism from neighborhood groups like Somos Logan Square and Humboldt Park No Se Vende has raised similar concerns, interrogating who gets to have a say in how neighborhoods develop economically and change culturally and how best to respect and make room for the complex adaptation processes communities live out in their attempts to exist with dignity amid the fraught urban social landscape. At the center of these considerations is yet another fundamental question: who is afforded claims of belonging in the city? Ultimately, I am concerned with the forms such claims take. In the above example, sonic and visual creative practices constitute a semiotic modality that both questions and curates who gets ratified as being of/from a place (barrio, neighborhood, or otherwise) and in what cascading order of importance those claims are seen and heard.

Anti-Black and anti-Latinx racism has been at the heart of official civic and economic processes constructing the "City of Neighborhoods"—as Chicago is often referred to—as far back as the 1940s.[3] By the 1960s and '70s, the forces of urban policy, electoral politics, financial (dis)investment, and city planning would succeed in largely containing the Mexican population in particular to the geography of the West and Southwest Sides and displacing Puerto Rican residents from North Side neighborhoods like Lincoln Park and Old Town to the city's Near Northwest Side.[4] In *Claiming Neighborhood: New Ways of Understanding Urban Change*, John J. Betancur and Janet L. Smith suggest the term "neighborhood" itself is fluid and unwieldy, a unit of analysis encompassing a broad range of material and immaterial designations of place. They write:

> Neighborhoods must be examined as a collection of spatially connected genealogies if we are to understand how they are constructed and what specific and intersecting structures are producing and reproducing them. Our a priori assumption is that neighborhoods are socially produced, relatively bounded arenas of ongoing struggle and that the struggle takes different forms depending on the societal regime.[5]

In Chicago, ethnic Mexican communities have historically settled in the Pilsen, Little Village, South Chicago, and Back of the Yards neighborhoods, in addition to the suburbs of Berwyn and Cicero. In the 1960s this population expanded significantly on the Southwest Side, which subsequently provided an opportunity to white real estate brokers and local politicians to reinforce neighborhood boundaries by allowing ethnic Mexicans to settle in areas impacted by white flight, as they occupied a more ambiguous—and thus preferable—racial position vis-à-vis African Americans and could act as a buffer to the settlement of the latter. Indeed, this is the process by which the housing stock in certain areas of South Lawndale, for instance, was kept viable—subsequently rebranded as "Little Village" by civic leaders—while the African American community of North Lawndale struggled economically.[6]

Similarly, by the late 1960s most Puerto Rican residents in Chicago had been relocated to the Near Northwest Side, at the intersection of the West Town, Humboldt Park, and Logan Square neighborhoods. Many Puerto Rican migrants came to the city in the wake of Operation Bootstrap—a series of rapid industrialization and economic development projects designed to transform the island of Puerto Rico from an agrarian to an industrial society, which subsequently displaced a perceived surplus population to the US mainland in a process intended to both clean up the island and improve the standard of living. By 1965 Puerto Ricans were experiencing intensified attacks by police in these Chicago neighborhoods, which culminated in the Division Street riots in June 1966, when civil unrest erupted in response to police antagonism and brutality.

Presently, most neighborhood-oriented policies "blame low-income people for [poor] conditions rather than structural factors such as racism and class bias," subsequently making "real estate development . . . a primary vehicle to improve low-income neighborhoods. As a result . . . the conditions that deprive low-income neighborhoods of opportunities are sidestepped, residents and their communities are often criminalized, and land is cleared to induce investment."[7] Yet, neighborhood residents consistently strive to hold those in power accountable in addressing unemployment, neglected infrastructure, crime, and poor schooling—struggles that also have much to do with shaping the representation of neighborhoods themselves. The dialectics of neighborhood change, thus, involve the historical interplay between structural forces and the efforts of resident leaders and community-based and civic organizations.

In this spirit, this chapter concerns Latinx modes of "sounding" in the city of Chicago—which as of 2018 was home to the fifth largest urban concentration of Latinxs in the United States—and does so by tracing how sound mobilizes physical and cultural claims of belonging amid the contentious politics of urban space.[8] This perspective opens up the possibility for amplifying sonic dimensions of place-making strategies particular to Latinxs. "Amplify," indeed, is a word that has specific material meanings, coupled with metaphorical significations. In literal terms, to amplify is to increase volume, yet the word's meanings extend beyond literal sonic intensification to include forms of enhanced circulation that widen spheres of social and cultural influence to broader publics. And so, this chapter situates sound in specific relation to the social metaphor of amplification, with attention to how Latinx artists and storytellers are voicing their presence in Chicago's sonic commons.[9]

Sound Politics

Fieldwork-based ethnography among Latinx youth, artists, and activists provides the empirical basis for my analysis of how sound forms a cultural model for understanding what previous scholars have termed "Latino Chicago." I consider sound as not just a sonorous phenomenon but as a cultural discourse shaped by the social reproduction of valuable forms of inequality that render Latinx communities disposable, deportable, and moveable in Chicago. I ask: What strategies and needs for "place-making" emerge given such profound and intersecting dislocations? How are such needs reflected in particular sounds? And, in turn, how do these sounds constitute broader processes of collective witness? For Latinxs are increasingly challenged to engage and reorganize the ways in which they identify as residents of Chicago, making their soundings places of dwelling, loci of politics, and aesthetic sites of citizenship—understood here beyond mere juridical designation, rather as a multifaceted social and cultural articulation of the right to collective space and belonging in contested contexts. This work therefore lends an "ethnographic ear" to the political mandates of contemporary Latinx sounds and how they are shaped by the racial politics of urban space in Chicago. I approach sound as a vernacular "vehicle for collective witness" and thus privilege an auditory field of inquiry for understanding localized strategies of emplacements, sonic processes of legibility, sensorial memory, sounded-semiotic constructions of place, and conditioned modes of listening that lend those sounds significance.[10] With this in mind, the sounds in question open up room for a mode of analysis that combines structural and semiotic-based approaches to the urban question, for Chicago reflects the socioeconomic and cultural consequences of the present neoliberal industrial order and its ever harsher regime of growing class inequality and disciplinary requirements.[11] For instance, this order of things reproduces and normalizes the disposability of racialized migrant labor—an allegorical figure that comes to represent all Latinxs as "forever foreign."[12] This very condition augments a generalizable moral panic about Latinxs, justifying their mass policing, deportation, and detention (irrespective of their status) in urban contexts (and certainly beyond them). The question therefore arises how a vernacular cultural political economy of place — a sonic semiosis in the present case — is leveraged amid the rapidly transforming neoliberal city to refuse these multiple lived displacements and continued intensified attacks (both discursive and related to long-standing public policy).

Chicago has been governed by three regimes since WWII, each enacting urban fiscal policy of various types: the Richard J. Daley Democratic Party machine from the 1950s to 1970s; the urban populism of Mayor Harold Washington in the 1980s; and the neoliberal approach of both mayors Richard M. Daley and Rahm Emanuel thereafter. Bennet, Garner, and Hague write:

> Over the past quarter-century, the City of Chicago has sought to entrepreneurialize government actions, create more responsible citizens and citizens who are more business-oriented, build a strong local business climate, encourage upmarket real estate development, and fashion a globally competitive consumption-oriented city.[13]

At a practical level, this philosophy has meant the aggressive privatization of public assets through public-private development partnerships, a reduction of the role of local government in service provision, the pursuit of land use policies designed to stimulate real estate markets that largely displace long-time residents, and an exponential increase in urban surveillance, security, and policing. These processes characterize Chicago's twenty-first-century racial geography of austerity, which exhibits long-standing (sound) neocolonial logics of dispossession and domination that now rely on deregulated financial instruments whose quick return on investment is contingent on rapid expropriation displacing vulnerable neighborhood residents. What, then, can be said about the textured sense of the everyday of neoliberalism in this regard? If indeed neighborhoods are materially experienced physical places, how are they also experienced symbolically amid the shrinking public commons and seemingly diminishing public sphere in the neoliberal era? And when you listen to this fraught social surround, what gets amplified?

Social Aesthetics

To narrate a landscape is to place oneself inside the story of a social surround; it is an interpretive practice—imaginative, relational, contingent, improvisational. It is an experiment wherein context is an enabling condition, not mere background. Aesthetic enactments, at their core, are discursive acts that both constitute and are constituted by social praxis and atmospheres of interaction. They amplify how people occupy lived-in worlds of attunements—at once representational and existential. In other words, art is a way of moving through the world and of being in it. Art both feels and is witness to how life happens as a relational world of individuated and collective experiences that together form the political subject. Art can be wielded as a weapon and a refuge—it is a place unto itself. Art maps what matters through social interventions of all kinds.

Diana Solís is a Chicago-based artist. She was born in Monterrey, Nuevo León, Mexico, in 1956 but was raised in the Pilsen neighborhood on Chicago's Southwest Side. Located just three miles from downtown, Pilsen has been home to a large proportion of the ethnic Mexican population in Chicago since the 1950s—a robust site of political mobilization, home to culturally significant spaces, and the symbolic center of the Latinx Midwest. Solís's family migrated to Chicago when she was only a few months old. A self-identified Mexicana-Chicana, Solís expresses themes of female empowerment as well as environmental and racial justice through her art and draws inspiration from both Mesoamerican and Latin American folklore. A photographer by training, she received a bachelor of fine arts from the University of Illinois at Chicago and transitioned to painting later in her career after having worked as a photojournalist internationally and for the *Chicago Tribune* and the *West Side Times*. As much an activist and educator as she is an artist, Solís has worked around social justice causes in the Pilsen neighborhood for decades, with her latest focus being on the issue of gentrification. From issuing calls for the provision of affordable housing and holding local elected officials accountable in the wake of development projects and rising rents, to protesting newcomer upscale business and luxury residential spaces and the destruction of public murals, Solís's efforts uniquely intersect with the subtler—though no less significant—work her art achieves when on display in local businesses accountable to the longstanding ethnic Mexican community in Pilsen. Sites displaying her work also include an art gallery/artist co-op called the Pilsen Outpost, which she founded with fellow artists Teresa Magaña and Pablo Ramirez. The gallery sells artwork, hosts monthly exhibition openings and workshops, and provides support for underrepresented local artists otherwise unable to exhibit their work in more formal settings. In an article published by Chicagovoz.org in March of 2015, Solís had this to say about the pressures of residential displacement:

> Gentrification is here. We all know that. But I think that stores owned by people of color, if they're conscientious, is also a way to not allow the gentrification to get to a point where you don't have a voice. I think we're fighting gentrification. I think we're staking our claim as born and bred Latino artists in the community. We can do this, and we don't have to depend on a hipster or someone from the outside to come in and do what we're doing.[14]

The situation is tense in the Pilsen neighborhood as of this writing. And local artists are deploying creative strategies to both refuse and negotiate around these pressures, part of which involves marking off the neighborhood through visual and sonic strategies in ways that signify the long-standing presence of the Latinx community that has been there for decades. In other words, they are doing the work of aesthetically mapping what matters.

Diana Solís and other artists of her generation have paved the way for the activism now taking place in Pilsen among a new crop of artists. In the remainder of this chapter, I focus on the work of a youth radio project based in the adjacent neighborhood of Little Village—or La Villita, as it is affectionately called—which is also facing gentrification. Yollocalli Arts Reach, a free youth arts program founded in 1997, typically comprises a group of a few dozen students ranging in age from thirteen to twenty headquartered at the Boys & Girls Club of America in Little Village. Some of these young people focus their talents and energy on sound-design. They produce audio narrative pieces available online, engage in creative multimedia projects that exhibit "their stories their way" (focused on youth issues, pop culture, as well as politics), and host on-air discussions on their live quarterly radio program *Wattz Up!* broadcast on local WLPN Lumpen Radio. After existing for a year as a web-only streaming station, Lumpen Radio made the transition to the radio airwaves in 2016. It is the latest outlet of the nonprofit Public Media Institute, founded by Bridgeport neighborhood native Edward Marszewski (or Ed Mar) in 2000. According to Ed Mar, in 2013, when regulatory and legislative changes made it feasible for small nonprofits to acquire low-power FM radio licenses, it was a "no-brainer" to set the wheels in motion. While big commercial operations often broadcast at 50,000 or even 100,000 watts of effective radiated power, LPFM (low power) signals are typically rated at 50 to 100 watts. Still, "we wanted to present marginalized voices and voices that aren't amplified on the FM mediascape," Ed Mar explained in a *Chicago Reader* article.[15] *Wattz Up!* has emerged as one of Lumpen Radio's most engaging programs, featuring the creative storytelling work of the Yollocalli youth. And one ongoing project that brings together their sound-design and production skills is centered around neighborhood sound-mapping.

Going forward, I consider these specific sound-design endeavors as a communicative platform through which these youth (many of them from mixed-status families and/or migrants themselves) participate in the public construction of their collective sensing of place in Chicago. As an emergent communicative modality, this localizing semiotic strategy exists as one of emplacement and thus engages with competing representations of Latinx personhood in the city. Indeed, the aesthetic mandates shaping the work of these youth are currently formed and informed by intensified attacks on Latinx migrant communities, including the rescinding of DACA, pressures on sanctuary cities, zero tolerance policies along the US-Mexico border, expansive deportation and migrant detention campaigns, and threats to rescind the birthright citizenship clause of the Fourteenth Amendment. Similar to the work of Diana Solís and the artists who organized *Peeling Off the Grey*, Yollocalli's artistic projects constitute and are constituted by social relations embodied in aesthetic practices, wherein they wield sound as a way of bearing witness to Latinx dwelling and place-making in Chicago.

Aural Ecologies

Mainstream scholarly perspectives on urbanism and neighborhoods emerged in the 1920s among human ecologists at the University of Chicago, no less. And while subsequent theories and research have moved well beyond the initial view of geographic differentiation and segregation as a reflection of the supposedly natural ordering of social groups across landscapes, I nevertheless invoke ecology because it draws our attention to the expressive grammar of the relationship between people and their environment. In the present discussion, aurality lends specificity to this always-changing relationship, a dynamic that is of particular importance when examining processes of urban renewal that transform neighborhoods. There is a cultural dissonance that undergirds gentrification as an urban strategy of displacement and renewal.[16] More specifically,

the disembodied use of urban spaces deeply inhabited by histories of segregation and racial violence "from below" are subject to processes of resignification
that empty out these vernacular geographies of lived life from their previous
meanings, in effect reducing the material residues of social injury to an attractive patina of "authenticity" so desired and inspirational to pioneers of urban
renewal—developers and their patrons, explicitly. In this way, the dialectical
interplay between sociospatial remove and simultaneity wherein gentrified
spaces are marked by erasure and desire is, in many ways, a quiet enchantment
with the architectural ruins of racism under the auspices of art, development,
and multiculturalism. This is a process transforming spaces and moving bodies
based on the very same logics of white supremacy that initially corralled non-
whites in the inner city in the mid-twentieth century. Betancur and Smith speak
to the current situation in Pilsen:

> Gentrification has helped to replace prior images of slum and blight with
> diversity, a bohemian lifestyle, and the promise of exclusivity when the
> replacement process is complete. Selling gentrification requires creating
> newer and newer enclaves by making the neighborhood space seemingly
> separate and distinct. This is the case of "East Pilsen," "East Pilsen Artist
> Colony" and "La 18" all being enclaves of Mexican Pilsen.[17]

The question arises: what have these places sounded and looked like (and continue to)? The answer is complex and requires attention to cultural histories and
struggles brought to bear over time.

My previous work around performativity and transgression among Mexican
migrants has focused on the multiple scales of space and time produced and
navigated through interpersonal stances and interactions in everyday poetics
and performance. The work I discuss in this chapter extends these concerns,
as I shift focus away from discourses about mobility toward emplacement, a
crucial component of the discursive framing of migration that stirs the most
alarmist reaction among racial conservatives: *migrants are settling in the United
States and they must therefore be forcibly removed.* The migrant presence, as it
were, animates institutional discursive strategies of boundary-making along the
lines of race and citizenship; yet this process is far more fluid, heterogeneous,
and porous, particularly at the vernacular level.[18] And so here I turn to what
Ana María Ochoa terms the "aural public sphere."[19] Ochoa's formulation echoes
R. Murray Schafer's "soundscape" in her attention to the material dimensions

of language, music, and the voice, while also remaining phenomenologically attuned to embodiment and the senses as central to the socially and culturally positioned forms of listening that constitute political subjectivities.[20] Most importantly, this construction brings together attention to both the sonic qualities and the ephemeral dimensions of sound in embodied experience. For sound is central to the signifying processes of place-making at the heart of everyday battles over political subjectivities in the city. In other words, emplacement involves the "sensuous interrelationship of body-mind-environment. This environment is both physical and social, as is well illustrated by the bundle of sensory and social values contained in the feeling of 'home.'"[21] We are thus challenged to take up the semiotic interplay between officialized toponymic designations of place and vernacular experiences of place-making constituted by physical and metaphysical swarmings of public meanings and embodied social relations, which are sonic *in nature*.

Soundscaping

Imagine you are blindfolded. What might you hear (or not) upon entering a neighborhood: who is talking and what about, in what languages, what musics are playing, what distinguishes noise from sound? Here is how the students from Yollocalli describe one recent sound-mapping project titled *Sounds of Little Village*:

> Thinking about various forms of deep listening, the students from Your story, Your way! were challenged to construct a sound impression of their experiences in a neighborhood, Little Village, through the act of hearing every possible sound and making site recordings. Little Village is a: vibrant, spontaneous, vivid, and colorful neighborhood. Having a high percentage of Hispanics residing in the community, and being the second largest commercial area in the city of Chicago, makes it unique. Students captured a series of sounds that narrate local stories, picturing the life in it. Have you ever imagined a sound for your house? The sounds of Little Village streets? The nature that surrounds it? Its habitants and the people who commute? The sounds of your own home?

The collection featured one hundred audio pieces of found and documented sound. The tracks included the sounds of air conditioning units; conversation in barber shops, at the hair dresser, and in nail salons; the rhythms of daily work in mechanic shops and restaurants; the cacophony of street traffic, car alarms, and neighborhood wildlife—from chickens to barking dogs. One piece titled "A Rainy Day on 26th" traces a youth's journey on the major corridor of Little Village, 26th Street, as they travel from sidewalk to sidewalk, storefront to storefront, seeking shelter from the summer rain. Along the way, we hear the sounds of the neighborhood—from conversations in Spanish, Mexican *ranchera* music, cars splashing through puddles, and neighbors carrying on across the street warning of potential basement flooding. Portions of this material were broadcast on WLPN Lumpen Radio.

Another Yollocalli audio project is *Portraits of Little Village*, which in their words focuses on neighborhood voices that offer "a glimpse into daily living." This collection included twenty-four produced audio pieces that layered neighborhood soundscapes with individual interviews and other sounds to aid in the storytelling effort—from music to found sound. In one such piece, students feature the voice of a storeowner, as she rings up customers and speaks about the neighborhood. She shares:

> *Bueno, fíjate que todo mundo sabemos que aquí es el corazón del barrio mexicano. Y aparte la economía aquí se puede decir que esta un poquito mejor que en otros barrios . . . hace aproximadamente quince años yo empecé a trabajar aquí . . . obviamente estuve como empleada, ya después de un tiempo mi hermano y yo pues ya agarramos este espacio pequeño. Esta pequeño, pero le estamos echando muchas ganas. Gracias a Dios tenemos nuestro local mi hermano y yo. Ahorita estaba acomodando para que comience el día para mi porque como fui a la mercancía pues tuve que acomodar ropa de hombre, mas que nada vaquera y casual. Bueno entre semana no tanto, pero fin de semana nos vienen de distintos estados podemos decir estados de Nueva York, Los Ángeles, Tejas, Iowa, Wisconsin, Indiana, etc. y obviamente los suburbios de donde aquí nosotros vivimos.*

Well, look, the whole world knows that this is the heart of the Mexican neighborhood. And apart from our economic standing, one can say that this neighborhood is a little better off than others. . . . I started working here approximately fifteen years ago. . . . Obviously, I first started out as an employee, then later after some time had passed my brother and I bought this small space. It's small, but we're giving it our all. Thanks to God we have our business, my brother and me. . . . Right now, to start off the day, I was arranging some clothes, since I went to source some of this merchandise, well, I was arranging some men's clothing, mainly western-wear. Well, not so much during the week, but definitely on the weekends folks from all over come out this way, from different states: New York, Los Angeles, Texas, Iowa, Wisconsin, Indiana, and obviously from the Chicago suburbs.

Her talk of economic activity and prosperity is in line with common knowledge that the 26th Street corridor in Little Village is indeed the most economically prosperous commercial area in the city, beating out the much-touted, tourist-centered Magnificent Mile in the River North area of Chicago. As she shares her story, we hear the sounds of the cash register, people chatting in the store, and the distant sounds of street traffic, all of which is overlaid with playful melancholic melodies played on a toy piano. The storeowner, like many of the people whose voices are featured on *Portraits of Little Village*, not only tells of the quotidian rhythms of the workaday but does so with attention to the geographic and social contexts that situate her place within a broader political economy of space.

At the heart of "your story, your way" are narratives of place documented with the aid of innovative sound-design methods. These documented stories of daily living amplify how sound is significant for Latinxs in *voicing* their place in Chicago, that is, in claiming space across the physical divides of segregation and social divides of economy and politics. The Yollocalli youths' sound-mapping skillfully traces the shifting social and economic configurations that make up the aural ecologies of the neighborhood. In this way, performativity emerges as central in understanding the participation frameworks constructed through sounded storytelling, and comprehending sound itself as a semiotic strategy that bears collective witness to the construction of place. Drawing on Brandon LaBelle's work on acoustic territories, J. Martin Daughtry introduces the analytic category of "radiant acoustic territories" to identify the "intersubjective places that are brought into existence through acts of sounding" whose acoustic nature is tethered to "the number of auditors who are interpellated into the unified field of acoustic power it projects."[22] While the somatic aspects of sound—which imply audition—are of importance in any context, of interest here is how acts of listening shape and are shaped by relations of power, such that acts of sounding (in contradistinction to the auditory) participate in the nexus of the acoustic, which is a "connotative field that emphasizes the relationship between sound, listening, and place."[23] In this (literal) sense, Yollocalli's mediatized aesthetic enactments trace localized sonic markers and processes of aurality that take place, that is, they (re)signify space in practice, such that sound is privileged as both tactile performance (in the Feldian phenomenological sense) and situated tactic of belonging. And so, we arrive at these fundamental questions: what happens when sound happens, who is listening, and how? Put another way, how do sound practices beyond the walls of institutional and normative conceptions—of citizenship, resident, legality—*perform* a vital role in disturbing the racialization of space and aural ecologies of othering? The Yollocalli youths' work engages with these concerns, they live them and as such are interceding in public constructions of their personhood by amplifying how *they* hear their own neighborhoods and sound in them, inciting modes of listening along the way that disturb existing configurations of belonging in the city.

In the summer of 2020, as communities across the United States rose up to protest the murderous consequences of policing after the killings of George Floyd and Breonna Taylor, Yollocalli produced a three-part series broadcast on *Wattz Up!* titled "Black Lives Matter. Period." The series featured conversations with Black activists, youth participants, and the experiences of Yollocalli youth at protests with the aim of highlighting "how to be active and the danger of silence." The series opened with the youth declaring that Black Lives Matter is "one of the most influential human rights movements of the twenty-first century" and that their own "voices matter," as they refused to be silent in the face of racial terror and injustice.[24] Youth producer Emmanuel Ramirez wrote about the program in a piece titled "Moment for Life: WE, Yollocalli" published on quarantinetimes.org—a web-based project featuring Chicago's creative responses to the COVID-19 public health crisis, which was designed by the previously mentioned Public Media Institute:

> Right before season 13 ended, downtown Chicago burned in an event that would live in history forever, and protests and riots soon spread all over the city. That was not a time to be tame and obedient, but to speak up and act out. Personally, that was one of the hardest shows to make, that challenged my team and I to push our pen and think deeply about the ways of our society. We used our remote radio platform to enhance the voices of those

who had been in the frontlines, youth perspectives, and black activists. Season 13 ended with our final show, "Black Lives Matter. Period," and we all couldn't have been prouder of ourselves.[25]

The program highlighted the sounds of Chicago in urban rebellion, the voices of communities fighting for justice and self-determination. From interviews and personal testimonials to the soundscapes of protest and police backlash, the series amplified the groundswell and social effervescence captivating the entire country, as activists and community stakeholders called for the reevaluation of how taxpayer dollars are allocated to police departments and security infrastructures, particularly in the neoliberal city. Further, the youth also spoke to the presence of anti-Black racism within the Latinx community and the need to uplift the struggles of Black communities in solidarity. In their analysis, a refusal to be silent means taking up the obligation to speak out against social injustice. At the level of performativity, they amplified this refusal by documenting the sounds of the city, applying thoughtful sound-design production, and subsequently broadcasting their message over the airwaves and online to listeners across Chicago (and beyond) in the hopes of enacting "the promise of shared cultural politics among Black and Brown communities."[26]

Sound Citizens and the Commons

The political, fundamentally, is a question of inclusion and exclusion, of belonging, of citizenship—a concept that scholars have augmented socially and culturally to extend its meanings beyond the political rights accorded by the state.[27] Their formulations instead privilege everyday practices and dimensions of identity through which people create community and fashion subjectivities. Relatedly, this question of citizenship among Latinx communities has taken on new meanings that center the political dimensions of both family and undocumented subjectivity within current activist movements concerning migrant rights in the United States. "The family" has emerged as a political unit of representation that challenges the "liberal political model that posits the polity as an aggregate of individuals."[28] Nevertheless, such claims rely on tensive and routinized performance of worthiness reliant on cultural, economic, and civic understandings of the ideal citizen—or "citizenship scripts" wherein the personhood of undocumented migrants is not enough (or even guaranteed or recognized). This paradox, according to Amalia Pallares, has the potential of simultaneously challenging the individualization of the undocumented migrant by privileging family ties, while also potentially relying on neoliberal frames of worthiness that represent Dreamers, for instance, as talented and innocent individuals who were brought to the United States through no fault of their own. This tensive relationship, nevertheless, calls attention to a politics of liminality and motion, "a politics that is both conforming and challenging, accepting and reinforcing state norms and categories of belonging, but also questioning and interrupting them."[29] In turn, this complexity also allows for critical attention to inventive political strategies and creative activism as everyday assertions of belonging. In the present instance, this is a question of listening and belonging, or in other words, *sound citizenship*, which in the context of Chicago demands attention to the material relationship between sound and space in the face of dispossession. Betancur and Smith expand upon David Harvey's formulation of the "spatial fix" to shed light on the relationship between displacement and neighborhood formation in Chicago.[30] They write:

> The production of cities, and by extension the production of neighbor-
> hoods, is driven by capital accumulation and social reproduction. Most
> relevant are [Harvey's] insights on the investment and disinvestment
> dynamic and differential class reproduction. The former are mechanisms
> of creative destruction that through devalorization and valorization
> processes, for instance, cause mass movement such as white flight while
> concurrently generating demand for suburban living and urban gentrifi-
> cation. Practices such as redlining and blockbusting are part and parcel of
> this process.[31]

This analysis aids in apprehending the actions government and private enter-prises have perpetrated against lower income residents of color in Chicago since the implementation of urban renewal policies in the 1940s.[32] At present, contin-ued displacements are unfolding within the context of the neoliberal reality of shrinking public space, that is, the intensified extension of commodity relations deep into the public sphere of the neighborhood, in turn generating an atmo-sphere of abjectivity for young people subsequently considered discardable.[33]

And so, we may begin to consider how sound constitutes a type of public performance revealing the complex social tensions that surround place-making in the city of Chicago. However, sound doesn't merely tell the story of displace-ment but is itself a dramatic expression at the heart of public battles over the claiming of space in the city. Within the context of gentrification and the neo-liberal reality of diminishing public space, sonic forms and practices that attest to histories of settlement and historical presence participate in the sanctifying of public space "in common." This provides an opportunity for conceptual-izing aesthetic models for understanding the history of Chicago's built envi-ronment—particularly the formation of its neighborhoods—but perhaps more importantly the interplay between the urban sonorous and a more particular sounding of Latinx Chicago. This dialectic expands into Harney and Moten's notion of an undercommons—the always existing space of oppositional knowl-edge and solidarity that refuses existing orders.[34] In turn, extending this to the realm of aurality, Bruce Odland and Sam Auinger define the sonic commons as "any space where many people share an acoustic environment and can hear the results of each other's activities, both intentional and unintentional."[35] I broaden their concept socially to include what we don't hear or choose not to hear, for the conditions that shape the aural public sphere involve listening, which is typically associated with the deliberate channeling of awareness toward sound. Yet, this mode of auditory attention is neither self-evident nor isolated; rather, it is shaped by culturally and context-specific sets of interpretive practices and involves a broad range of nonauditory dispositions, all of which necessitate attention to experiences of space and memory. Therefore, listening reveals it-self as a political act comprising culturally and historically situated modes of attention. Thus, the sounds of the neighborhood—otherwise deemed illegible or heard as noise—come to index another sociopolitical and cultural order for the Yollocalli youth. Their manner of listening emerges as a way of sanctifying public space "in common," attesting as it does to deep and continued experiences of settlement, integration, segregation, and community.[36] An alternative public emerges through their aesthetic rendering of the sounds that make up the social aesthetic of "the neighborhood" experience. Alternative imaginings of this type have elsewhere been termed "counter-publics," or publics self-aware of their subordinate positionality in relation to other more dominant publics believed to possess greater relative social worth.[37] Yet, and of particular relevance with respect to Chicago, beyond existing as mere parallel arenas of oppositional dis-course, the conflicts embodied in counterpublics extend also to the modalities of address that constitute the public.[38] In other words, beyond content alone, the performative is also a site of struggle and refusal over the resignification (and thus contestations) of public space, much of which is tethered to manifestations of ethnoracial identity as a resource articulated in place.

Admittedly, there exists a tension here, for such manifestations—understood generically as "culture" or "cultural"—operate as a type of socially constituted "boundary of difference" that may be mobilized for various political ends, for example acting as a marketable object to attract industry and newcomers, or as the discriminatory bases for justifying urban spatial fixes, or as their utter disavowal in claims for equity.[39] These different uses of culture, to be sure, have been central to Latinxs' historical struggles "between developers and residents' resistance practices for space."[40] Arlene Dávila comments on the contemporary moment, in which "processes of gentrification and neoliberal policies pose challenging questions about the operations of culture in the spatial politics of contemporary cities, and about the growing interplay between culture as ethnicity and as marketable industry."[41] Nevertheless, this logic too is undergirded by ideologies of vacancy, wherein the "blight" (vacant land, buildings, homes) in Latinx neighborhoods is seen as symptomatic of a problematic urban condition that in turn must be vacated as a way of remedying economic crisis. To further invoke David Harvey, this physical reality must be fixed, for it is deficient, lacks order, stability. However, such myopic conceptions of urban blight ignore local strategies of collective witness. And in the present case, these imaginative possibilities are *taking place* amid the complex processes of residential displacements in the throes of urban restructuring, fraught relations between law enforcement and neighborhoods of color, and processes of globalization that are remaking the city of Chicago in the guise of both transnational migration and residential gentrification.

Sounds of the Future, Citizens in the Present, or Home Is Where the Heart Is[42]

John Holloway writes, "in the beginning is the scream," a critical vibration which is the starting point of negation, "a refusal to accept . . . the inevitability of increasing inequality, misery, exploitation and violence . . . a refusal to accept closure." The scream rejects "a world that we feel to be wrong."[43] The scream is embodied dissonance. It is a sound that bears witness and asserts presence. Sound's more capacious and figurative power is in enacting forms of social legibility and amplifying them amid the violences of displacement, dispossession, and surveillance. Bringing "culture" to bear, in this way, has political implications with respect to citizenship. For in the face of the officialized nexus of discourse and public policy that labors to exclude, segregate, and define neighborhoods in the city on the basis of race, the present generation of artists and storytellers is wielding art as a type of creative refusal by documenting the sonics of both extraordinary struggles and ordinary living bearing collective witness to the politics of belonging. This expressive grammar is a site of citizenship capable of reimagining the borders of urban territory, policy, and of who is allowed to maintain a semblance of home, which has everything to do with *how* "we" understand the city, *how* we hear its neighborhoods, and *who* we hear in them. Or as the Yollocalli youth put it in a statement celebrating their twentieth anniversary:

> In 1997 the National Museum of Mexican Art launched a new home onto Pilsen. A home where young people could create art alongside artists and explore the art and themselves freely. This home was named Yollocalli, because like the nahuatl word Yolotl it had a lot of heart. Over the years Yollocalli has become the place for those that lived in the margins, those that needed a community of their own, that wanted to be different, sad, ridiculous, rebellious, sassy and make some art. Like the Afro futurists looking to see their realities reflected in space and the future, Yollo has been the place for youth to see themselves beyond their everyday. A humble home has become a way of being and learning. Yollocali has built a planet of its own here on earth where youth of color can be weird, cosmic, and ephemeral. The people who inhabit this home have built an abstract dream that waits for your smiling. Let's celebrate the journey so far and imagine a galaxy not so far away.

This is an embrace of what is not quite audible, of another possible world in the offing, of an abstract future on the horizon, yet presently in process—in time, in space, and through sound. Returning to Holloway, Yollocalli's cosmic, wondrous, polyphonic scream—in all its embodied soundedness and refusal— "is ecstatic, in the literal sense of standing out ahead of itself towards an open future."[44]

Notes

1. "Peeling Off the Grey," National Museum of Mexican Art, accessed October 10, 2021, http://nationalmuseumofmexicanart.org/exhibits/peeling-grey#.

2. Mashuska, "Our Response to Peeling Off the Grey," Plus Gallery Chicago, May 12, 2018, https://plusgallerychicago.com/2018/05/12/our-response -to-peeling-off-the-grey/.

3. Van Cleve 2016.

4. Pérez 2004.

5. Betancur and Smith 2016, 200.

6. Vargas 2016.

7. Betancur and Smith 2016, viii.

8. Luis Noe-Bustamante, Mark Hugo Lopez, and Jens Manuel Krogstad, "U.S. Hispanic Population Surpassed 60 Million in 2019, but Growth Has Slowed," Pew Research Center, July 7, 2020, https://www.pewresearch.org/fact-tank /2019/07/08/u-s-hispanic-population-reached-new-high-in-2018-but-growth -has-slowed/.

9. Previous research has focused separately on Latinx expressive culture (Cintron 1997; Farr 2004, 2006; Rosa 2019), the settlement of Latinxs in Chicago (Amezcua forthcoming; De Genova 2005; De Genova and Ramos-Zayas 2003; Innis-Jiménez 2013; Pérez 2004), or on political activism (Pallares 2014; Pallares and Flores-González 2010; Ramírez and Yenelli Flores 2011), rather than the articulations between these domains as proposed here. And so, this chapter calls for an integration of sound studies (Johnson 2013; Novak and Sakakeeny 2015; Samuels et al. 2010; Taussig 2018) and an anthropology of place (Arnason 2012; Feld and Basso 1996; Stewart 1996) toward a perspective on Latinx urbanism (Dávila 2004; Díaz and Torres 2012; Wacquant 2008).

10. Lipsitz 2007.

11. Victor Valle and Rodolfo D. Torres (2012) reaffirm the "centrality of capitalist formations in the study of the Latino urban question by embedding social and cultural categories in the lived spaces of our macroeconomic order" (181).

12. Lipsitz 2006.

13. Bennet, Garner, and Hague 2017, 2.

14. "Women of Pilsen Diana Solis," *Chicagovoz.org*, March 16, 2015, http://chicagov-oz.org/2015/03/16/women-of-pilsen-diana-solis/.

15. Erin Osmon, "Lumpen Radio Amplifies Voices from the Margins," January 18, 2017, https://www.chicagoreader.com/chicago/lumpen-radio-wlpn-bridgeport -community-marsziewski-logan/Content?oid=25135932.

16. This includes the works of Lees, Slater, and Wyly 2008; Maurrasse 2006; and Wacquant 2008.

17. Betancur and Smith 2016, 202.

18. Perrino and Wortham 2017.

19. Ochoa 2006.

20. Schafer 1997.

21. Howes 2005, 7.

22. LaBelle 2010; Daughtry 2015, 193.

23. Daughtry 2015, 125.

24. Yollocalli, "Wattz Up! Special Edition – Black Lives Matter. Period," Soundcloud, June 6, 2020, https://soundcloud.com/yollocalli/sets/wattz-up-special-edition -black-lives-matter-period.

25. https://quarantinetimes.org/news/kfb1jj5069atsxin6qgta7cnv8rdb2.

26. Johnson 2013, xiii.

27. Del Castillo 2007; Gálvez 2013; Rosaldo 1994.

28. Pallares 2014, 93.

29. Ibid., 17.

30. This process takes on two general forms. First, there is the literal durable positioning of capital in specific places; second, the metaphorical fix refers to an interim solution to capitalist crisis achieved through spatial strategies (i.e., deindustrialization in one area and the simultaneous reindustrialization in another so as to absorb labor and capital surplus, which in turn braces the spatial movement of mobile forms of capital necessary for continued accumulation).

31. Betancur and Smith 2016, 13.

32. One egregious example is the ethnic Mexican neighborhood of Pilsen, whose residents were forced into that space as a result of targeted arson and eminent domain inactions around the area that would eventually become the University of Illinois at Chicago University Village.

33. Gonzales and Chavez 2012.

34. Harney Moten 2013.

35. Odland Auinger 2009.

36. Bruce 2016.

37. Warner 2002.

38. Warner 2002.

39. Appadurai in Dávila 2004, 10.

40.   Dávila 2004, 3.

41.   Ibid.

42.   Torres, Rizzini, and Del Río 2013.

43.   Holloway 2002, 1, 6, 2.

44.   Ibid., 6.

CHAPTER FOUR

Diasporic Signs

Puerto Rican Place-Making, Latinx Artivism, and the Aesthetics of Resistance

JONATHAN ROSA AND DAVID FLORES

> *Yo te doy la gracia por poner este sign—es una belleza,*
> *lo que tú has hecho aquí para nuestra ciudad de Holyoke.*
>
> *[I thank you for putting up this sign—it is beautiful*
> *what you have done for our city of Holyoke.]*
>
> —Holyoke, MA, resident commenting
> on the display of a mural celebrating Holyoke's Puerto Rican
> diaspora next to city hall in October 2014

In June 2015, four years after moving to the small New England city of Holyoke, Massachusetts, we—a US-born Puerto Rican anthropologist (Jonathan) and US-born Mexican artist, designer, and activist (David)—finished loading a moving truck and prepared to drive to Chicago, where we were both relocating for new opportunities. The only remaining item was a box of a couple dozen T-shirts displaying the image of a Puerto Rican license plate dedicated to Holyoke (see fig. 4.1). The image on the T-shirt corresponded to a mural featuring an oversized Puerto Rican Holyoke license plate that David had played a leading role in designing and creating, and whose public display had become the object of considerable controversy in Holyoke just a few months prior. This debate inspired many Puerto Rican residents and allies throughout Holyoke and beyond to embrace the mural and its various replicas, including the T-shirts designed as part of a community art fundraiser that David organized. As we finished packing the truck, the box of leftover T-shirts ended up sharing precious cabin space with us. The plan was to distribute the shirts among Puerto

Rican Chicagoans who had begun collaborating with Puerto Rican Holyokers on various political campaigns, including the effort to secure the release of Puerto Rican political prisoner Oscar López Rivera.[1]

While preparing to depart we noticed that our neighbors—a multigenerational Puerto Rican family—a couple of doors down were having a party in front of their home and wondered whether they might appreciate a few of the T-shirts. We carried the box over, exchanged greetings, and discussed our moving plans before opening the box to offer the shirts to them. Smiling widely, they passed the box around and returned it to us completely empty in what seemed like an instant. After saying goodbye and beginning our journey, we watched in the rearview mirror as this beautiful family of children, parents, grandparents, great-grandparents, and friends excitedly transformed their front yard into an impromptu fitting room, with several of the kids running around in oversized Puerto Rican Holyoke shirts that nearly completely enveloped them. This image of public, outsized Puerto Rican diasporic pride, which galvanized not only these youth but also an entire community, was in many ways an apt beginning to our journey along the I-90 corridor connecting so many postindustrial cities with often small, but profoundly proud Puerto Rican populations. What from some perspectives might seem like curiously emphatic expressions of Puerto Rican pride in these communities, located in and around Boston, Springfield, Albany, Syracuse, Rochester, Buffalo, Cleveland, Lorain, and Chicago, demonstrate how multiscalar aesthetic practices can become powerful enactments of ingenuity and survivance in the face of ongoing displacement and marginalization across the Puerto Rican diaspora.

In fall 2014, when the public display of artwork celebrating Puerto Rican Holyokers' diasporic identities sparked a local controversy that became the focus of widespread conversation and debate, Holyoke was the US city with the largest concentration of Puerto Ricans outside of Puerto Rico.[2] Despite these demographics, efforts to display affirming public representations of Holyoke Puerto Ricans were continually met with challenges from the city's white ethnic—predominantly Irish—power structure. This phenomenon can be understood as part of broader internal colonial dynamics through which various ethnoracially minoritized US populations face marginalization and erasure across spheres of everyday life, including electoral politics, education, housing, and claims to public space.[3] For Puerto Ricans throughout the diaspora, struggles in response to myriad forms of marginalization require ongoing endurance in the face of perpetually deferred decolonization.[4] This chapter analyzes efforts to disrupt

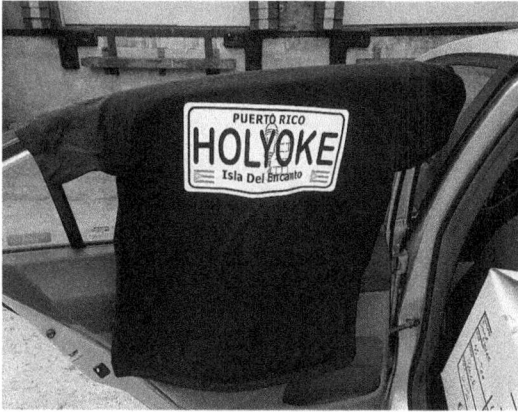

FIGURE 4.1 Puerto Rican Holyoke T-shirt. Photo by David Flores.

this marginalization in the context of controversy surrounding Holyoke residents' collaborative creation of a celebratory diasporic Puerto Rican public art installation, which became a contentious claim to space in a deeply stratified community. This effort, resulting in a broader debate about the public display of artwork affirming Puerto Ricanness within Holyoke, received national media attention focused on the censorship of Puerto Rican identity and eventually led to a citywide ban on public art.[5] However, through the collaborative efforts of local artists and activists, the installation is currently displayed outside of Holyoke's city hall and represents a momentous victory for the city's Puerto Rican community. Thus, artivism—the interplay between political struggles and aesthetic practices—can become a powerful vehicle for social change, underscoring Baca's point that public art consists not only of design elements such as "line, form and color but all the environmental and social factors that are inherent in the space and that cannot be separated from it."[6] We build from this insight to explore a set of ethnographic refusals through Puerto Rican place-making and Latinx artivism, which we suggest become crucial sites for redefining diasporic community, solidarity, and political belonging.

Entering Holyoke

Nicknamed the "Paper City" due to its reputation as the world's largest paper producer in the late nineteenth and early twentieth centuries, Holyoke was the first planned industrial city in the United States.[7] The paper mills brought waves of migrant and immigrant groups to the area starting in the mid-nineteenth century, beginning with the Irish and followed by French-Canadians, Germans, and Poles. These groups initially worked low-wage factory jobs and faced various forms of marginalization; over generations, however, they were able to achieve upward mobility through participation in labor unions and increased access to employment in the public sector. In the mid-twentieth century, as factory jobs began to disappear, an influx of Puerto Ricans and other Latinx subgroups began to arrive in Holyoke.[8] According to the 2017 American Community Survey, Latinxs composed the largest ethnoracial group in Holyoke; the city of approximately forty thousand residents is 51 percent Latinx and 43 percent non-Hispanic white.[9] The Puerto Rican community composed nearly 50 percent of the population of Holyoke, the highest concentration of Puerto Ricans in any US community.[10] Unlike Holyoke's previous (im)migrant groups, Latinxs have not experienced upward socioeconomic mobility or increased employment opportunities across sectors over generations. The Puerto Rican population in particular is concentrated in the downtown area and South Holyoke, the city's most stigmatized and socioeconomically marginalized areas.

Puerto Rican marginalization in Holyoke underscores Flores's broader point that "the search for Latino identity and community, the ongoing articulation of a pan-ethnic and transnational imaginary, is also a search for a new map, a new ethos, a new América."[11] When we first began living and working in Holyoke, we were struck by our perception of a Latinx space with so few visual markers and affirmations of identity typically associated with "barrio urbanism" and its "jardines, color, calles, árboles, tiendas, arte public, y la vida de la calle."[12] Instead, the public streets of Holyoke were covered in giant green shamrocks representing the city's Irish community (see figs. 4.2 and 4.3). Importantly, these shamrocks were concentrated primarily in the predominantly Puerto Rican downtown area rather than the areas where the large majority of Irish and other white residents reside.

Disparities between visual affirmations of Irish and Puerto Rican identity are perhaps most starkly evident during the annual St. Patrick's Day and Puerto Rican Day Parades. During the St. Patrick's celebration, held annually in March on the Sunday following St. Patrick's Day, downtown Holyoke is essentially shut down, the streets are closed, traffic is rerouted, and an entire 6.2 mile stretch of road is reserved for the parade and 10k road race. The widescale preparations throughout Holyoke reflect the fact that the city hosts one of the largest St. Patrick's Day Parades in the United States, attracting hundreds of thousands of people from across the Northeast.[13] The approximately 6,400 Irish residents

FIGURE 4.2 Shamrock in downtown Holyoke. Photo by David Flores.

FIGURE 4.3 Shamrocks on High Street downtown in front of city hall.
Photo by David Flores.

constitute 16 percent of the city's population.[14] Recall the aforementioned statistic that Puerto Ricans constitute nearly 50 percent of Holyoke's population, the largest concentration of Puerto Ricans anywhere in the mainland United States. Yet, in contrast to the St. Patrick's Day Parade, the Puerto Rican Day Parade, held annually in July, covers a mile-long stretch of road, attracts around four thousand people, and takes place in a park on the outskirts of the downtown area.[15]

Despite a Puerto Rican population that is three times larger than the Irish one and sunny summer weather as compared to the typically brisk climate in late winter/early spring, the annual Puerto Rican festivities are thus strikingly outsized by Holyoke's St. Patrick's celebration. These two very distinctive celebrations of identity demonstrate Holyoke's Irish dominance and Puerto Rican subordination. Similar to racial dynamics across the country, the fraught politics of space and place within Holyoke privilege populations stereotypically associated with normative American whiteness, empowering them to define the landscape and — by extension — the city's identity. This underscores Breitbart's point that "one of the clearest demarcations of power, wealth and influence in the urban landscape has always been the ability to invest one's living space with meaning — to literally occupy, define and decorate one's surroundings."[16] Breitbart's use of the colonial language of "occupation" is fitting not only because of the longstanding displacement and eradication of Indigenous populations in US communities like Holyoke but also because of Irish immigrants' access to whiteness and by extension white land occupation facilitated through various twentieth-century policies and because of Puerto Ricans' colonial displacement prompted by US occupation of the island.[17] In this sense, Holyoke's highly stratified contemporary relationships between Irish and Puerto Rican residents are rearticulations of long-standing colonial systems that stipulate the locations where and the conditions under which different ethnoracial populations can reside in the United States.

The reproduction of Holyoke's spatial and ethnoracial boundaries has continuously repressed its minoritized residents and contributed to striking forms of political and economic marginalization. These boundaries enact and institutionalize white supremacy by structuring inequality in domains such as electoral politics and public education. Puerto Ricans are clustered in fewer wards than other population groups in Holyoke, which reduces their representation in the city council: the city's Latinx population outnumbers its non-Hispanic white population, yet at the time of the public art controversy discussed in this chapter, only three of the fifteen city counselors were Latinx, with the rest being non-Hispanic white. In public schools there is a reverse effect: Latinxs compose roughly half of Holyoke's population, yet they make up nearly 80 percent of its public-school students. Indeed, in some Holyoke public schools, the student body is more than 90 percent Latinx.

Latinx political underrepresentation and educational underachievement is often problematically viewed as the product of a "pathological culture," which is how one non-Hispanic white city council member described Holyoke's Puerto Rican community at a community literacy event. This thinking, in conjunction with the marginalization of Puerto Ricans throughout Holyoke, can be understood as a part of broader patterns of stigmatization and exclusion. As Baca states, "if you deny the presence of another people and their culture and you deny them their traditions, you are basically committing cultural genocide."[18] More recently, scholars have conceptualized the abject marginalization that racialized communities face as a form of "social death" that renders particular populations disposable by denying their personhood and justifying the forms of marginalization they face.[19] As demonstrated by the thinking of the city councilor quoted above, social death and cultural genocide are rationalized by attributing a "culture of poverty" to Puerto Ricans that renders them fundamentally illegitimate and in need of containment. Pérez shows how long-standing stereotypes about a Puerto Rican "culture of poverty" emerged as deceptive behavioral rationalizations that obscured political and economic shifts taking place in a particular historical moment.[20] Massive Puerto Rican migration to northern US urban centers in the mid-twentieth century corresponded to initial access to stable jobs that quickly and dramatically declined as part of broader patterns of deindustrialization. Rather than understanding Puerto Rican poverty that resulted from these conditions as the product of a shifting political economy, culture of poverty logics blamed Puerto Ricans' experiences of extreme economic marginalization on their cultural behaviors. The notion that Puerto Ricans suffer from a culture of poverty becomes a way of framing inequality as the product of individual choices rather than forms of structural exclusion and institutional racism—including access to education, childcare, health care, employment, stable housing, and transportation. Structural inequalities require structural interventions, but the problems that plague Holyoke are continually attributed to stereotypes about a deviant Puerto Rican culture, erasing the ingenuity and resilience Puerto Ricans have continually been forced to cultivate in response to a rigidly stratified community.

A purported cure for the "culture of poverty" that plagues Holyoke is the recruitment of middle-class and wealthy newcomers to the city. An opinion piece titled "Holyoke Needs Middle-Class Housing," published in a prominent local media outlet, states:

> Nationwide, there is a tremendous untapped market for middle class, market-rate housing in vibrant, walkable urban areas. So far, Holyoke has been unsuccessful at turning this market to its advantage. Instead, it has watched a valuable asset stagnate into a bleak cityscape of social service offices, in effect prioritizing a government-led economy over a more productive, more dynamic privately-led economy for the city's historic business center.[21]

This perspective, voiced by one of Holyoke's most prominent developers, reflects some middle-class and wealthy Holyokers' interest in consolidating their privilege and power, while leaving socioeconomically marginalized residents to fend for themselves. This coincides with efforts elsewhere toward establishing residential tax abatement zones in gateway cities, which would serve as a tool to bring about gentrification and displace the existing residents in downtown neighborhoods through increased rents.[22] Through such efforts, Holyoke has sought to create more cafés, restaurants, bars, and condos in predominantly Puerto Rican areas. While the case for such development is articulated socioeconomically and culturally, the invocation of "a bleak cityscape of social service offices" signals a set of racialized assumptions about populations that are stereotypically productive versus those alleged to be parasitic. This involves a distinction between a dynamic, racially unmarked "creative class" imagined as generating its own prosperity on the one hand and a stagnant, racialized Puerto Rican underclass necessitating perpetual public aid on the other.[23] Whereas the former is represented as an engine of cultural and economic development, the latter is framed as a burdensome, welfare-dependent population incapable of sustaining itself. Narrative contrasts between allegedly individually generated economic prosperity and purportedly pathological state dependence serve as a justification for neoliberal revitalization efforts organized around disinvestment in social services and incentivization of private development.[24] This championing of individual development and scapegoating of marginalized Puerto Rican communities obscures ongoing structural inequalities that have systematically reproduced both an institutionally empowered—that is, state-dependent!—non-Hispanic white population and an economically precarious, welfare-dependent Puerto Rican population; it also ignores the incredible cultural and economic ingenuity that Holyoke's Puerto Rican community has developed to survive abject marginalization, which could be reimagined as a space from which to redesign the city by prioritizing the well-being of its most marginalized residents. As a result of this erasure, Holyoke Puerto Ricans are rendered fundamentally problematic and disposable. Characteristic of many communities targeted for gentrification, proponents of development demonstrate little to no concern for long-standing residents' individual well-being and collective cultural lifeways in these neighborhoods of Holyoke.[25] Instead, the primary goal is to push for economic development by attracting outside developers and investors, and, by extension, displacing Puerto Rican residents. The following section highlights the deceptive ways that apparent efforts to overcome Holyoke's inequalities through revitalization and multicultural unity can in fact contribute to the reproduction of disparity.

Revitalization and Neoliberal Multiculturalism in Community-Based Design

In 2014 the Holyoke Alleyway Revitalization Project (HARP) emerged as an effort "to bring people together from all wards of the city to clean up and transform an urban alley for daily use as an attractive, connecting walkway/bikeway, including plantings and art."[26] Its director stated her hope that the alley would provide space for events and activities for Holyoke's residents and visitors alike.[27] The development of the project was to include input sessions with residents, collaboration with and consent from property and business owners, and applications for public funds. Despite this purported commitment to widespread community engagement and the location of the HARP alleyway in Holyoke's predominantly Puerto Rican downtown area, all but one of the proposed HARP public art designs were ethnoracially unmarked, apolitical urban decorations (e.g., paintings of a peace sign, yin yang, and silhouettes of figures dancing). The lack of ethnoracial specificity in these designs was part of a broader politics of neoliberal multiculturalism in which cultural differences are strategically represented in ways that privilege marketability.[28] Rather than promoting progressive community transformation by creating representations that honor the unique experiences of marginalized populations, neoliberal multiculturalism downplays issues of power and inequality in favor of depoliticized invocations of difference.

In contrast, after conducting information-gathering sessions with Puerto Rican Holyoke residents in conjunction with his initial collaboration with HARP, David Flores proposed a design explicitly intended to affirm Puerto Rican identity and avoid a situation in which "any population could move through the place without being reflected in it."[29] Inspired by his previous work with Chicago's Puerto Rican Cultural Center and its celebration of nationalist Puerto Rican public art and architecture, Flores's design consisted of a large-scale art installation that would resemble a giant Puerto Rican flag made of chain-link fencing draped on the side of a building.[30] The fencing would hold thousands of bells, which would create a soothing sonic effect in the wind or rain. This design reflects Flores's commitment to creating "art that will ask people to use all of their senses."[31] The fencing and the bells would be painted light blue, red, and white as a tribute to the anticolonial version of the Puerto Rican flag. The project was to take around three months to complete. HARP agreed to fund the project entirely through grants and fundraisers and Flores was to be in charge of the actual execution.

Flores collaborated with a Holyoke city council member and a local career center to identify Puerto Rican youth to work as paid interns and assistants on this project. His commitment to community collaboration is similar to that of other Latinx place-makers, for whom bringing "talented young people into the design crew fits the goals of the project . . . it's part of the leadership development aspect of the program, giving kids more and more power to meet and enhance their growth."[32] Participation in the creation of public art can have a powerful impact on youth. In Breitbart's analysis of her own public art collaboration with youth in Holyoke, she explains that "when young people are encouraged to re-examine the strengths and weaknesses of their surroundings and then act creatively to transform them, the experience can alter young people's attitudes towards each other and their future."[33]

Hoping to spark this transformation through his work with youth in Holyoke, Flores collaborated with one such group of young people for several weeks to realize his design. He sought to exchange knowledge, share skills, and empower youth through action. This approach to art and the design itself reflects Flores's rejection of neoliberal multicultural aesthetic approaches. As a Chicago-born Mexican artist who had previously worked with Chicago's radical nationalist Puerto Rican Cultural Center, Flores worked from a position of Latinx political solidarity. In opposition to neoliberal multicultural sensibilities that might celebrate the homogenization of Mexicanness and Puerto Ricanness into a

FIGURE 4.4 The creation of the Puerto Rican license plate mural.
Photos by Jonathan Rosa.

FIGURE 4.5 Holyoke license plate mural outside of city hall. Photo by Rob Deza.

whitewashed Latinidad, Flores's Latinx artivism emphasized political solidarity through a Mexican–Puerto Rican collaboration that centered Puerto Rican empowerment.[34] This effort can be understood as part of a broader "Latinx artivist movement" that "may represent a significant break and intervention away from the dominant 'Latino' projects . . . that promote assimilationist and conservative representations of Latinos as 'model minorities.'"[35] Flores's Latinx artivism involved a complex insider-outsider positionality that presented him with the opportunity to enact solidarity with Holyoke Puerto Ricans as a Holyoke resident, but a newcomer, and as Latinx, but not Puerto Rican.[36]

However, several weeks into the project, HARP informed Flores that they needed to cut the originally agreed upon budget by more than 75 percent. Flores went back to the drawing board and developed a less costly, but no less affirmatively Puerto Rican, design based on one of the community consultation sessions that he had previously conducted. He proposed to create a mural consisting of a Puerto Rican license plate with HOLYOKE written across the center. The following section explores the diasporic thinking that informed this design.

Latinx Artivism and Diasporic Puerto Rican Place-Making

Reflecting a commitment to creating a site-specific art piece that would affirm Puerto Rican identity, David Flores designed an 8' × 16' mural of a Puerto Rican license plate that reads HOLYOKE (see fig. 4.4). Whereas many Puerto Ricans throughout Holyoke proudly display similar license plates that point to their hometowns on the island, Flores's piece intended to claim that Holyoke is part of Puerto Rico. By drawing on a local diasporic practice and projecting it onto a larger scale, Flores sought to engage in what Juan Flores characterizes as "thinking diaspora from below":

> The grassroots, vernacular, "from below" approach helps to point up the many diaspora experiences that diverge from those of the relatively privileged, entrepreneurial or professional transnational connections that have tended to carry the greatest appeal in scholarly and journalistic coverage. That approach, guided by a concern for subaltern and everyday life struggles of poor and disenfranchised people, also allows for special insights into ongoing issues of racial identity and gender inequalities that are so often ignored or minimized in the grand narratives of transnational hegemony.[37]

The display of Puerto Rican license plates throughout Holyoke can be understood as a practice of "diaspora from below" that reflects the symbolic value associated with the Puerto Rican flag among a people whose flag was outlawed by the US colonial government from 1898 to 1952.[38] By drawing on the imagery of the license plate and the flag, Flores invoked Puerto Ricans' resistance against colonial experiences on the island as well as in the United States generally and Holyoke specifically. The broader goal was to imagine an alternative Holyoke in which Puerto Ricans would have a legitimate claim to place. As Sommer explains, "Without imagining the world otherwise, change is unthinkable . . . and thinking otherwise is an invitation to play."[39] In this case, to "play" would mean to creatively reconstruct a more inclusive Holyoke. For Sommer, "exemplary creative agents can spark recognition of agency in others who artfully engage the world."[40] The effort to draw on subaltern cosmopolitan themes to spark progressive action reflects Flores's aspiration as a Latinx artivist.[41]

The planned size of the mural was informed by Flores's intuition that "changing scale . . . makes people perceive things differently."[42] That is, "by taking a small object and transforming it into a giant image, you teach people to look at it in a different way."[43] This semiotic claim to space would serve to intervene in Holyoke's status quo, wherein the majority of Puerto Ricans, specifically in the downtown and South Holyoke areas, are repressed to the point of being erased. However, this erasure is countered with tremendous pride in symbols of Puerto Rican culture and identity. This situation, in which visual symbols are very important to populations even if they are marginalized in public space, is similar to Baca's description of the Los Angeles context in the 1960s and 1970s:

> The group of people I was working with was very connected to and influenced by visual symbols—in tattoos, in the kind of writing that went on in the street—but there was no visible reflection of themselves in the larger community. Nothing of the architecture or visual symbols reflected the presence of the people—other than the graffiti.[44]

Flores was similarly dismayed by the dearth of visual affirmations of identity in a community with the largest concentration of Puerto Ricans anywhere outside of Puerto Rico. He sought to create a mural with this community that would resonate with and reimagine cultural symbols that residents value. For Baca, the representation of these symbols has a unique power:

> Symbols already had significance in this community, and it made sense to create another set of symbols acknowledging the people's commonality, the fact that they came from the same place and had a common culture. It seemed to me this could break down the divisions among these people, give them information, and change their environment. The murals have been clear forms of expressions, reflecting issues and needs as they see them. I think decorative murals are a waste of time in urban areas. They're urban decoration, Band-Aids on cancer.[45]

Similarly, for Flores, this mural was intended to be more than urban decoration or simply a Puerto Rican license plate that reads "Holyoke." Instead, he intended to challenge the terms of belonging in a community where several generations of Puerto Ricans have made their lives yet face continued marginalization. Flores's politically provocative semiotics of Latinx place-making involved reclaiming Holyoke as part of Puerto Rico and emphatically asserting the primacy of Puerto Ricans' claim to Holyoke.[46] By engaging with deeply vernacular practices that might seem to have little normative material value and projecting these practices onto a significantly larger scale, Flores also drew on a Chicano aesthetic of *rasquachismo* that embraces resilience, resourcefulness, and boldness.[47] Flores's effort not only recognizes the basic presence of Puerto Ricans in Holyoke—it reclaims the city as a uniquely transnational and translocal Puerto Rican space while at the same time symbolizing broader, long-standing struggles for Latinx rights and resources across various diasporas.

From Reclamation to Repression

In September 2014 Flores's mural celebrating Holyoke's Puerto Rican community was scheduled for installation as part of a set of pieces created in conjunction with HARP, a public art initiative funded by a grant from the Massachusetts Cultural Council/Holyoke Local Cultural Council. Before the piece could go up, however, the owner of the building on which it was to be installed decided that it could not be displayed on any of the exterior walls of her property. In explaining her decision, she said she thought, when giving initial permission, that Flores's piece was going to be "about the community" and "for every ethnic group;" she further suggested that the mural would do more harm than good to Holyoke's Hispanic community. She proposed hanging it on the inside of the garage; in order to display it outside, she stipulated that Flores would have to change it to make it "more diverse." Holyoke's public streets are covered year-round with giant green shamrocks that represent the city's Irish population and yet these displays are not met with the same demands for "diversity." The notion that Flores's mural should be displayed inside rather than outside is similar to the spatial marginalization demonstrated by the aforementioned Puerto Rican festival, which is minimized and relegated to the margins of the city. Worse, although the building owner had previously approved of Flores's design and seen the finished project well in advance of the scheduled installation, she responded affirmatively to pressure from nearby business owners and other residents seeking to prohibit public displays of Puerto Ricanness in Holyoke. While HARP purportedly supported Flores's mural, the decision to collaborate on this project with a building owner who opposed public affirmations of Puerto Ricanness reflects problems that are characteristic of various revitalization initiatives. In fact, like revitalization efforts in Puerto Rican neighborhoods and communities of color throughout the United States and beyond, such projects can often contribute to processes of gentrification despite their organizers' expressed intentions.[48] The other artwork funded through the grant, which was regarded as more inclusive than Flores's mural, was displayed on the building whose owner discriminated against Flores's piece based on its affirmation of Puerto Rican identity.

The guidelines of the public grant that funded HARP state: "In accordance with state law, local councils may not discriminate against applicants on the basis of race, gender, religious creed, color, national origin, ancestry, disability, sexual orientation or age, nor may they fund projects that discriminate on the basis of these attributes."[49] Reflecting on the violation of the grant's guidelines and the broader discrimination against Puerto Ricanness in Holyoke, Flores embarked on a mission to find a home for his mural. For Flores, this mural represented the Puerto Rican community that had been systematically pushed aside, so it was important for it to be displayed in a highly visible and prominent location. He passed out flyers to passersby and local business owners and hung them on buildings whose owners allowed him to do so. The bilingual flyer, which read, "ADOPT MY MURAL/ADOPTA MI MURAL," briefly recounted of the series of events surrounding the mural's exclusion from the public art initiative. Many people were immediately receptive and offered to display it on the outside of their buildings and homes. While Flores was excited about the outpouring of support, most of the spaces that people offered were not in prominent locations; they were neither high traffic nor highly visible. Still, community members' overwhelmingly positive response to the mural not only encouraged Flores to continue seeking the right home for it but also demonstrated the ways that public art can galvanize a community that might otherwise appear fractured or docile.

Transforming Place

After news of the controversy surrounding the mural began circulating on social media, it made headlines in several local and even national news outlets.[50] This helped Flores secure a meeting with Holyoke's then-mayor, Alex Morse, who expressed support for the mural and broader efforts toward affirming Puerto Rican identity. Moving from words to action, Morse sent representatives from Holyoke's Department of Public Works to collect the mural from Flores's residence and began to build a frame for it that would allow it to be displayed outside of city hall, which it was on the following day (see fig. 4.5). The mayor released a public statement:

I'm happy to announce that David Flores' mural will be displayed outside City Hall. This mural is not only an impressive work of art; it is also a fitting symbol of the city's values and commitments. The story of Holyoke has always been the story of people from varying backgrounds and different cultures making their homes here—a story of diverse people sharing a common dwelling and striving to share a common purpose. At its best, that's what the city of Holyoke stands for.

Today, nearly 45% of Holyoke residents claim Puerto Rican heritage—a higher percentage of Puerto Rican residents than any other community in the United States. And while our Puerto Rican residents have too often been marginalized, and have too often failed to enjoy the full benefits of membership in our community, they have nonetheless contributed to the life and vibrancy of our city in incalculable ways. Puerto Rican culture is just as much a part of Holyoke's history as Irish, Polish, or French culture, or any of the other expressions of identity that enrich our civic life. Our differences should not be denied or ignored, nor should an affirmation of one culture be considered threatening to any other. And if an artist wants to celebrate a marginalized group, that should be welcomed by all Holy-okers as an invitation to appreciate difference, to question the assumptions we make about others, and to imagine a more just community for us all to share.

Over the past two weeks, I have closely followed the debate surrounding HARP and David Flores' mural. I was saddened and disappointed by what happened to Mr. Flores, and believed—and still believe—that he deserved better. But I also think this controversy and the debate that ensued may provide a valuable opportunity for our community to grow. Very important issues have been raised—issues such as the systemic nature of racism, the problem of assimilation, and the value of celebrating cultural difference—and I would hate for our city to miss a chance to discuss them.

In the coming weeks, I will be announcing a series of steps to address, and to facilitate dialogue about, issues of race, class, and culture in Holy-oke. For now, I am happy that this mural has found a home, and grateful to Mr. Flores for agreeing to display his art at City Hall.[51]

After the mayor had the mural installed next to city hall, it was met with a tremendously positive reception from the community. Holyoke residents began taking pictures in front of the installation and using images of it in their social media profiles.[52] One man recorded a video next to the mural which was circulated on social media: "David Flores, yo te doy la gracia por poner este sign . . . esta es una belleza lo que tu has hecho aquí para la ciudad de Holyoke . . . te agredezco de corazón y Cristo te ama" ("David Flores, thank you for putting up this sign, what you have done for the city of Holyoke is beautiful . . . thank you from my heart and Christ loves you"). This powerful community response demonstrates how the claim to place and identity represented by the mural can be understood as an enactment of Latinx cultural citizenship affirming Holyoke Puerto Ricans and rejecting their marginalized status. Cultural citizenship involves the fashioning of alternative modes of political relationality beyond normative models of state-recognized citizenship. Rosaldo suggests that "in effect, new citizens have come into being as new categories of persons who make claims on both their fellow citizens and the state."[53] However, the assertion of diasporic identities that at once transcend the nation-state and stake a claim to hyperlocal experiences demonstrates that Puerto Rican Holyokers simultaneously experience, contest, and forge new forms of citizenship and noncitizenship.[54] The widespread embrace of Flores's project reflects the ways that art can become a platform for the expression of cultural citizenship and noncitizenship by breaking "habit by 'defamiliarization.'"[55] For Lippard, "the power of art is subversive rather than authoritarian, lying in its connection of the ability to make with the ability to see—and then in its power to make others see that they too can make something of what they see . . . and so on."[56] The widespread circulation of residents' pictures with the mural signaled not only the potential for art to stir the imagination but also the inability to contain Holyoke Puerto Ricanness.

Conclusion: The Aesthetics of Resistance

While Flores's mural was embraced by residents from throughout Holyoke's Puerto Rican community, it was also met with significant pushback. The strongest opposition came in the form of a ban on public art that Holyoke's city council issued in October 2014.[57] Within a month of Holyoke attracting national attention because of the exclusion of a Puerto Rican–themed art piece, the Holyoke city council instituted an indefinite ban on public art. Flores's mural was part of a city-funded public arts initiative in the city with the largest concentration of Puerto Ricans in the United States. If this had taken place in another context, one might have expected the city council to respond by denouncing this discriminatory use of public funds rather than doubling down on the repression of public displays of Puerto Ricanness in Holyoke.[58] However, in this Western Massachusetts city, situated in a state in which a ban on bilingual education functioned from 2002 to 2017, racism and xenophobia are perhaps more readily legible as the law than in other contexts in which this is functionally the case.[59]

In response to the various controversies surrounding his mural, Flores launched a "Más Color, Más Poder" (More Color, More Power) initiative to promote visual representations of marginalized communities, cultures, and peoples. Más Color, Más Poder emerged as a fourfold vision to (1) create more Puerto Rican/Latinx public art; (2) create a Puerto Rican/Latinx arts and cultural center in Holyoke; (3) contribute toward efforts to put marginalized people in positions of power, especially in low-income communities of color; and (4) empower youth in these communities and establish a pipeline to positions of power and higher education by providing safe spaces, resources, and programming that contributes to self-empowerment. As an aforementioned fundraiser for this initiative, Flores created T-shirts that would fund future public art projects. The image of the mural began to circulate not only on T-shirts but also on license plate placards that Puerto Rican residents display proudly in their vehicles, homes, and public spaces.

Holyoke's public art ban on the one hand, and widespread celebration of Flores's mural on the other, demonstrate the fraught politics of space, place, and identity. Without recognition of the profound nature of Puerto Rican place-making represented in symbols such as Flores's mural, the mayor's effort toward "reinventing Holyoke" will reproduce the long-standing marginalization of Holyoke's Puerto Rican residents.[60] This tendency is reflected in the gentrifying public arts initiative that sparked this debate, which promoted a whitewashed vision for public art in Holyoke, with limited participation of long-standing Puerto Rican residents and affirmations of Puerto Rican identity. This debate about public art and Puerto Rican identity is indicative of the broader need to abolish the city's white, Irish-dominated power structure—from city council to the cultural council to the school committee to the police department. Then-mayor Alex Morse used his platform to bring attention to diversity issues and highlight the need to address Puerto Rican marginalization in Holyoke, which suggests that there is at least some political vision for guaranteeing rights and resources for Puerto Rican residents. However, diversity and inclusion are a far cry from decolonization and abolition in a city whose Puerto Rican residents face profound structural violence that deeply constrains their everyday lives. Engaging with these broader antagonisms and visions of change, Latinx artivists throughout the United States have responded to the realities of structural violence by creating representations that transform how marginalized populations understand and respect their histories and communities. This analysis of one such effort and the controversy surrounding it, examined together with a defiant diasporic community's embrace of affirming representations, demonstrates how Latinx artivism can contribute to broader social and spatial change.

Notes

1. In one of his last acts as president, Barack Obama pardoned Oscar López Rivera in January 2017. For a discussion of the debate surrounding Puerto Rican Holyokers' efforts to advocate for the release of López Rivera, see Mike Plaisance, "Holyoke Council Committee to Debate Oscar Lopez Rivera, Federal Trans-Pacific Partnership Trade Deal April 4," *MassLive*, March 4, 2016, https://www.masslive.com/news/2016/03/holyoke_council_committee_to_d_3.html.

2. These numbers shifted dramatically following the displacement of hundreds of thousands of Puerto Ricans to the mainland United States in the years following Hurricane María in September 2017; see Meléndez and Hinojosa 2017.

3. Pérez, Guridy, and Burgos 2010.

4. Ruiz 2019; see also Bonilla 2020.

5. Erica Y. Lopez, "Dispute over Public Art Celebrating Latino Heritage Drives a Wedge in Massachusetts Town," Fox News, October 2, 2014, https://www.foxnews.com/lifestyle/dispute-over-public-art-celebrating-latino-heritage-drives-a-wedge-in-massachusetts-town.

6. Neumaier 1990, 270.

7. Della Penna 1997.

8. Throughout this chapter I use "Latinx" as a nonbinary alternative to the masculine "Latino" and feminine "Latina," in reference to people who (im)migrated or whose families (im)migrated to the United States from Latin America. I use gender-specific terms in direct quotations.

9. "Quick Facts: Holyoke City, Massachusetts," accessed October 22, 2019, https://www.census.gov/quickfacts/holyokecitymassachusetts.

10. "Puerto Ricans in Massachusetts: Demographic Profile and Fact Sheet," Massachusetts Parents United and University of Massachusetts Donahue Institute for Economic and Public Policy Research, October 2017, accessed October 22, 2019, http://www.donahue.umassp.edu/documents/MPU_MA_Puerto_Rican

_Fact_Sheet.pdf; "Puerto Rican Influence in Holyoke," Greater Holyoke Chamber, accessed October 22, 2019, http://www.holyokechamber.com/puerto -rican-influence.

11. Flores 2000, 191.

12. Díaz and Torres 2012, 4.

13. Michelle Williams, "Holyoke St. Patrick's Day Parade Highlighted by USA Today as Place to Celebrate," *MassLive*, March 12, 2015, https://www.masslive .com/st-patricks-day/2015/03/holyoke_st_patricks_day_parade_1.html.

14. "Holyoke, MA Population and Races," accessed October 22, 2019, http://www. usa.com/holyoke-ma-population-and-races.htm#PopulationbyRaces. Note also that, by concentration of Irish population, Holyoke ranks 207th in Massachusetts. See "Massachusetts Irish as First Ancestry Population Percentage City Rank," accessed September 23, 2021, http://www.usa.com/rank/massachusetts -state--irish-as-first-ancestry-population-percentage--city-rank.htm?hl =Spencer&hlst=MA&yr=9000.

15. "About Us," La Familia Hispana, http://www.lafamiliahispana.org/aboutus.html, accessed October 22, 2019; Brian Steele, "Puerto Rican Parade and Family Festival Shows Growth, Pride of Holyoke's Hispanic Community," *MassLive*, July 10, 2011, http://www.masslive.com/news/index.ssf/2011/07/puerto_rican_parade _and_family.html.

16. Breitbart 1998, 306.

17. Ignatiev 1995; Grosfoguel 2003.

18. Neumaier 1990, 256.

19. Cacho 2012.

20. Pérez 2004; Lewis 1969.

21. John Aubin, "Viewpoint: Holyoke Needs Middle-Class Housing," *MassLive*, October 20, 2013, http://www.masslive.com/opinion/index.ssf/2013/10 /viewpoint_holyoke_needs_middle.html.

22. http://www.holyoke.org/cchip/, accessed October 22, 2019.

23. Dávila 2012.

24. V. Rosa 2018.

25. Dávila 2004.

26. https://www.facebook.com/HARPupdates/info?tab=page_info, accessed October 22, 2019.

27. Ibid.

28. Londoño 2010.

29. Neumaier 1990, 262.

30. Ramos-Zayas 2003; Patrick O'Connor, "Holyoke's Alleyways Become Canvas for Paper City's Story," *MassLive*, July 21, 2014, http://www.masslive.com/living /index.ssf/2014/07/holyokes_alley_ways_become_can vas_for_paper_citys _story.html.

31. Neumaier 1990, 258.

32. Ibid., 267.

33. Breitbart 1998, 321.

34. Dávila 2008.

35. Dávila 2020.

36. For more on solidarity see Pérez, this volume; for more on insider researcher positionalities, see Villareal, this volume.

37. Flores 2009, 25.

38. Ayala and Bernabe 2007; Wilkinson 2004.

39. Sommer 2005, 264.

40. Ibid., 265.

41. Dávila 2020.

42. Neumaier 1990, 259.

43. Ibid., 263.

44. Ibid., 261.

45. Ibid., 262.

46. For more on the semiotics of Latinx place-making, see Chávez, this volume.

47. Ybarra-Frausto 1991.

48. V. Rosa 2018.

49. "Local Cultural Council Program," accessed October 22, 2019, https://www .mass-culture.org/lcc_public_applicant_guidelines.aspx.

50. E.g., J. Kyle Sullivan, "HARP Mural Controversy," New England Public Radio, November 14, 2014, https://digital.nepr.net/audiofiles/2014/11/14/harp-mural -controversy/.

51. "'Isla del Encanto' Public Art Mural Finally Finds a Home in Holyoke, Massa-chusetts," *Latino Rebels*, October 8, 2014, http://www.latinorebels.com/2014 /10/08/isla-de-encanto-public-art-mural-finally-finds-a-home-in-holyoke -massachusetts/; "Reflections on Public Art and the Community," accessed May 18, 2015, http://www.holyoke.org/news/reflections-on-public-art-and -the-community/.

52. Dozens of people changed their Facebook profile picture to the image of the mural.

53. Rosaldo 1997, 30.

54. Pallares 2014.

55. Sommer 2005, 270.

56. Lippard 2009, 199.

57. "A Temporary Ban on Public Art in Holyoke, Massachusetts," *Latino Rebels*, October 22, 2014, http://www.latinorebels.com/2014/10/22/a-temporary -ban-on-public-art-in-holyoke-massachusetts/.

58. Based on previous debates about public art in Holyoke, the city council's response was not entirely surprising. Many long-standing community members reported that the situation with Flores's art piece reminded them of the debate surrounding a mural created by Puerto Rican youth in Holyoke in 1996. Because the mural included a Puerto Rican flag and an upside-down US flag, a city counselor threatened to paint over the piece. In their analysis of the controversy surrounding the 1996 mural, Delgado and Barton show how "the obstacles faced in doing this mural project galvanized the Puerto Rican community" (1998, 354). Thus, debates surrounding public art have the potential to unify communi-ties and spark action.

59. For a related discussion of the Massachusetts bilingual education ban and responses to it, see J. Rosa 2018.

60. Alex Morse and Greg Bialecki, "Reinventing Holyoke," *Boston Globe*, May 29, 2014, http://www.bostonglobe.com/opinion/2014/05/29/reinventing-holyoke /CgGEojczPz4W2liUVYOlXO/story.html.

CHAPTER FIVE

Race, Trash Talk, and Dissent in Contemporary Suburbia

ANA APARICIO

In the mid-twentieth century, as suburban sprawl began to redefine America's real estate landscape, developers also manufactured and oriented the country's new middle class. A vision of prefabricated homes for nuclear families and streets designed with a particularly pedestrian and unvaried aesthetic was engineered by the likes of Abraham Levitt and his company, Levitt and Sons. As they developed their first Levittown, on a tract of land on Long Island close to New York City, they excluded from their vision Black and Latina/o populations. Many other real estate developers, supported by regulations and the policies of the Federal Housing Administration, followed suit, formally denying Black and Latina/o families the opportunity to purchase property in prime suburban developments. The justifications that such developers gave at the time centered on maintaining homes' property value. This quintessential piece of the American Dream, à la mid-twentieth century, was foreclosed to people of color, despite Supreme Court rulings that segregation in real estate stipulations was "unenforceable as law and contrary to public policy."[1] Functionally, as these mid-century developers continued to manufacture the new white middle-class, they determined policy that shaped the demographics and politics of suburbia for generations to come.

While Latinas/os were denied access to Levittowns and other similar suburban communities, they nonetheless created their own paths to suburbia, inspired by dreams of upward mobility and lives away from congested urban life. Indeed, many of these families gathered resources and tools, purchased plots of undeveloped land, and built their own homes, block by block. The site on which I base this chapter, Riverville, is one such suburb.[2] Puerto Ricans began moving from Brooklyn to this quiet, nature-filled hamlet on Long Island in the 1950s to fill jobs in the local lumber mills, hospitals, and manufacturing industry.

By the 1980s, they were joined by Dominicans, Central Americans (primarily from El Salvador), and South Americans (primarily from Colombia). This Latina/o suburb, filled with bodegas, botanicas, cuchifrito and pupusa spots, and numerous nonprofit organizations, has defined a different vision of suburbia and upward mobility. But its Latina/o and Black residents have continuously faced various forms of racialization, racism, and marginalization—at both the interpersonal and structural levels—that shape the way they are depicted in the public sphere and, subsequently, the way they are treated by politicians, via policy, and in everyday spaces. Since the 1980s, as the diversity of this Latina/o suburb grew, local elected officials, neighboring white suburbanites, and local media expanded critiques of these Latina/o newcomers. Much of the circulating narrative is what I refer to in this chapter as "trash talk"—xenophobic and racist at its core and operating with an assumption of a shared common knowledge among suburbanites in the region.

This chapter considers two interrelated processes: the way that "trash talk" in the public sphere and in politics solidifies a particularly negative narrative of brown and Black populations on the one hand, and the creative ways that Latinas/os are developing meaningful forms of dissent on the other. Scholars like Leo Chavez and Otto Santa Ana have analyzed the profound and persistent manner in which white publics have created stigmatizing narratives of Latina/o populations in the United States, as well as the consequences of the investment in the tropes they produce.[3] The production and circulation of what Chavez calls the "Latino threat narrative" is evidenced in magazines, news, other media, as well as in the work of scholars and elected officials. The bombardment of particularly negative and stereotypical images of Latinas/os in the public sphere over time has allowed for the dehumanization of Latina/o populations and for the justification of racist and xenophobic policies (e.g., the forced separation of immigrant families and detention of minors at the US-Mexico border).[4] Such processes are not unique to the twenty-first century, as they have clearly been at work throughout US history. However, what we are experiencing now is a return to overt forms of xenophobia and vilification of Black and brown populations, as well as an accelerated circulation and consumption of the stereotypical tropes that are at the heart of the Latino threat narrative. To borrow from Deborah Vargas, stereotypes and imagery of Black and brown bodies as "sucio" abound, and they continue to draw upon long-weaponized tropes like that of the "dirty immigrant" either polluting or draining the nation.[5]

It is within this context of heightened "trash talk" and accompanying forms of structural racism that contemporary Latinas/os develop diverse strategies to combat racist tropes and policies. Here, I build on the work of Deborah Vargas and José Esteban Muñoz to offer an analysis of the way these activists refuse to conform to dominant narratives while simultaneously imagining a more beautiful reality for themselves and their neighborhood.[6] As I will argue in this chapter, in their attempts to reframe images of Latinas/os in the public sphere, local activists in Riverville are not simply performing the "good citizen" or hyperperforming respectability—they are challenging processes that deem Latinas/os disposable, unfit, and not deserving recognition as part of the nation. In her work on a JROTC program in a predominantly Latina/o high school in Ohio, Gina Pérez highlights the complex ways that Latina/o families work to craft a sense of citizenship too often denied them.[7] Through their participation in military programs like JROTC, they seek not simply to prove they belong by hyperperforming the "respectable citizen" but also to demonstrate belonging with the tools most readily available to them. As they develop their own sense of self and ways of moving through their neighborhoods and social spaces, they do so with an understanding of the white gaze and, equally, with an understanding of the diverse ways in which one can belong. In reframing themselves, the Latina/o activists in the suburb of Riverville are very much like the Latina/o youth in the JROTC program and like the young Latinas described in Lorena Garcia's work;[8] they are crafting citizenship in a context in which they have been systematically denied that access, where there is an uneven recognition of personhood, and where their citizenship is indeed fragile, even disposable. It is within this context that they develop diverse projects that defy simplistic analyses of dissent. I now turn my attention to Riverville, environmental and structural racism, and local activists' beautification campaigns.

Vignette 1: Suburbia's Environmental Nightmare

In early spring 1987, *Mobro 4000*—a barge carrying three thousand tons of garbage—set sail from Long Island, from the larger town of which Riverville is a part. The local landfill, which processed garbage from across Long Island and New York City, was nearly full and the town needed to find another site to accept its trash. Because local landfills were dwindling in number and the United States was facing a waste crisis (with some municipalities predicting that by 1990 they would no longer be able to accept new trash), businessman Lowell Harrelson developed a recycling plan for New York's garbage. Convinced of the plan's sound business and environmental considerations, he brokered a deal with North Carolina for the first barge test run leaving Long Island. The barge was set to dock in North Carolina, where its contents were supposed to be converted to methane, which would then be used to heat and power homes. Once it arrived at its proposed destination, however, a local reporter claimed that New York's rats and diseases abounded in the cargo, prompting government officials to refuse to allow the barge to be unloaded.

For a period of five months, the barge traveled six thousand miles, as six other states and three countries also turned away the dirty cargo. "If it wasn't bad enough that North Carolina, Louisiana, Alabama, Mississippi, Florida [NY] and New Jersey refused to take the Mobro's rotting cargo," reported a Long Island paper, "it became an international incident when Mexico, Belize and the Bahamas followed suit."[9]

The reason given for refusing the trash was that it was an environmental and health hazard, with rumors spreading that the barge contained bedpans and potentially contaminated needles from multiple New York hospitals.[10] Nobody wanted to accept what appeared to be tons of infectious or hazardous waste from New York. And, of course, part of what alarmed people was who they perceived produced the garbage—namely, Black, brown, LGBT, and impoverished populations from NYC, whom they knew only from the stereotypes that circulated widely in the news and in the public sphere. At the center of such trash talk were warnings about poverty, crime, rape, HIV, and the crack epidemic, almost always in the coded language that Dana Davis refers to as "race-mute."[11] The refusal of NYC's garbage was the result of the power of the circulation of this trash talk in the public sphere. The decision to turn away the barge from US ports was, indeed, an investment in the protection—presumably, the physical protection—of white bodies. News outlets labeled it "the barge to nowhere" and chronicled its daily crisis, the negotiations surrounding it, and its messy politics. It became a national embarrassment and ultimately returned to the Long Island suburb from where it had originated.[12]

Vignette 2: Fractured Suburbs

More recently, this same Long Island suburb received attention once again due to a different kind of "trash talk" and waste management crisis. In early 2014, following the unregulated dumping of toxic construction and demolition waste on an undeveloped area on the western half of the suburb's largest public park—the material included wire, brick, wood, and broken glass containing asbestos and heavy metals—the State of New York closed the park, declaring it a crime scene as it conducted its investigation. Long Island's largest newspaper declared the illegal dumping of thirty-two thousand tons of asbestos-ridden waste and the town's mishandling of it an "environmental nightmare." Alongside this incident, Riverville was also the site to which the garbage of the wealthier Hamptons was transported in the summer of 2014, just months after the discovery of the toxic waste; even more recently, it is the site where the county is seeking to rezone a section of the neighborhood to allow for the development of a scrap metal processing facility. Local residents have been drawing attention to these individual cases, pointing out that environmental racism is on the rise in Black and brown neighborhoods.

In my current work, which draws on over four years of ethnographic and archival data collection in the majority Latina/o Riverville and its neighboring suburbs, I analyze how such crises are occurring in increasingly poor suburbs where people of color are the majority, as well as how local residents respond to these negative circumstances. Here, I contextualize and examine two differing forms of environmental justice activism, analyzing how and why seemingly diverging types of dissent develop around similar issues in Riverville. I focus on two initiatives in which young people organized around environmental issues. A series of questions motivate this work: How do we define and understand dissent, and can we imagine that it emanates from work that appears, on the surface, to be complying with neoliberal frameworks? What consequences—beyond policy change or reform—do we value when assessing the efficacy or value of particular forms of collective action? Finally, what does an analysis of such issues suggest about the changing landscape of grassroots politics in the neoliberal context? In what follows, I provide a brief overview of the site, then highlight examples of suburban racial projects—namely, the "trash talk" that circulates about local residents and the kinds of violence that result—and finally, analyze the two forms of collective action that local residents have developed around environmental justice concerns.

The Site, or Why Suburbia?

Since the turn of the nineteenth to early twentieth century when the "first suburbs" were developed, and certainly as a result of the mid-twentieth-century postwar suburban sprawl, these sites have signified class ascendancy and the achievement of the "American Dream." And as Karen Brodkin and others have explained, mid-century suburbs were manufactured to produce a new middle class, to which white ethnics had access and from which people of color were excluded.[13]

In the contemporary era, however, contestations over notions of "belonging," the aesthetics of private and public suburban and urban spaces (see Rosa and Flores, this volume), and resource allocation are classed and raced in different ways. Today's suburbs look dramatically different from the Levittowns of the mid-twentieth century. In recent decades, suburbs across the United States have borne the consequences of major political, economic, and demographic shifts: a dramatic increase in foreclosure rates, a sharp and sudden decrease in labor prospects (in the service sector, in construction, and in white-collar professions), an influx of more people of color, and an increase in neoliberal bureaucracies and policies, particularly devolution. Among the consequences of these various shifts is a scapegoating of the most vulnerable populations. In Riverville, public discourse often vilifies local Black and brown youth, as well as immigrants more generally. The narrative that circulates most aggressively includes language about Latina/o gangs, overcrowded homes, and ESL instruction as a tax payers' burden. And despite the diversity of this neighborhood's Latina/o population—Central American, Puerto Rican, Dominican, Colombian, white, Indigenous, Afro-Latina/o, newly arrived, third- and fourth-generation, citizen and noncitizen—the stereotypes paint a very homogenous picture of Latina/o residents, with every story or complaint leveled equally at all Latinas/os. The widespread circulation of "trash talk"—racist tropes and the "Latino threat narrative"—allows elected officials and others to justify the kinds of policies and/or programs that further marginalize or endanger people of color and immigrants.

Since the 1950s, working-class Latinas/os began to move out of major cities in the Northeast in search of economic opportunities in smaller cities and suburbs.[14] Puerto Rican families who moved from places like Brooklyn to Riverville in the 1950s and 1960s did so often as a result of businesses—like lumber yards and a large medical facility—recruiting Latina/o blue collar workers and because there were real estate opportunities that allowed families to buy an undeveloped acre for a couple hundred dollars. In the 1980s and 1990s immigrants from Latin America and the Caribbean—both newly arrived and those already living in US cities—moved to secondary cities and suburbs in search of work in the growing service and manufacturing sectors. In suburban New York these new arrivals filled the demand for low-wage labor in industries such as construction, landscaping, and health care.[15]

Today, more than 50 percent of immigrants in the United States live outside of major cities. And as gentrification in cities like New York continues to displace the working poor, many are moving to nearby suburbs. According to the 2010 Census, immigrant populations increased more than 60 percent in rural and suburban areas where immigrants had made up less than 5 percent of the population in 2000, a trend that continues a decade later.[16] In New York State, suburbs have witnessed vast population increases; according to the same 2010 Census, while the state's general population grew 26 percent, the number of Latina/o residents in New York's suburban counties grew, on average, 55 percent.[17] And the suburbs to which immigrants are now moving are increasingly working poor.[18]

As a diverse Long Island suburb that is nearly 70 percent Latina/o, Riverville continues to receive newly arrived immigrants of varying immigration status, as well as immigrant and nonimmigrant families moving from other US sites, all with various racial and class positions. Together with long-standing Puerto Rican, Dominican, and Salvadoran residents, this Latina/o suburb more closely resembles the diverse urban neighborhoods of places like Queens and Los Angeles.[19]

Trash Talk

Riverville is among a handful of Latina/o-majority suburbs in the same geographical area and like others, it is experiencing increasing poverty, foreclosures, and the dwindling of public resources and services. Given the heightened awareness in the media of such problems, public perception of the neighborhood has been negative, to put it mildly. The range of comments made to online newspaper accounts about the site and its residents are illustrative of mainstream public sphere depictions of them, and are often blatantly xenophobic and racist, no matter the focus or tone of the story.

Take, for example, online comments to a local paper's story on the expansion of the local free breakfast program (an initiative that was funded by private corporate sponsors):

Thomasmollo: It's really disgraceful to see so many children of illegal immigrants living off the hard earned [*sic*] tax money supplied by law abiding Americans. . . . This country is going broke supporting these people who pay nothing into the tax rolls and live off cash jobs yet benefit from liberal bribe money designed to create more Democrat voters. These people mostly have NO loyalty to this country and take every opportunity to wave their flags in our faces and spit on ours. And we wonder why America is falling apart ? We need not look further than the people who disrespect our laws and who are invading our neighborhoods.

Thomasmollo: Great !! More of hard working [*sic*] American taxpayer $$$ on children of illegal immigrants who make their money in CASH and never pay taxes. When will it end ???

Megkathleem217 *Thomasmollo* Not paid for with tax dollars . . . read the entire article. It came from a grant from Walmart.

Such commentary, in addition to its incendiary xenophobia, always flattens this population; that is, all Latinas/os fit into the same nativist trope. The logic behind this kind of trash talk in the public sphere also motivates racist and xenophobic action in public spaces. In the early 2000s, coinciding with increasing poverty and the influx of immigrants to suburbs across Long Island, there was a dramatic increase in incidents of physical attacks against immigrants. One well-known case was that of Marcelo Lucero. In 2008 a group of seven teens attacked Lucero and his friend as they were walking home, yelling racist slurs and ultimately, stabbing Lucero to death. The *New York Times* reported, "The authorities said the teenagers . . . were on the hunt for Hispanic men to beat up, a kind of sport that they referred to as 'Mexican hopping' and 'beaner hopping.'"[20] The attackers eventually pleaded guilty to gang assault, conspiracy, and attempted assault as a hate crime after confessing that they had participated in an ongoing series of attacks against Hispanics, which ultimately resulted in the 2008 stabbing death of Lucero. There have been other similar attacks but, unlike this one, the assailants are rarely brought to trial, often because the victims are afraid of reporting crime to local authorities, as they fear being questioned about their immigration status or that of their family members. Local activists have drawn attention to the ways in which elected officials have allowed—and in some ways, encouraged—a climate of racism and xenophobia to take root on Long Island. In 2009 the Southern Poverty Law Center issued a report concluding that "Latina/o immigrants in Suffolk County were regularly harassed and beaten, and that the anti-Hispanic rhetoric of local politicians had contributed 'to an atmosphere conducive to racial violence.'"[21]

Such trash talk moves in a circular manner between elected officials and other leadership, comments in the public sphere, and everyday spaces. As the 2018 midterm elections got under way, local leaders vying for office took clear positions on issues related to immigration and Latinas/os. In one 2018 ad supporting Jack Martins's campaign for county executive, the New York Republican State Committee (an affiliate organization of the national GOP) used fear tactics and the long-enduring trope of Latino men as criminals to align a Democratic candidate with the Salvadoran gang MS-13.[22] The ad focused on three brown, bare-chested, and heavily tattooed men staring menacingly at the viewer, their bodies seeming to both appear from and recede into darkness (see fig. 5.1). Along the top of the poster big bold red letters proclaimed, "MEET YOUR NEW NEIGHBORS! Laura Curran will roll out the welcome mat for violent gangs like MS-13!" It continued with less alarming font, albeit with equally disturbing language: "Laura Curran's campaign is supported and funded by New York City special interest groups. These groups want to make . . . [this] a sanctuary county for illegal immigrants and protect those convicted of violent crimes from deportation." It closes with another set of colored letters in bold, "MS-13 wins. Taxpayers lose. Laura Curran: She's MS-13's choice for County Executive. She shouldn't be yours."

The image and language used here rely on the long-circulating stereotypes of Latino men as savage, menacing, and criminal. These bodies are, as Vargas points out in her work, *sucios*, unruly bodies that threaten to pollute the sanctity of white suburbia. This image also capitalized on strong sentiments about two dominant media stories regarding different Latina/o immigrant groups at that time: hysteria and outrage about unaccompanied minors from Central America being placed on Long Island by the tens of thousands, which was far from the reality of the crisis that began in 2014; and a fear of encroaching violence from a Salvadoran gang, which, contrary to public perception, mostly affected the well-being of fellow Salvadorans. All of this reflected a broader trend in which the complexity or nuance of this diverse population gets erased, as all Latinas/os are lumped into one monolith of brown sucios, in all their supposed menacing criminality.

These kinds of examples are not new, unique, or innocuous. They travel with

FIGURE 5.1
New York
Republican
State Committee
political ad, 2018.

the heft of white investment in such tropes (particularly in suburbia's white spaces), the support of local leaders, and the reality that they work to shape local sentiment and policy that affects immigrants and Latinas/os. This was the reason that the forty-fifth president of the United States (hereafter referred to as "45") launched his campaign in 2015 with racist and xenophobic language targeting Mexican immigrants. For those trafficking in this kind of rhetoric, immigrants and Latinas/os with origins in different countries in Latin America are one and the same. In New York suburbs, a wave of new stories about MS-13, a transnational Salvadoran gang, has worked to further solidify a white fear of brown bodies, particularly brown men. While the violence enacted by the group has been real, the targets have been Latinas/os. But the narrative that is continuously evolving is one where these brown men are invading the safety and peaceful aesthetic of white suburbia. The political ad referenced above does precisely that, but it can only do so because a fear of the Latina/o presence — one that is very gendered and marked as savage, hypermasculine, menacing, and vicious — has been ever-present and operates as shared knowledge in the public sphere.[23] The narratives such ads rely on, as well as those of white suburbanites who have internalized this xenophobic and racist fear, do not distinguish Salvadorans from Puerto Ricans, Dominicans, or Colombians. Nor do they distinguish between citizen, permanent resident, and undocumented, as they traffic with a vicious shorthand that paints all Black and brown populations with one broad stroke.

And so, it was no surprise when, after his election, 45 traveled to Long Island twice within a year and a half of taking office to speak about the MS-13 gang, to justify a proposal to end the visa lottery and chain migration as well as to secure additional funding for local law enforcement and to build a wall along the

US-Mexico border. (He drew on the same trope that tied immigrants to criminality during his first State of the Union speech.) During his first visit to Long Island in July 2017, 45 delivered his speech from a stage where he was surrounded by and primarily speaking to local law enforcement. He spoke at length about the gang and the way they have caused pain and violence in suburbs across New York, how they've polluted the country as a whole. And he warned about their continued arrival, which he claimed was the result of what he understood to be "lax immigration enforcement." Building on the grotesque trope of the Latino sucio, he detailed vile acts of violence perpetrated by gang members, including language about how they have "transformed peaceful parks and beautiful, quiet neighborhoods into bloodstained killing fields. They're animals." And he empathized with local communities whom he sees as the victims, telling them he will be "liberating them":

> One by one, we're liberating our American towns. Can you believe that I'm saying that? I'm talking about liberating our towns. This is like I'd see in a movie: They're liberating the town, like in the old Wild West, right? We're liberating our towns. I never thought I'd be standing up here talking about liberating the towns on Long Island where I grew up.

Though he talked about the gang, his discussion of immigration policy and the influx of immigrants easily and purposefully slipped into a narrative about all Latinas/os in the United States of every age group, the supposed threat they pose, and how his administration was cracking down on it/them all.

> We're also working . . . on a series of enforcement measures. . . . That includes cracking down on sanctuary cities that defy federal law, shield visa overstays, and that release dangerous criminals back into the United States' communities. . . . The previous administration enacted an open-door policy to illegal migrants from Central America. "Welcome in. Come in, please, please." As a result, MS-13 surged into the country and scoured, and just absolutely destroyed, so much in front of it. . . . In the three years before I took office, more than 150,000 unaccompanied alien minors arrived at the border and were released all throughout our country into United States' communities—at a tremendous monetary cost to local taxpayers and also a great cost to life and safety. . . . Failure to enforce our immigration laws had predictable results: drugs, gangs and violence.

But that's all changing now. . . . We will defend our country, protect our communities, and put the safety of the American people first.

The president's delivery and policy positions built on long-standing narratives of Latinas/os, black populations, and immigrants as interlopers who ultimately sap local resources and increase crime rates. In the context of suburban politics, these narratives are explicit in outlining how these populations bring down local property values and destroy the safety and tidiness of an otherwise presumably sanitized and peaceful white suburbia. His speech on Long Island was but one example of how politicians position Latinas/os as the threat and white suburbanites as the victims in need of rescue. This dehumanizing language of the sucia/o has been equally leveled against all Latinas/os—Black, Indigenous, white, man, woman, child, citizen and noncitizen. Inflammatory speeches of politicians, such as those of the forty-fifth president, do not address either the actual victims of violence in the region or the resources and support they need. The example of the speech offered above is only a more recent instance of the kind of political rhetoric that numerous politicians and local leaders have used to frame Latinas/os around Long Island.

What I'm suggesting is that if during the mid-twentieth-century suburban boom/sprawl, developers and town officials worked to manufacture a middle-class utopia, at the start of the twenty-first century, there is another reality. As more immigrants and people of color move into suburbs, as suburbanites experience poverty and foreclosures at high rates (higher than those in cities), and as the wealthy and development dollars flock to city centers, developers and town officials seem to be manufacturing dystopic wastelands. Oftentimes obscured by more celebratory endeavors—such as suburban downtown development projects or Fourth of July parades and Octoberfest-type festivals—the reality is that suburbanites in places such as Riverville are experiencing a dramatic form of racialized structural violence.

The town officials and developers who allowed for the toxic dumping, the park closure, the importation of the east end elites' garbage (i.e., the Hamptons' shit), and who in 2015 easily considered a different kind of waste processing site in Riverville, have been able to imagine these projects because of the perception they have of the diverse Latina/o suburb and its residents. The circulation of the Latino threat narrative has allowed for that trope to become the raison d'être for dismissing this population and abandoning concern for their well-being. Such trash talk allows for the discursive and literal "dumping" on Riverville.

The spectacle that has been the management of material waste and the mismanagement of municipal resources in Riverville speaks to the ways in which suburban spaces are now imagined, as well as how certain suburbanites are imagined as belonging or not, deserving or a menace, a resource or a drain. The processes inherent in producing suburban spaces are, at their core, racial projects. The various projects and processes I outline here point to the material destruction of suburban landscapes—physical as well as economic and material. As such, it is important to analyze suburbia as contested and racialized space, and, building on Henri Lefebvre's work, a space that has always been produced in profoundly material ways.[24]

The pattern of "trash talk" I documented in Riverville seeks to blame immigrants and other people of color for a variety of problems—including overcrowded and underfunded schools, plummeting property values, increasing property taxes, and crime. This "trash talk" is ubiquitous in mainstream public discourse and is unmistakable in official town meetings—whether of the town board or the school board. Within this context, what forms of activism are possible, sustainable, and/or effective? In what ways do Latina/o activists working in an increasingly impoverished and racialized suburb such as Riverville attempt to critique local policies and programs?

Environmental Racism and Collective Action in Racialized Suburban Spaces

In early spring 2010, following a series of well-publicized incidents of crime, particularly the murders of Latina/o youth in the area, residents in Riverville called for a public forum to voice their frustrations. They were concerned about the way they perceived local government was addressing a recent wave of violence. The discussions held during and after these forums led to a barrage of new activist efforts; among them was the "Keepin' It Clean Project." This grassroots project brings together area youth and families to pick up trash in public spaces and to paint graffiti-riddled fences. Now an annual event, it draws anywhere between three hundred to five hundred volunteers every spring and garners the support of area businesses, the local police precinct, and elected officials.

Two cousins in their twenties launched the Keepin' It Clean Project. They envisioned an all-day, neighborhood-wide project focused on getting people—especially young people—to "Do Something," establish community partnerships, reduce negative perceptions of the neighborhood and its residents, increase neighborhood awareness, and create a cleaner environment. They

organize volunteers to remove trash from the streets and empty lots (they usually remove around one ton) and paint over as much graffiti as they can from
local homes and businesses. In the past, they've received support from local
government to buy paint and supplies. Their goals include the following:

> In the process we will save our residents and business owner's time and
> money, and take a stand again those who wish to deface and pollute our
> property. Our objective is to enlist neighborhood residents in a campaign
> to take back their streets and to remain active in taking care of our neigh-
> borhood, which will in turn reduce the negative behaviors that correlate
> to the recent spike in crime around town. We want to promote self-respect
> and neighborhood awareness by providing this hands-on opportunity
> to clean up neighborhood blight. . . . It is our hope that with a campaign
> focused on immediately addressing litter and graffiti . . . [and] that . . .
> vandals will feel hopeless in their efforts to pollute and deface property.
> This in turn could reduce the recidivism rate of this segment of the popu-
> lation; in other words, they may find something better to do. During our
> event we plan on taking before and after shots of homes and businesses
> that have been rehabilitated through our volunteer's efforts as a way of
> documenting the entire process. We will also use social media sites such as
> Facebook, local print media, and local television stations to promote the
> event and track progress.

I quote extensively from their material to point out a few themes: self-policing, respectability, changing public perception and public space, and finally, local
and youth civic responsibility. Within this agenda, they are involved in some
complicated and, at times, contradictory, politics. They seem to be modeling
a form of self-policing that would adhere to a neoliberal stance on addressing
poverty and crime in neighborhoods such as this one. That is, address behavioral
issues among local residents and you will see crime dwindle. It would be easy
to dismiss their agenda as a form of neoliberal civic engagement that does not
fully address structural issues. However, doing so would do a great disservice to
such projects and our theorizing around contemporary forms of dissent. I argue,
instead, that these young people are aware of (1) the stigma attached to youth
of color in the site; (2) the need to obtain the support of local elected officials to
effect change; and (3) the need to demonstrate and perform "good citizenship"
in order for changes to occur with respect to public perceptions and policies
that affect local residents, particularly impoverished and people of color. And

their project is also one that seeks to create a particular environment for local residents—one in which they enact a sense of ownership of their neighborhood. Theirs is a practice of envisioning community that moves far from dominant stereotypes—while fully aware of the white gaze—and works to redefine community for its residents.

These volunteers' attempt to clean up the physical landscape, to beautify public space, is very much connected to cleaning up the image of youth and people of color in the area. One also cannot ignore the possibility that they seek to create an environment that is cleaner, safer, and more beautiful, work that many believe should be done by the town. Their public campaign and program focuses, in part, on demanding that elected officials respect and support local residents. Signaling success in this area, one of the organizers explained why a local congressman bought into and offered resources to the project: "There we were, and we weren't a bunch of sp**s and n****s asking what you can do for us, but here's what we're going to do for ourselves."

In private conversations and in their planning, organizers also discuss their frustrations with local government and media. They critique the way that elected officials ignore the residents of the site, the poorest of their electoral district, how they shuffle more resources to the part of their district on the other side of the proverbial track, where the population is majority white. They talk about meetings and attending local hearings to address what they consider to be local representatives' incompetency and racism. When I've attended public hearings, local residents—particularly people of color—who speak publicly do so in a way that obviously involves hyperperforming respectability, both in their physical and oral presentations. I've attended school board and town council meetings where elected members call local residents "illegals" and decry Latina/o gangs, poverty, the increasing rate of overcrowding due to multifamily households, etc. In short, public officials are regularly engaged in the type of blaming discourse (at times blatantly so, more often subtly and in a "race-mutedly" manner) one encounters from the public on blogs and newspaper commentary. Local activists believe that they must address and fight both the public discourse that vilifies people of color and the policies and budget decisions that continue to leave their residents at a loss.

In its first year of programming, the Keepin' It Clean Project brought together nearly six hundred people to help "Paint Back the Streets." Their events continue to draw hundreds of volunteers, most of them young people. They advertise for the event and then publicize the successes of the volunteer effort on social media, in the local and region-wide newspapers, and through their network of community-based organizations.

The goal is not just an aesthetic one; it is about changing the perception others have about youth and people of color in the suburb, changing how local residents see and act on their frustrations with local issues, and developing a base of home-grown activists, which they hope will lead to more productive changes in the neighborhood. This event and organization are among many new initiatives in the neighborhood that seek to address local "trash talk," environmental racism, xenophobia, and politics.[25]

Many of these same "homegrown" activists were at the center of another environmental justice project that began in 2014. The work they initiated was a result of two major incidents of environmental racism. As noted in one of the opening vignettes, in early 2014 someone in Riverville complained about what turned out to be the illegal dumping of toxic waste in the suburb's main public park. Contaminated construction debris from NYC was dumped and then covered up by bulldozers in this park. According to media reports, "In addition to asbestos, the garbage was contaminated with toxic metals, petroleum products, and hazardous pesticides."[26] Further, at "another site where illegal dumping occurred, the same contaminants were found and the asbestos there was 10 times the legal limit . . . alongside other contaminants that have been banned in the U.S. because they are unsafe. [An investigator] warned that anyone who used the park since dumping began [the previous] spring until it was shut down [in 2014] could be at risk. . . . [Furthermore,] the contaminants . . . can find their way into the groundwater and linger for decades."[27] Local residents who attended town meetings, press conferences, and community forums believed this latest issue to be the result of the way the town council and people outside of Riverville racialize and "trash" the majority Latina/o, immigrant, and working poor suburb. The smoke had not yet settled from this crisis of the illegal toxic dumping in Riverville's largest park—in fact, the investigation had not been finalized yet—when, in the summer of 2014, in a deal struck with the governor of the State of New York, elected officials governing Riverville agreed to allow garbage from the wealthy and ultraposh Hamptons to be transported into and processed in the community. Although the garbage would not remain in the suburb, as it was to be transported via rail—first to Queens, NYC, and then to Kentucky—the truckloads of garbage were transported through Riverville as they made their way to the processing site. Trucks hauling tons of the Hamptons' garbage made it through miles of residential streets, ending up at a processing site at the end of a major residential street that already saw more than its fair share of industrial traffic. There, the garbage (some of it poorly sealed), awaited freight trains that somehow got rerouted, causing the tons of trash to sit for longer than planned in Riverville over the summer months.

Amid the investigations into the illegal toxic dumping, and as the wealthier Hamptons' garbage arrived, a group of neighborhood activists worked to inform and mobilize local residents around what they understood to be environmental racism. They organized meetings on street corners and at a local community garden; these meetings included some of the same people who organized and participated in the cleanup event. They also held rallies where they used their bodies to block trucks hauling trash into the neighborhood (see figs. 5.2 and 5.3).

These public protests usually involved a group of thirty to forty residents. They worked with a nonprofit organization to create flyers, canvas the neighborhood, set up meetings with the Department of Environmental Conservation (DEC), and demanded a special town forum. Their efforts did not stop the Hamptons garbage from being hauled into the neighborhood that summer. But they did lead to a deal with the town, brokered in consultation with the DEC, that such garbage hauling would not be permitted again. Just as important were the ways in which the activists brought different residents together to discuss the issues and to develop a network of concerned citizens. The kind of organizing work they did is familiar from scholarship on social justice work: they held meetings and planned rallies, committed acts of civil disobedience, and met with elected official and other representatives of the state to issue demands, including having a seat at the table when major policy changes were to be decided.

Trash Talk and Latina/o Dissent in Suburbia

So what do these two different initiatives tell us about the power of the circulation of anti-Latina/o narratives, environmental racism, and about dissent? In many ways, the Keepin' It Clean project and the 2014 environmental justice group are beginning to function as powerful rituals for Riverville's Latina/o population. The cleanup day happens annually and the activists in the environmental justice group help organize many other forums and projects in the neighborhood, including a public garden and weekly radio show. David Kertzer defines ritual as a rhetorical act, capable of creating change within and beyond communities. "Far from simply propping up the status quo," he writes, "ritual provides an important weapon in political struggle . . . [furthermore,] ritual is

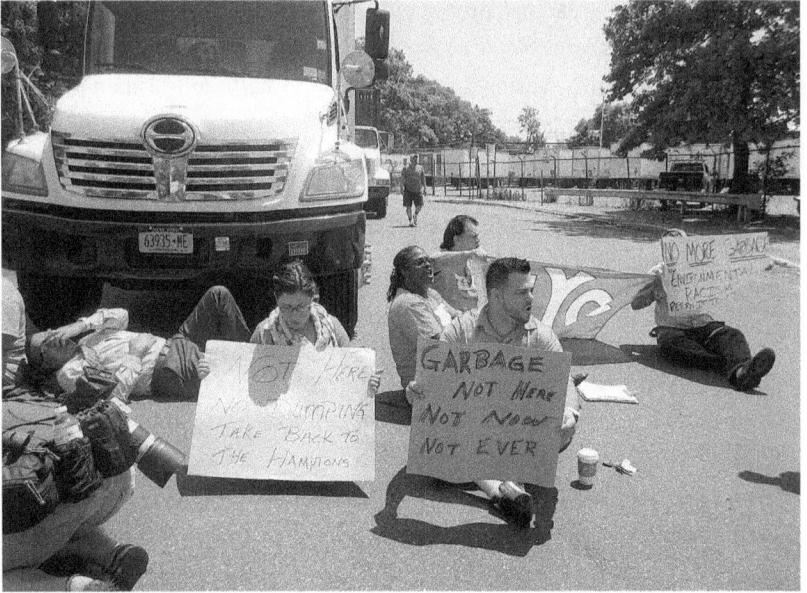

FIGURE 5.2 Local residents and organizers block trucks carrying Hamptons garbage. Photo by Ana Aparicio.

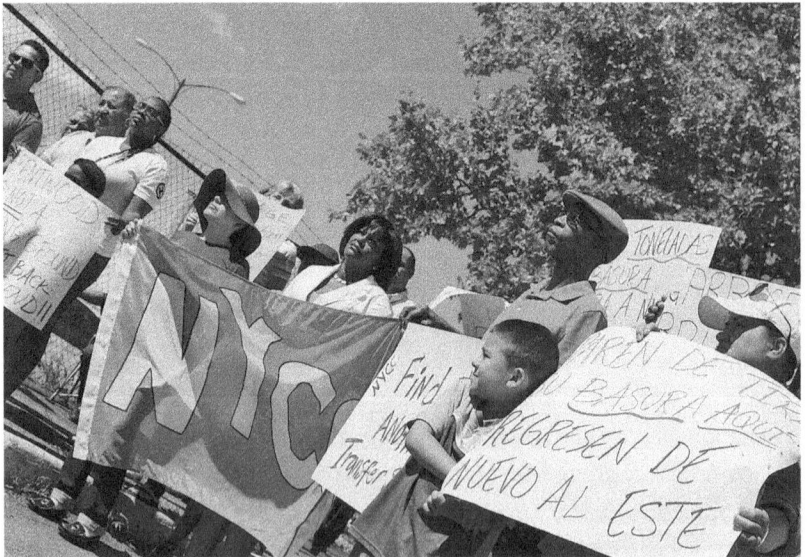

FIGURE 5.3 Local residents and organizers protest the arrival of Hamptons garbage. Photo by Ana Aparicio.

used both to make claims to power and to send messages to the public."[28] As performances and claims to public space, these "rites can take on a much more systematic and self-conscious role in bringing about political change."[29] This takes on new meaning in suburban sites experiencing dramatic economic and demographic transformations and rising nativist discourse. In highlighting the role of youth of color in "painting back the streets," or in blocking trucks from entering the neighborhood, we can see how they are challenging the ways in which mainstream political and social discourse portrays and/or incorporates them. The work of the Keepin' It Clean Project has been the catalyst for many other endeavors, including an extensive community gardens movement, various campaigns for local elected positions, and subsequently, the environmental justice work that developed in the summer of 2014.

In the efforts of both groups of activists to take control of public spaces, the actors are all clearly aware of the power inherent in changing the suburb's physical landscape. Neil Smith and Setha Low's interpretation of the importance of such sites is appropriate here: "Public spaces are simultaneously an expression of social power and a force themselves that help shape social relations."[30] These spaces are "socially produced . . . [they are] a matter of intense political struggle, and an object of historical change."[31] Events and projects such as those organized by the Keepin' It Clean Project and the group that formed in 2014 are important parts of an ongoing struggle for social inclusion, recognition, and power in suburbia. It's clear that these projects—much like those analyzed by Rosa and Flores, as well as others in this anthology—are involved in reshaping civic engagement, as well as furthering social and racial justice in the suburb.

The two Riverville groups I've documented here are engaging in the kind of activist work that is becoming the norm in this neoliberal age. They have a profound and painful recognition of racism, xenophobia, and of the material consequences of the decades-long circulation of negative and stereotypical images that continue to paint Black and brown bodies as sucios, interlopers, criminals. And while the work of the activists analyzed here does not always neatly fit into facile understandings of dissent—or of what dissent "should" look like—they are, nonetheless, working to confront and combat processes that relegate them as disposable, undeserving, noncitizens. They are acutely aware of how their efforts are necessary in creating the kind of suburban reality that the Latina/o resident population deserves; in the absence of resources and just policy from elected officials, they work to actively transform the neighborhood while simultaneously challenging various forms of structural violence. Theirs is a critical politics of dissent that is challenging "trash talk," reshaping contemporary suburbs, and imagining a new Latina/o suburbia.

Notes

1. *Shelley v. Kraemer*, 334 U.S. 1 (1948).

2. Except for elected officials, unless otherwise noted, names of individuals and places are pseudonyms.

3. See Chavez 2013 and Santa Ana 2002.

4. See Pallares 2014. See also Rosas 2012.

5. Vargas 2014.

6. See Vargas 2014 and Esteban Muñoz 2009.

7. Pérez 2015.

8. Garcia 2012.

9. Timothy Bolger, "How the Islip Garbage Barge Saga Compares to the Town's Toxic Dumping Scandal," *Long Island Press*, March 23, 2015, https://maketheroadny.org/how-the-islip-garbage-barge-saga-compares-to-the-town%C2%92s-toxic-dumping-scandal/.

10. When the barge docked in Florida, the Environmental Protection Agency examined the barge. They found hospital waste but determined that it did not carry infectious material and was, therefore, not hazardous and posed no health or environmental concerns.

11. Davis 2007.

12. Ultimately, the garbage was transported to local landfills after being incinerated in Brooklyn. Before the garbage was burned, Greenpeace activists hung a banner across the length of the barge; it read "Next Time . . . Try Recycling." In fact, when the waste was finally processed, one official indicated that much of the material was paper. In the years after the "barge to nowhere" voyage, recycling in the United States tripled. The barge's odyssey and the debates it generated drew attention to the increasing problem of the nation's garbage. It also was the first step in launching new ways of handling solid waste, including recycling. Riverville was thus at the center of what has since become a profitable and more environmentally sound trash management process (i.e., recycling).

13. Brodkin 1998.

14. See Torres 2006.

15. See Niedt 2013.

16. Sabrina Tavernise and Robert Gebeloff, "Census Data Show Immigrants Making Path to Suburbs," *New York Times*, December 15, 2010, https://www.nytimes.com/2010/12/15/us/15census.html. See also Frank Donnelly, "New York's Population and Migration Trends in the 2010s," Weissman Center for International Business Occasional Paper Series.

17. David Chen, "Hispanic Influx Slowly Altering a Town Veneer," *New York Times*, April 16, 2001, https://www.nytimes.com/2001/04/16/nyregion/hispanic-influx-slowly-altering-a-town-veneer.html.

18. See Hanlon and Vicino 2007.

19. See Ricourt and Danta 2003. See also De Lara 2018 and Cheng 2013.

20. Manny Fernandez, "Mourning Victim but Liking Accused in L. I. Killing," *New York Times*, April 5, 2010, https://www.nytimes.com/2010/04/05/nyregion/05patchogue.html.

21. Manny Fernandez, "Estate of Marcelo Lucero, Slain Immigrant, Sues Suffolk," *New York Times*, November 22, 2010, https://www.nytimes.com/2010/11/23/nyregion/23lucero.html.

22. MS-13, or Mara Salvatrucha, is a transnational gang that was established in California and now operates within and between the United States and El Salvador. See Ward 2012. Also, Wheeler 2020.

23. See Aparicio 2018.

24. Lefebvre 1991.

25. Aparicio 2018. In other work, I describe the way Latina women in the neighborhood have been at the heart of a burgeoning gardening and politics movement in recent years. The work they do addresses some of the same forms of structural inequality, beautification efforts, and community-building as the Keepin' It Clean project. But they do so with different strategies and a different awareness of the way gender and race politics affects them.

26. "DA: Illegal Dumping Investigation Reveals Banned Pesticides, Dangerous Metals at 2 Suffolk County Locations," CBS New York, May 29, 2014.

27. Ibid.

28. Kertzer 1988, 104.

29. Ibid., 150.

30. Smith and Low 2006, vii.

31. Ibid., 7.

CHAPTER SIX

Trans Latina Fantasías

Creating Trans Latina Selves, Families, and Futures

ANDREA BOLIVAR

Jesenia is a thirty-six-year-old Puerto Rican transgender woman. She was kicked out of her parents' home when she was twenty years old because of her gender and has been engaging in sex work and living on and off the streets ever since. She has applied to numerous jobs but has never been hired, which she suspects is because of her gender, race, and appearance as a trans Latina woman.[1] As she explained to me,

> We live in a society where there is no law to really protect us and everyone is declining us for work, where it's OK to attack us on the street and to even kill us. Ninety-nine percent of men only want us for their sexual fantasies. Yet they don't want to commit to a serious relationship. *Somos una fantasía.* So we are smart enough to use you before you use us. But then, that's really dangerous too. We are just out here trying to survive. It's *complicada, mi hija.* People don't understand.

Jesenia's sage words indicate the various levels at which violence against trans Latinas is manifested: from societal attitudes and laws to employment discrimination, intimate partner abuse, and everyday acts of random violence—which can be fatal. Her statement that trans Latina women are a "fantasía" acknowledges that because they exceed the limits of white cisheteronormativity, they are racially and sexually objectified by men, and thus larger society, in dangerous ways. At the same time, Jesenia points out that trans Latina women strategically engage with these harmful fantasies, capitalizing on them to create and sustain alternative economies of labor ("So we are smart enough to use you before you use us"). In other words, fantasía is not solely imposed upon them. Jesenia's use of fantasía, like that of many other sex-working transgender Latinas in Chicago, raises a number of questions. How might trans Latinas critically embody, rearticulate, and resist fantasía, or the ways they are fantasized? Moreover, how might sex-working trans Latinas actively fantasize alternative ways of being, working, and living? What potentialities does being a fantasía—an im/possibility—allow? What other fantasías beyond normative configurations of gender, sex, race, and class are possible?

Ethnographically illuminating sex-working trans Latinas' daily lives and how they endeavor (im)possibilities against and above normative frameworks is necessary, as sex-working trans women of color are commonly presented as the ultimate victims. In the last few years, increasing attention has been given to the murder of transgender people, and especially trans women of color in the United States.[2] As a result, they are often associated with death. While drawing attention to lethal violence against trans women of color is important, we must also recognize them in life and their fantasías in the present and for the future.

Furthermore, I argue that alongside the figure of the hypervictim that only allows visibility via violence and death, a second and equally flattening figure is emerging in both popular discourses and some queer circles: the trans woman of color activist. She is embodied by celebrities such as Janet Mock and newly (and strategically) celebrated historical figures such as Sylvia Rivera and Marsha P. Johnson, and she is unfairly expected to transform society and save us all. However, fantasías involved in trans Latina ways of being, which are enabled by sexual economies, are not necessarily grandiose, romantic, or activist in nature. Instead, I show how fantasías are often quiet and mundane, such as living in bodies that feel right, loving family members beyond death, practicing Afro-diasporic faiths, and just being. The women's quotidian acts of future-making, however, do not fail to trouble the white cisgenderist status quo.[3] As sex-working trans Latina fantasías resist sexualized dehumanization and death, they also refuse equally limiting and dehumanizing stereotypes of trans color activists, and the larger systems that impose both constructions. This chapter highlights trans Latina ways of being and the understudied, and at times unpredictable, ways that Latinxs refuse multiple layers of political, economic, and social marginalization.

Being a "fantasía" is akin to being a "sucia" as theorized by Deborah Vargas. *Sucias* defy "hetero and homonormative racial projects of citizenship formation, projects that seek to sanitize the world of filth and grime."[4] *Suciedad*, which is embraced and flaunted by sucias, persists in surplus despite multiple efforts to destroy it; it also offers the possibility for queer sustenance and alternative imaginaries of work, intimacy, and care. Queer spaces, Vargas points out, are critical for expressing suciedad, and the bars, dance halls, homes, or other places where people feel safe are treasured sites. Trans Latina sex workers may indeed be considered sucias. In this chapter, I show how women organize and enact resistant forms of labor, care, kinship, and space-making, while navigating constant violences that seek to erase them.

Yet it is trans Latinas' suciedad that also makes them sexually attractive, both to clients in sexual economies of labor and to US society more broadly. They are both simultaneously abject and alluring, repulsive and attractive. Therefore, they are not just sucias, but also fantasías, possible impossibilities within white cisheteronormative structures. Their transgenderhood poses a particularly formidable threat to white cisheteronormative ontologies, evident in the fact that they experience higher rates of murder than cisgender queer sucias. From a state of ontological impossibility, they are able to fantasize about the future and present, offering dangerous potentialities in and around sexual economies of labor. Therefore, fantasía as a racialized trans analytic indexes much more than sexual/racial/societal abjection and allure: it conjures a world free of racial capitalism, settler colonialism, and gender/sex normativities. Moreover, it speaks to how these two processes are intricately intertwined. From the margins of the margins, sex-working trans Latinas are able to work toward liberation.

Building upon Vargas and other queer theorists who have acknowledged the importance of fantasizing for queer folx and futures, I show that trans Latinas fantasize, while also being critical of fantasies of themselves and the larger systems of racism and cisgenderism that produce such fantasies.[5] Their own fantasías, I reveal, make up complex countereconomies, epistemologies, and ontologies. The women fantasize and manifest trans Latina bodies, selves, families, and communities. As they do so, they refuse binary stereotypes that present trans women of color as either hypervictims or activists and defy simplistic understandings of sex work, contestation, and the current political moment.

Ethnographically focusing on trans Latinxs—including brown and Black Latinxs—also answers calls for more work on the experiences of people of color within trans studies and trans people within Latinx Studies.[6] Therefore, it deepens our understandings of how trans people of color are racialized and gendered, and of how they refuse both disciplinary processes in the United States. Such work is urgent in the current political moment, when Latinxs and gender nonconforming individuals are increasingly under attack. Yet, the women with whom I work also refuse punitive regimes of transnormativity and normative

Latinidad. They are sex workers, and live and work in the *calle*. Many don't "pass." Some have dark skin, are fat, queer, and disabled. They live and love in excess of white, Euro-centric, cisheteronormative mandates of family and spirituality, thus offering radical potentialities beyond the current racist-cisgenderist reality as well as the transnormative and normative Latinx status quo.

Trans Latina Methodology

I conducted the bulk of research continuously between June 2015 and August 2016 on the West Side of Chicago, where the majority of the city's Latinx population resides. Most of my time was spent in Humboldt Park, which is the heart of Puerto Rican Chicago, and Little Village, a pillar of Mexican Chicago. I collected data across several sites, including interlocutors' homes and workplaces, LGBTQ and HIV/AIDS organizations, and streets, bars, and clubs where sexual services are sold. My methods included semistructured in-depth interviews, life history interviews, and participant observation with twenty-four sex-working trans women of color. Reflecting Chicago's Latinx population on the whole, most participants were Mexican or Puerto Rican, and some were Cuban and Ecuadorian. Two Puerto Rican women identified as Black, and two Mexican women identified as Indigenous. One woman, who hung out with the rest of the interlocutors, was non-Latinx Black.

I would be remiss if I did not address how my positionality—as a cisgender Latina woman—affected the research. Firstly, I would like to acknowledge the privileges I possess that distinguish my experiences from those of my interlocutors. I am cisgender, a US citizen, and at the time of research was a doctoral student at a prestigious private university that offered a modest yet stable source of income. These privileges are significant. At the same time, however, I am a Latina femme and the first in my family to graduate high school. I grew up in the hood and have family members involved in alternative economies. Many in the project shared these characteristics. Yet, I assumed that our differences would outweigh our similarities and make it hard for the women to trust me. I was surprised when this was not necessarily the case.

Instead of merely acknowledging and weighing the similarities and differences between myself and my interlocutors, I was forced to move beyond such binary thinking and develop a trans Latina analytical approach to power dynamics that "moves beyond narrow politics of gender identity."[7] A trans Latina methodological approach draws from Kai M. Green, who suggests that "trans* is a disruptive orientation but it is not for me specific to transgender bodies, it is rather a method or mode of engaging time, history, people, things, places with an openness and an acceptance of the excesses that are constantly being created and unaccounted for."[8] While important to examine how I am similar to and different from my interlocutors, it is also crucial to honor trans Latina epistemologies and ontologies. Doing so reveals that during the course of my research, power moved in multiple, complex, at times contradictory ways. Moreover, it was constantly negotiated and renegotiated by all parties in the research encounter with openness and acceptance. For example, the fact that my brother was in prison and was going up for parole was the reason why many of the women shared their spiritual beliefs with me, which until then (about eight months into the research) were strategically hidden from me. One woman revealed she was a Santera and very generously offered to do a reading for my brother the night before his parole hearing, even though she had just completed a long day of work. She predicted my brother would be granted parole, to my great relief, and the next day he was. Every time I saw her after that it was clear that she was my spiritual superior and had done me—and my family—a powerful favor. I was graciously indebted to her. Taking Santería, a major component of trans Latina epistemologies and ontologies, seriously means appreciating the ways in which the women sometimes had power over me.

At the risk of overemphasizing our similarities and underemphasizing my privileges as a cisgender citizen, because I look a lot like my interlocuters (as a small, young, brown Latina femme) I often blended in when we were out in public. I was subject to some of the same more immediate and superficial violences. For instance, one night as we were all hanging out on the stroll, a passerby hurled broken glass at all of us. This does not compare to a lifetime of such attacks, and I do not mean to suggest that our experiences in that moment were the same. Yet, sharing this experience with them, coupled with my own history of trauma as brown femme in the United States, allowed me to "accompany" the women with whom I worked, in the way Pérez (this volume) describes. Accompaniment means to be with and to intentionally build coalition with differentially located people in order to work together to create a better world.

Trans Latina Sexual Economies of Labor

Trans Latina sexual economies of labor are long-established spaces for trans Latina creativity and potentiality. Within them, women are able to fantasize and materialize their genders, cultivate queer spaces of resistance, and nurture complex networks of kinship and care—some of which extend beyond this lifetime. Before discussing trans Latina fantasizing, I must introduce trans Latina sexual economies of labor more broadly. The powerful and fantastical image of the hypersexual trans Latina intersects with extreme economic exclusion to result in the development of a robust sexual economy of labor among trans Latinas. Women capitalize on the figure of hypersexual trans Latina within the sexual economy; yet they are also deeply critical of it and the larger societal structures responsible for its production and circulation.

While trans Latina sexual economies of labor afford opportunities otherwise denied for personal growth and political contestation, all of my interlocutors state that they do sex work because they cannot secure employment elsewhere. For example, Katalina, a twenty-eight-year-old Puerto Rican who easily "passes" for a cis woman, had a job interview at a factory, arranged by one of her clients who knew the supervisor.[9] The interview went well, and Katalina was excited when her potential boss took her identification into the next room to make copies. Because a wall with a large window separated the two rooms, Katalina saw everything that transpired. When the potential employer looked at her ID before placing it in the copy machine, he noticed that although Katalina has a very feminine appearance, the name on her license was still the one she was given at birth: "Justin." There were a few other cisgender male workers in the room. The boss passed Katalina's ID around and they all took turns looking at it and laughing.

Katalina was born in Puerto Rico and is therefore a US citizen. Barriers to employment are heightened for undocumented individuals.[10] When an undocumented Mexican transgender woman was venting to me about her desire to quit sex work, I asked her what type of work she would like to do. She replied, "Something not too manly." As scholars have pointed out, manual labor in the United States is racialized (as brown) and gendered (as masculine).[11] Undocumented trans women, many of whom are pushed out of formal education, find themselves with two employment options upon arrival to the United States: manual labor or sex work. Domestic work is an option for undocumented cisgender women, but trans women are unwelcome in domestic spheres because of their nonnormative femininity. Between manual labor and sex work, the former may seem like the less desirable option because of its threat to femininity. Therefore, many turn to sex work despite its criminality and the possibility of violence from various sources, including clients, police officers, etc. Criminal records decrease employability in the formal sector, creating cycles of marginalization. For example, Josefina began doing sex work precisely because she was detained for being undocumented. When she was released from the detention center, she found herself in an unfamiliar rural area where she had no money and nowhere to go. In order to have food and eventually a place to sleep that wasn't on the streets, she turned to sex work. State sanctioned and socially acceptable forms of racism, classism, and cisgenderism work against trans Latina women in ways that only reinforce their racial, sexual, political, social, and economic marginalization.

Trans Latina sexual economies of labor are built around fantasies of the hypersexual transgender Latina. Indeed, fantasies about gender deviance comingle seamlessly with racialized ideas about Latinas, their bodies, and their morality. Frances Aparicio and Susana Chávez-Silverman describe how Latin Americans and Latinxs are subject to "hegemonic tropicalizations" or "instances in a long history of Western representations of the exotic, primitive Other," which are deployed through certain discursive strategies.[12] Stereotypes of Latinas as hypersexual have been propagated throughout US history via popular discourses claiming that Latinxs, and especially women, are sexually promiscuous or *caliente*, and therefore out of control of their bodies and emotions. This is also evidenced in the figure of the *loca* or "crazy" Latina. According to popular stereotypes, Latinas are deeply feeling, sensual, overemotional, and moody. All of these qualities make Latina women naturally skilled "lovers" or sexual partners. Scholars have argued that Latina women are constructed as hypersexual and overly romantic in order to distance them from, and thus bolster, the white heteronormative family and nation.[13] Racialized/sexualized stereotypes also justify violence, including sexual violence, against Latinas and other women of color.

Alongside the hypersexual Latina is the hyperfertile immigrant who "illegally" crosses the border to birth "anchor babies" in order to exploit US resources. Racist beliefs about Latinas' hyperfertility have been solidified into numerous policies aimed at controlling and suppressing their reproduction.[14] Like fantasies of hypersexuality, stereotypes of hyperfertility produce and protect symbolic and physical borders that distinguish Latinxs from white Americans, who are presented as sexually appropriate, morally superior, and thus deserving of citizenship and its benefits.[15] Racist portrayals of Latinxs as inherently hypersexual and hyperfertile are still rampant in contemporary US society, becoming more widespread under the presidency of Donald J. Trump.

Transgender Latinas, however, are not believed to biologically reproduce needy, brown offspring and thus are not threatening to the nation in the same way as the cisgender mother of the "anchor baby" (though, as I will soon show, trans women do mother and socially reproduce). Leo Chavez has pointed out that despite nationalist discourses that condemn Latina reproductivity, the economy is dependent on the re/production of Latinx laborers. It is perhaps because trans Latinas' sex(uality) is not re/productive that it is viewed as exceptionally hedonistic and excessive of the norms of capitalist white cisheteronormativity. In sexual economies of labor, trans Latinas' racial, sexual, and gendered extravagances are commodified and desired by clients. The women I interviewed frequently theorized that their customers wanted to have sex with them because they were Latina and thus construed as "exotic" and "freaky," and even "extra," and "dirty" in ways that gives them "sex appeal . . . that maybe other races would not have."

For example, after a meeting at an HIV organization, Jackie, a forty-five-year-old Mexican trans woman, explained why clients desire trans Latinas, sharing the story of her experience working as a maid for a white cisgender man. He demanded that she wear a short skirt around the house, with nothing underneath, so he could see her penis throughout the day as she cleaned. The tone of the room, previously party-like, immediately became somber. The man's hypersexualization of a woman with a penis, an impossibility according to cisnormativity, was deeply racialized via the stereotype of the domestic worker, in a way that was ultimately demeaning. Therefore, while I draw on Vargas's incredibly useful concept of *lo sucio*, I argue that trans Latinas are more than just sucias, because their transgender bodies pose a particular threat to white cisnormativity in the United States that transcends that of queerness, which may still be mapped onto cisgender bodies. Both their race and their gender, and moreover how the two come together and inform each other, are sexually fantastic.

While trans Latinas are exoticized by virtue of their nonnormative gender *and* race, the primary way the women I interviewed were fetishized had to do with their being transgender. Serena, a forty-six-year-old Peruvian immigrant, explained why trans Latinas are fantasías: "When you hire a cis woman sex worker you always know you will penetrate her; when you hire a gay male sex worker you know he'll always penetrate you. But when you hire a trans you never know." Serena's words reflect the larger sentiment that trans women are sexually desirable to clients precisely because they transgress gender boundaries and challenge heteronormative—and notably also homonormative and transnormative—sexual expectations as women with penises who may both penetrate and be penetrated. Such fantastic possibilities are turned into paid transactions and commoditized.

As the meeting at the HIV organization continued, Jackie elaborated on what it means to be a fantasia: "They are paying you so much not because you are so good at sex, but because they are so enfermo. Cuz they have a wife at home; she just doesn't have a pene." Everyone nodded in agreement. Jackie's statement that clients are "enfermo" because of their desire for erotic encounters with trans women and their penises can be interpreted in a few ways. It can be read as an assertion of cisnormativity, heteronormativity, transnormativity, and even internalized self-hatred based on transphobia. The logic being: a man should not want to have sex with a trans woman, someone with a penis, if he has a cisgender wife at home. I argue, however, that Jackie's words critique the client not because he is sexually attracted to transgender women but because he is attracted to them by virtue of their sexual deviance according to gender norms (represented by the wife). Jackie is critiquing the fantastical and dehumanizing discourses about transgender women that shape clients' interests, which oscillate between fear and disgust, and curiosity and pleasure. Ultimately, her words can be interpreted as a sophisticated critique of the larger system of racist cisgenderism that produces such desire. To say that he—and thus cisgenderism—is "enfermo" suggests that there is the possibility for healing, a future without the exotification of trans women of color and its accompanying violences. As the women creatively utilize the racist/cisgenderist discourses about themselves to make a living, they are critical of them. By critically engaging with harmful discourses, they can fantasize and manifest trans Latina bodies/selves, spaces, and communities and thus work toward a future free of "sick" cisgenderism.

Fantasizing Trans Latina Bodies/Selves

Before their annual fashion show in 2018, the chief marketing officer of Victoria's Secret, Ed Razek, said in an interview that transgender women should not be models for the brand or appear on their runaway. When asked why he felt this way he replied, "Shouldn't you have transsexuals in the show? No. No, I don't think we should. Well, why not? Because the show is a fantasy. It's a forty-two-minute entertainment special. That's what it is."[16] Razek's use of fantasy highlights the difference between normative sexualized fantasies, which are permitted in mainstream society, and nonnormative fantasies, which are taboo. The "fantasy" created by the Victoria Secret brand, and the annual fashion show in particular, is one that celebrates white, upper-class, cisheteronormative bodies and sexuality. The celebration of this normative fantasy directly fuels the taboo trans fantasy, where transgender women are othered, fetishized, and dehumanized.

In response to Razek's devaluation and stigmatization of transgender women and their bodies, trans actress Rain Valdez created a calendar featuring "multicultural women of transgender experience." The theme is "fantasy." Each month features a picture of a different scantily clad trans woman in a sexually alluring, though tasteful pose, and a quote explaining what "fantasy" means to them. Valdez and the other women in the catalogue reclaim the ways in which trans women are fantasized by dominant society. Important dates in LGBTQ history are also highlighted throughout the year. A portion of the proceeds goes to the Trans Latina Coalition.[17] In an interview with Gay Star News, Valdez says about the calendar: "The calendar is called The Fantasy because if anyone knows the power of fantasy, it is trans people. Without fantasy there may not be understanding between my then, my now and my future. Because I fantasized a future for myself, it helped me become the hardworking woman I am today."[18] According to Valdez, fantasy is a process that bridges past, present, and future to imagine and achieve an improved self. How the other women featured in the calendar understand and articulate "fantasy" reflects Valdez's approach. In their explanations of "fantasy," many focus on the fantasizing that was required to dream and create their trans feminine bodies, as well as better present realities and futures for themselves.

However, the women's understanding of fantasizing and manifesting better presents and futures involves not just themselves as individuals but also the larger trans community. The two are intertwined—one builds the self and a better world for the self as one also builds trans community and a better world for all. Carolina wishes that everyone could "transform their own fantasy into reality," and Maria points out how as she realized her womanhood she also became a role model for others who push "social norms." The creation of the calendar itself is an attempt to bring increased safety, dignity, pride, and humanity to the trans feminine community.

The semipornographic calendar not only evidences the importance of fantasizing against cisgenderist fantasies of transgender women but also underlines the significance of trans fantasizing of the body in order to achieve trans selfhood, community, and futurity. My research affirms the importance of the body, and being in the body, for trans Latina world-making. Moreover, trans Latina *fantasías* of the body challenge binary approaches to sex workers, which view them as either victims or agents, and to trans women of color, which position them as either hypervictims or super-activists. In what follows, I show that their own desires fulfill neither stereotypical extreme. Instead, I reveal how fantasías can be mundane: they can be to just exist in a body that feels right. This does not mean, however, that they are not radical, as their bodies surpass the confines of white cisheteronormativity, transnormativity, and normative Latinidad.

In my initial interview with Katalina, after a few basic demographic questions, she interjected with, "I just feel like I don't love myself," and then burst into tears. When I asked why she felt this way, she couldn't quite articulate her reasons. No doubt, her lack of self-love is a complicated issue that was influenced by systemic transphobia and the countless acts of violence—both structural and intimate—committed against her throughout her life. A few weeks later, as I was waiting for a meeting at an HIV organization to begin, Katalina excitedly rushed through the door once she saw me inside. She was glowing. She exclaimed, "I got my boobs! I feel like I love myself now!" She had just returned from Florida, where she got DD-sized breast implants via a doctor who travels from Mexico to Florida to provide surgeries to transgender women at discounted prices. She paid the entire bill with money earned from sex work.[19]

While explaining the prevalence of sex work in the trans Latina community and its connection to surgery and the pressure to transition, one collaborator said, "What would you do if you felt trapped in a cage? What would you do to feel alive? Work at McDonalds and make minimum wage and wait twenty years to transition . . . or maybe even wait forever?" This challenges the popular assumption that in accepting cash for sexual services they are "selling their bodies" and thus "selling their selves."[20] Quite the contrary, women use money earned in trans Latina sexual economies to honor and build the body and thus produce the self. Here we see how an ethnographic look at trans Latina fantasías troubles binary approaches to sex workers that present them as either victims or agents. For trans Latinas who are systemically excluded from other means of making money, sex work can ensure survival and make their greatest fantasías a reality.

When I asked my interlocutors about their wishes for the future, most of their responses focused on receiving feminizing surgical procedures for their own bodies/selves, and surviving. I admit I expected answers that included the larger community, reached farther into the future, and were more stereotypically activist in nature. And, in fact, in my research I have encountered an assumption that traditional activism is seen as a priority by trans Latinas. Indeed, it is important to elevate the activist efforts of those who are multiply marginalized and excluded from both normative society and popular histories of activism, even queer activism, such as trans Latinas. And to be clear, some of the women in the project were activists—among other roles—and a few prioritized traditional forms of activism in their daily life (as I will discuss later). Yet, much like hypervictimizing sex-working trans women of color, romanticizing them as activists runs the risk of simplification and objectification. Moreover, it elides other actions and ways of being that trouble the cisgenderist status quo.

While the women's dreams of obtaining gender-affirming medical procedures and surviving may seem individualistic and short-sighted, I argue that such fantasías are anything but. Living in a body that affirms one's transgender self, as a woman of color in the United States, directly defies white cisgenderism as an ontology, epistemology, and political system. It is too dangerous for the Victoria's Secret runway—a pillar of white, thin, ableist, capitalist, cishetero patriarchy. Moreover, the trans Latina body is the heart of trans Latina sexual economies, which house resistant forms of space-making, care-taking, and kin-creating. All of the latter are examples of work toward more radical futures, none of which would be possible without the development of the trans Latina body and self. A fantasía is to just exist in a body that feels right. This fantasía and the trans vernacular desire to "just survive," which is enabled by sexual economies, show that fantasies are not always grandiose or romantic but can be to simply live. However, just being and living as a sex-working transgender Latina in the United States is radical.

Cultivating Trans Latina Families, Spaces, and Spiritualities

A key site for fantasía-making in Chicago is La Hueca, one of the oldest LGBT clubs in the nation.[21] Located on the Southwest Side of the city, La Hueca was founded in the 1970s by trans Latina women, the majority involved in sexual labor, who sold tamales and records on the streets to open the club. Vargas explains how sucias maintain the association with abjection by reconfiguring spaces deemed inferior to sustain queer Latina worlds. La Hueca is a space of suciedad and of trans Latina sustenance and investment in "what is not yet here." The club is most popularly known for its incredible "drag" performances and the selling of sexual services. Yet instead of describing those here, I will address alternative kinships and spiritualities fostered in the club, two examples of future-making in the present. I show that in addition to housing resistant economies, the club also nurtures trans Latina ontologies and epistemologies.

Before discussing earthly and otherworldly trans mother-daughter relationships within the club, I will explain trans motherhood more generally. Sex-working and transitioning are often done with the help of a trans mother. Trans mothers provide emotional care and support, and oftentimes food and shelter, to their daughters. They teach them how to be trans women and offer advice about makeup, hormones, silicon injections, and surgeries. They also teach them how to get started in the sex trade. If the daughters have already begun doing sex work, the mothers encourage safer sex practices and share tips for getting more clients. Interlocutors found their trans mothers on the "stroll," in clubs, and while living on the streets after being kicked out of their parents' homes. Some actively seek out and court potential trans mothers. Popular culture suggests one can only fantasize about a relationship if it is romantic and/ or sexual in nature. Yet, some women ardently desired trans mothers, and the fantasies that they help make reality.

Katalina hung out in Humboldt Park, where fifty-five-year-old HIV counselor and former sex worker Mariana passed out condoms to sex workers and drug users. Katalina heard from others that Mariana is like a *madrina* to Chicago's trans Latina sex working community. Lacking stable parental figures in her life since she was about eighteen years old, when her biological parents violently kicked her out of the house because of her gender nonconformity, Katalina yearned for a trans mother. After a few months of hanging out with Mariana, Katalina nervously gave her a card on Mother's Day. The front of the card read, "Isn't it amazing how one little person can change your whole world?" The inside said, "Celebrating you on your 1st Mother's Day!" Katalina then wrote her own message on in the inside: "I love and enjoy being around you. I want to better my life because one day I wanna be like you." Mariana accepted the card and from then on started treating Katalina like her daughter.

Many interlocutors found their trans mothers in queer clubs, such as La Hueca. Brittni was twenty years old and confused about her gender when she met her trans mother, Isabella, who was forty years old, a performer at La Hueca. Before she offered to be Brittni's mother, Brittni spent many months helping Isabella prepare for performances. Throughout this time, Isabella taught Brittni about transgender and helped her transition. Isabella sometimes stayed on the phone with Britnni all night, as she cried about difficulties with her transition and her fear that her biological family would reject her. In addition to teaching her about trans womanhood, Isabella taught Brittni how to be a successful sex worker. Isabella's own trans mother did the same for her. La Hueca, where all three mother/daughter dyads I interviewed met, allows for the creative development of trans Latina selves and trans Latina families, and thus the larger trans Latina community. It is a historical example of trans love and resistance.

An additional form of trans motherhood exists, a trans feminist kinship that has not only persisted over generations but traverses spiritual realms. In La Hueca, some women met godmothers in Santería, who are also sex-working trans Latina women. Santería is an African diasporic religion that originated in the Caribbean and that, drawing from Yoruba and Catholic religious practices, revolves around santos or orishas, who are different manifestations of God.[22] Santería allows for gender fluidity and bodily transformation among santos and practitioners. And, as Beliso–De Jesús points out in her stunning ethnography, Santería also allows for a multiplicity of being, in body, space, and time.[23] Brenda learned about both transgender and Santería—the two most important aspects of herself and her life—at La Hueca. An important aspect of trans Latina sexual economies of labor, Santería is central to trans Latina epistemologies and ontologies.

Brenda went to La Hueca as an effeminate "gay boy" and saw the trans women performing on stage, knowing immediately that she wanted to "be like them." She got close with all the "girls," especially Sadia, who was slightly older and would become her godmother via Santería. Another woman would become her official trans mother. Thus she would have two mothers, who were both sex-working trans Latina women. Importantly, many of the women also maintained close relationships with their biological mothers. Like the groundbreaking work on lesbian and bisexual Latinas by Acosta, this finding disputes the potentially racist stereotype that Latinx parents are exceptionally homophobic and transphobic and are more likely than white parents to disown queer children. [24] Quite the contrary, some women had three mothers: biological, trans, Santera. Such kinship configurations racially, sexually, and spiritually exceed the limits of white cisheteronormative notions of family.

One night at the club, Sadia received the news that a close friend, also a trans Latina woman, was arrested for drug-related activities and could go to prison for a very long time. Sacrificing opportunities to service clients and perform on stage, she rushed into La Hueca's tiny women's bathroom and pulled Brenda with her. Sadia did an impromptu reading to ascertain her friend's fate. In a reading, the Santera communicates with the santos via a ritual of rolling, throwing, and reading of *caracoles*. Elegguá, the owner of all crossroads, acts as an intermediary, communicating with the rest of the saints and then relaying their messages to the Santera via the shells. Sadia argued with Elegguá, yelled at and pleaded with him in English, Spanish, and Yoruba. She got sweatier and the small bathroom got hotter. Eventually, the santos told Sadia that their friend would be charged with a crime that carried a potential sentencing of forty years, but that she would only serve less than one year. Sadia and Brenda were relieved. The friend would go on to serve six months in prison.

It was then that Brenda knew she wanted to be a Santera. Sadia initiated her and thus became her godmother. Now, Brenda's main sources of income are sex work and readings. It is also important to note that Brenda was granted asylum, despite the fact that she had a number of drug-related charges and was deported three times.[25] Unable to believe she was awarded asylum, I once exclaimed, "But how!?" She assuredly replied that it was because of the saints. Her logic may eschew white Western epistemologies but was accepted and lauded within trans Latina sexual economies. According to Brenda, she would have perhaps never found her gender, her faith, her two jobs—sex work and her work as a Santera—or her "freedom" if she had not started going to La Hueca. In sum, La Hueca, an example of trans Latina space-making, nurtures not only the development of the self but also various kinds of trans Latina community, in this world and beyond. Sex working, trans mothering, and practicing Santería are all interrelated community-building activities that draw from centuries of resistant queer, Latinx knowledge and ways of being. As the women engage in ancient practices passed from generation to generation, they strive toward a more radical queer, Latinx future.

"Business as Usual": Trans Latina Activisms and Futures

In the previous sections, I have argued that activism is not the only way in which trans Latinas challenge white cisgenderism. They can also do so in mundane ways, by just being, loving, and practicing their faith, all of which are examples of a trans Latina vernacular rooted in everyday living and offering ontological impossibilities within white, Eurocentric cisgenderist structures (see Chávez, this volume).[26] Yet, some women did engage in activism to fantasize possibilities beyond the current political and social order. Even those who did, however, cautioned that there are many forms of "activism" and ways of supporting trans Latina life. The women's diverse activist activities continue to defy simplistic and binary notions of political contestation, transgender women of color, and the current political moment. For many US-Americans, the level of violence against Latinxs and trans folx feels unprecedented. Yet trans Latinas have long been living under the threat of multiple intersecting violences: in the words of Jesenia, they have "always been at the bottom." Therefore, their strategies of contestation echo the astute observations of Yarimar Bonilla and Jonathan Rosa and suggest that some aspects of current political situation are not new.[27] The insights of Jesenia, and others, demonstrate that they are acutely aware of the complexities of the current moment and the ways it is novel and not. Their varied strategies of refusal reflect their deep knowledge of the political reality, a commitment to the abolishment of gender and race normativity and the political institutions that uphold them, and work toward a world where trans Latina ways of being are affirmed and celebrated.

After the inauguration of the forty-fifth president in 2016, some sex-working trans Latinas maintained that neither their everyday lives nor activist efforts would change much. They viewed the widespread racism, sexism, xenophobia, and cisgenderism embodied by the administration as "business as usual" in America. To be clear, however, many women have expressed that Trump encouraged them to fight harder. Brenda said:

> He's the enemy. He's been creating hate. He's given people the tools and the right to hate the trans Latina community. And we already had so many communities against us. On the other hand, what doesn't kill you makes you stronger. I think we are in a trans revolution all over the country, trans women of color are standing up. We are fighting against Trump. The community is creating and building spaces, even underground. We are standing up for justice.

Brenda recognizes that while the administration may be encouraging more violence against trans Latinas, trans Latina communities around the country are organizing and resisting.

Brenda then excitedly reminded me of the "1st Trans-Gay Migrant Caravan," or "Rainbow 17," which consisted of eleven trans women and six gay men from Central America who crossed the border and surrendered themselves to officials after holding up a colorful sign that read "Primera Caravan Trans-Gay 2017." Before crossing at Nogales, they all met each other after being denied asylum in Mexico and bonded over similar experiences of gendered violence in Central

America. They then brainstormed and reached out to numerous legal organizations specializing in asylum in the United States. Attorneys and volunteers flew to Mexico and provided legal advice and some even crossed with them. Protestors showed support on both sides of the border. After they turned themselves in, the Rainbow 17 were detained in Milan, New Mexico.

Brenda, who crossed the border twelve years ago, was deported three times, and detained for many months, could relate to the members of the caravan, especially the trans women. She felt so compelled to help them. She said she knew that they were getting legal counsel, but she "knew from experience." She had lived it, she asserted. She contacted one of the legal organizations traveling to New Mexico and asked if she could come along. They said yes. They flew her to New Mexico and she met many of the trans women. She proudly recounted to me that she "coached" them on how to be brave in front of asylum officers.[28] I was reminded of something Jesenia said to me when I began conducting research: "Activism isn't just being loud on the streets, but also the small quiet moments of caring for a sister." Jesenia's insistence on helping the Rainbow 17 seemed to fall somewhere between the two modalities of activism. The sharing of embodied and experiential knowledge and involvement in various types of activism and care among trans Latina women can also be considered "business as usual."

After two months in detention, the labors of activists and lawyers were fruitful: all of the transgender women were granted parole. They will no longer have to endure the horrors of being in a man's detention center while pursuing their asylum cases. While this is a victory, the battle is far from over. Historically fewer than one-third of cases are granted asylum, and now the Department of Homeland Security tends to approve even fewer. Asylum seekers must wait months or years for permission to work, as well as for access to housing or food support. This is precisely why some undocumented trans Latinas turn to sex work in the first place. Ironically, sex work, a crime of "moral turpitude," can make applicants ineligible for asylum.

Brenda and I sat in silence with this harsh reality for a few moments. Yet, I am still heartened that Brenda, a poor sex worker in Chicago, found a way to support her sisters over a thousand miles away. In addition to this one act, Brenda has been finding as many fora as possible to share her "knowledge from experience." Despite centuries of political, economic, racial, and social marginalization, Brenda, like many other Latinxs and transgender folx before her, develops and shares unique epistemologies and various forms of trans Latina refusal, from "being loud on the streets" to "caring for a sister" in "those small quiet moments." Against the backdrop of extreme violence, the fantasizing of trans Latina selves, families, and futures is also "business as usual" in America.

Notes

1. When referring to transgender women, I, of course, use "Latina." When referring to the larger community, I use "Latinx" in order to recognize nonbinary individuals and to combat pervasive and often internalized cisgenderism among Latinxs. I am also inspired by Alan Pelaez Lopez's (2008) use of Latinx "as a wound" to signify the violences of colonization, slavery, displacement, and feminicide that make Latinx identity impossible to easily articulate.

2. Snorton and Haritaworn 2014.

3. Muñoz 2009.

4. Vargas 2014, 718.

5. Butler 2004; Muñoz 2009; Rodríguez 2014.

6. Ellison et al. 2017; Galarte 2014.

7. Stryker, Currah, and Moore 2011.

8. Green 2017, 448.

9. This shows the diverse ways that clients compensate sex workers (see also Brennan 2004 and Cabezas 2009).

10. Chavez 1998; Zavella 2011.

11. De Genova and Ramos-Zayas 2003; Gomberg-Muñoz 2010.

12. Aparicio and Chávez-Silverman 1997, 8.

13. Chavez 1998; Gutierrez 2008; López 2008.

14. For example, the government has funded the widespread forced sterilization of Mexican-American and Puerto Rican women across the country at various points in history (Gutiérrez 2008; López 2008). The forced sterilization of Puerto Rican women by officials from the mainland was a way to control the population, "modernize" the island, and thus justify the US intervention.

15. Chavez 2013.

16. Nicole Phelps, "'We're Nobody's Third Love, We're Their First Love'— The Architects of the Victoria's Secret Fashion Show Are Still Banking on

Bombshells." November 8, 2018, https://www.vogue.com/article/victorias
-secret-ed-razek-monica-mitro-interview.

17. A nationwide organization that organizes and advocates for the needs of Trans
     Latin@s around the country: https://www.translatinacoalition.org/.

18. David Hudson, "Naked Trans Women Calendar Showcases Beauty and 'Fanta-
     sy,'" *Gay Star News*, December 18, 2018, https://www.gaystarnews.com/article
     /naked-trans-women-calendar-fantasy/.

19. Notably, however, not all transgender people feel the need to change their
     bodies, and those who do may not understand such changes via the concept
     of "transition." Yet those who do encounter a number of legal, medical,
     and financial barriers to feeling comfortable in their own bodies. In fact,
     dissatisfaction with one's body and appearance has been linked with diminished
     mental health and quality of life (e.g., Ainsworth and Spiegel 2010).

20. Barry 1996; MacKinnon 1991; Pateman 1988.

21. Pseudonym.

22. Beliso–De Jesús 2015; Vidal-Ortíz 2006.

23. Beliso–De Jesús 2015.

24. Acosta 2014.

25. This is incredibly rare and likely never happened under the Trump
     administration.

26. Chávez, this volume.

27. Rosa and Bonilla 2017.

28. I was hesitant to include the language of "coaching" because I did not want to
     inadvertently contribute to the erroneous, and racist, belief that refugees lie to
     immigration officials. However, I ultimately chose to include Brenda's words in
     order to highlight her knowledge and honor the labor and care she enacted to
     prepare her sisters for continual encounters with the inherently violent immi-
     gration system.

CHAPTER SEVEN

The Drug War, Drug Reform, and the Latinx Community

An Ethnographic Perspective
from the Texas-Mexico Border and Colorado

SANTIAGO IVAN GUERRA

It's October 21, 2014, and I am sitting alongside Aaron Smith, the cofounder and executive director of the National Cannabis Industry Association. We are about to engage in a debate on marijuana legalization on the campus of Arizona State University (ASU) with two antilegalization advocates, one an Arizona prosecutor, the other a psychology professor at ASU. As the debate commences, Aaron stakes his position in support of marijuana legalization: "What this debate is about is whether we should continue a policy of arresting consumers of cannabis and then leaving the control of the market of this popular product under the control of black market drug dealers, violent gangs and cartels, and really bad people, or should we change directions and do what Washington and Colorado voters have been successful at doing, and put this popular product behind a regulated counter, similar to the way that we treat alcohol so that it is available to adults over 21 through a strict regulated regime."[1] We have much to learn from the marijuana legalization movement, and the above quote is a glimpse into the complexities surrounding the movement and the logics and material realities that it informs, especially in the case of Mexicans and Mexican Americans.

In November 2012, Colorado citizens voted to pass Amendment 64 to the Colorado state constitution, making Colorado the first state to "legalize" the recreational consumption, possession, and production of marijuana for adults over the age of twenty-one. On January 1, 2014, the law officially went into effect and recreational marijuana shops opened in Colorado. In the lead-up to this historic moment, recreational marijuana proponents relied on troubling and concerning racial and class discourse. Specifically, the Colorado Campaign to Regulate

Marijuana Like Alcohol and other marijuana advocates increasingly leaned on rhetoric that positioned Mexicans as criminals in contrast to the respectable medical (and recreational) marijuana business owners. As part of a "Yes on 64" TV ad, a comforting female voice declares, "Let's vote for the good guys and against the bad guys. Let's have marijuana tax money go to our schools, rather than criminals in Mexico."[2] In the same ad, Melissa Etheridge states, "It's wrong to let gangs and cartels profit from marijuana." Another radio ad featured Tom Tancredo—a notorious Colorado congressmen, former Republican presidential candidate, and anti-immigrant/anti-Latino figure—declaring that marijuana prohibition "steers Colorado money to criminals in Mexico."[3]

As the aforementioned proponents of cannabis legalization make clear, the reasons for moving toward legalization are twofold: protected, decriminalized consumption and regulated, legitimate production and sales. In this legalization narrative—in the case of marijuana—there are good guys and there are bad guys. If we've learned anything from the media, it's that cartels (i.e., Mexicans and other Latin Americans) are the bad guys while marginalized American (white) drug consumers are the victims in the War on Cannabis. The villain-ization of Mexicans, Latin Americans, and the US Latinx population through an association with drug trafficking and organized crime has become a central mechanism in characterizing this population as a threat to the United States and is a larger extension of the Latino Threat narrative highlighted by the work of Leo Chavez.[4] While Chavez does not explicitly engage with discussions of Lat-inx criminality, instead focusing primarily on undocumented immigration and Latinx sexuality, fertility, and reproduction, the framing of the Latinx population as predatory criminals in both popular culture and news media via the figures of the narcos and *cholos/maras* (delinquent youth/gang members) has become central to the Latino Threat narrative in the last two decades. The image of the narco, and of Mexicans as narcos in particular, gained particular notoriety in the racist proclamations of the 2016 Republican presidential candidate (later pres-ident) Donald J. Trump. Narcos, the omnipresent bad hombres, have become linked to Latinidad through political discourse and popular culture, creating a perception of the Latinx/Latin American population as criminal and unruly, and thereby policeable.

As a proponent of drug policy reform—marijuana legalization specifically—and as a Chicano anthropologist and ethnic studies scholar, I have witnessed firsthand the problematic racist and classist attitudes that inform the drug re-form and marijuana legalization movement. This chapter, therefore, offers a critique of US drug policy reform work and its invocation of anti-Mexican, anti-Latinx, and anti–Latin American sentiments, typically unrecognized due to the strong emphasis on social justice–focused frameworks invoked by legalization proponents. In doing so, it also offers a way to understand current legalization efforts that would avoid reproducing practices of oppression and discrimination inherent to our current systems of drug prohibition.

Making Cannabis Mexican: Marijuana and the Rise of the Drug War

For the last century, Americans' relationship with marijuana has been shaped by the presence of Mexicans in the southwest US border region. The association of the cannabis plant with Mexicans—in smokable cigarette form and as a foreign menace with an unfamiliar name (marijuana)—increased anxieties over Mexican migration, criminality, and led to cannabis becoming a pressing policy and policing concern in the United States, resulting in the rise of the drug war. In the lead-up to marijuana prohibition, Mexicans were villainized as crazed consumers; today, Mexicans are once again criminalized as treacherous traffickers through regulation and legalization.[5]

Since 1848 the border communities of Starr County, Texas, have had to deal with national, global, and local pressures to survive. For many families, smuggling and the informal economy became a supplemental, and in some cases main, source of income. The contemporary international drug trade at the United States–Mexico border is an outgrowth of earlier forms of smuggling. Indeed, by the early twentieth century, border smugglers were able to diversify their operations to include several psychoactive substances as a result of policies prohibiting these popular intoxicants. The 1914 Harrison Narcotics Tax Act initiated the United States' targeting and regulation of coca and opiates. The primary function of the Harrison act was to implement two different taxes on coca and opiates to better control and regulate access to these substances. However, within a short time this legislation effectively diminished the supply of legally available coca and opiates, resulting in the growth of an illicit market. Initially, enforcement of this particular legislation was carried out by the Department of the Treasury, but in 1930 Congress created the Federal Bureau of Narcotics (FBN) to deal with the drug problem.[6]

While the effective prohibition of coca and opiates as a result of the Harrison act was a gradual benefit for border smugglers, the prohibition of alcohol in the United States had profound effects on the intensification of border "drug" smuggling.[7] In 1919 the Eighteenth Amendment, coupled with the National Prohibition Act, banned the manufacture, sale, and consumption of alcohol in the United States. Prohibition, however, could not decrease demand and very quickly elaborated criminal networks formed to supply alcohol to a growing illicit market. While most Americans are familiar with the bootleggers in the South and the Chicago organized crime group famously led by Al Capone, border smugglers—known as *tequileros*—played a significant role in delivering alcohol to American consumers.

The South Texas border was a major site of liquor smuggling during Prohibition. According to Maude T. Gilliland's interviews with many of the customs officers charged with policing the Rio Grande Valley, three major smuggling routes cut through Starr County; in contrast, only one route was identified in each of the neighboring counties. Gilliland states that "their [liquor smugglers'] main crossing strip along the southern part of the border below Laredo was around San Ygnacio, in Zapata County, and on down to about La Grulla, in Starr County, Texas."[8] Once the tequileros crossed the Rio Grande/Río Bravo, they rode through the brush country of Starr County, resting intermittently before reaching their rendezvous point with rum runners in the South Texas towns of San Diego, Freer, and Benavides, which were at least one hundred miles north of the border. Upon purchasing the liquor from the tequileros, the rum runners would transport the liquor to the urban markets of the interior United States, such as Dallas and Chicago. In 1933, after over a decade of contending with illicit liquor smuggling, manufacture, and sales, the United States repealed the prohibition of alcohol with the passing of the Twenty-First Amendment. Shortly thereafter the US government continued its prohibitionist drug policies with the implementation of the Marijuana Tax Act of 1937. Similar to the Harrison Act, the Marijuana Tax Act was prohibition through taxation; the legislation effectively made it impossible to be in possession of marijuana without violating the law, resulting in stiff penalties of up to five years in prison and a fine of up $2000. Along the Texas-Mexico border, smugglers quickly adapted to the unexpected shift. After having lost revenue through the repeal of alcohol prohibition, drug smugglers solidified their control over the supply of the emerging American drug trinity of opiates, cocaine, and marijuana.

The Garcias of Starr County are one among many local families that have dedicated themselves to cross-border smuggling as both a primary and supplementary form of income. Salvador Garcia, born in 1846, became the first in his family to engage in cross-border smuggling for reliable income, evading the new tariffs imposed by both the United States and Mexico as part of their efforts at assuming control over the newly established Mexico–United States boundary. By the 1960s, however, Salvador Garcia's grandsons devoted their smuggling practices—by now their primary sources of income—to the importation of marijuana.

The Garcia brothers created a marijuana smuggling cooperative that allowed them to amass small fortunes prior to the onset of the War on Drugs, which was ushered in along the border initially in 1969 with Operation Intercept and later expanded with the full force of the 1970 Controlled Substances Act. On September 21, 1969, the United States engaged in a concentrated large-scale drug interdiction effort that targeted border crossings for increased inspection and surveillance of marijuana smuggling.[9] The operation only lasted until October 2, 1969, but it signaled a new strategy in dealing with the growing concern surrounding drug consumption in the United States, a strategy now focused on targeting source and transit countries for drug interdiction. However, as Lawrence Gooberman has argued, Operation Intercept also had unintended consequences, especially with respect to the response by drug smugglers. Gooberman suggests that the operation's drastic surveillance and interdiction strategy effectively prompted the growth of organized illegal drug smuggling along the border. In fact, Operation Intercept was part of the preliminary phase of the contemporary War on Drugs, which the Nixon administration declared as a direct result of the interdiction tactic's perceived success. These efforts were part of a global policy shift in drug policing escalation that had its roots in the 1912 International Opium Convention and resulted in more sweeping global drug prohibition with the 1961 United Nations Single Convention on Narcotic Drugs and the 1971 United Nations Convention on Psychotropic Substances.

It was in the midst of these global drug policy initiatives that contemporary US narcopolitical initiatives took shape. In 1970 the United States passed the Controlled Substances Act to implement its federal drug prohibition strategy in accordance with the UN convention on narcotic drugs. In an effort to enforce this new sweeping drug prohibition, the Nixon administration established the Drug Enforcement Administration on July 1, 1973. By the late 1990s, border militarization, the rise of mass incarceration, and the restructuring of the domestic and international marijuana market had significantly affected the lives of the fifth generation of Garcia smugglers. In the following, I present some stories of this family in the wake of the legalization movement.

Marijuana Smuggling During the Marijuana Legalization Movement

Popular dramatizations of narco life have created the image of a ruthless class of Mexican, Latin American, and Latinx drug smugglers that often obfuscates the mundane lived experiences of low-level drug workers who make up a significant segment of the illicit drug economy. Throughout Mexico, and on both sides of the United States–Mexico border, young to middle-aged Mexican people have relied on the omnipresent opportunities within the drug trade to generate income at the margins of these two countries. For many border residents, the drug economy has offered the potential to work in transporting, packaging, and surveillance as part of marijuana smuggling operations. Here, I discuss some of these workers' experiences.

It's December 31, 2003, in the rural border community of El Canton, Texas, and Joker Garcia is preparing to celebrate New Year's Eve alongside his girlfriend and close friends. Joker is twenty-one and has been involved in the drug trade since the age of seventeen, dropping out of high school because severe dyslexia made it impossible for him to continue to the next grade level. Though he had experience as a transporter driving drugs up to *conectas* in Houston, most of his work in the drug trade centered around being a marijuana packer. In 2003, he lived in a small one-room cinderblock building behind his uncle's house, where he compressed marijuana into blocks of various sizes. The purpose of Joker's work was to repackage large, hundred-pound marijuana bundles into smaller strategically packaged blocks that could be stashed in *clavos*, hidden automobile compartments. Joker and some of his associates also tried to devise new ways of packaging drugs to ship past the Border Patrol checkpoints located within one hundred miles of the South Texas border, in order to reach the lucrative drug markets to the north.

That New Year's, as Joker went out to celebrate, he left a large load of marijuana unattended in his *cuartito*. When he returned in the early morning, he found that someone had broken in and taken the marijuana. Later that afternoon, Joker's bosses (former business partners and close relatives of his uncle Juan Garcia) picked him up and took him to a secluded ranch. They tortured him and beat him for several hours, expecting that he would confess to stealing the marijuana or at least turn in whomever he suspected of the theft. His bosses also accused Joker's brother Jay of having stolen the shipment, to which Joker replied: "Trayte a es culero pa' ca y si se las robo el, yo mismo me trueno al bastardo."[10] The bosses did eventually bring Jay to the ranch and tortured him as well. However, they could not prove that either Joker or Jay had stolen the pot. Joker and Jay were eventually released, with the admonition "si no hubiera sido tan buen amigo del difunto Blas, aqui me trueno a los dos."[11] Joker, however, was charged with the responsibility of packing marijuana for most of 2004 without pay in order to make up for the "lost" shipment. It was eventually revealed that Joker's own bosses had taken the "lost" shipment to teach him a lesson. This unfortunate incident served to keep Joker entangled in the complicated web of the drug trade; it also kept him in a state of constant fear and distrust.

Since dropping out of high school, Joker has attempted to support himself in a variety of ways ranging from construction work to oil drilling. His experience with drug violence reveals the most recent transformation of power within larger systems of organized crime in Mexico and along the US-Mexico border. As part of this process, drug trafficking organizations have centralized power into militarized corporate entities that rely on expendable laborers and the "outsourcing" of violence into Mexico. This outsourcing along the border relies on the cartels' impunity in Mexico as well as the targeting of drug workers through tactical violence.

The story of Adan Garcia highlights the effects of this phenomenon. Adan was still a teenager when, in early 2010, he began working as a mule for a representative of Los Zetas, operating out of the Ciudad Camargo, Tamaulipas–Rio Grande City, Texas, drug corridor. Much like his cousin Joker, Adan was a low-level drug worker and his expendability was an integral factor in drug trafficking operations along the border. As such, Adan would experience a similar tactic of violence that Joker was subjected to, with some salient distinguishing circumstances. During a smuggling attempt gone wrong, Adan was intercepted by border policing agents. A pursuit ensued. In possession of several hundred pounds of marijuana, Adan made a quick decision to evade the agents and flee to Mexico. In the process, he abandoned the vehicle and the marijuana. When he arrived in Mexico, Adan was *levantado* (abducted) and held hostage for the loss of the marijuana and the vehicle. The members of the organization sent a message to Adan's mother: if she and her family could not pay off Adan's debt from the botched smuggling attempt, Adan would be executed. After a series of bake sales, car washes, and other fundraising activities, Adan's family was eventually able to gather the funds for his release. In the week that passed, however, Adan was subjected to both physical and psychological torture at the hands of his captors. Still, Adan, much like Joker, was lucky. He escaped the drug trade with his life. As evident from several recent cases, many drug trafficking operatives have not been so fortunate. In the year following Adan's release from captivity, forty-nine decapitated bodies were dumped near Cadereyta-Jiménez, Nuevo León, on the highway leading from Ciudad Miguel Alemán, Tamaulipas, to Monterey, Nuevo León.[12] The site of the carnage was within a few miles of where Adan was held prior to his release.

Connecting Colorado: Marijuana Legalization's Impact on Illicit Marijuana

How do the stories of these border marijuana smugglers relate to the marijuana legalization movement? We need to revisit the rhetoric of the legalization proponents that I began with. The lives of these smugglers offer a look into the complexities of marijuana legalization. First, they are vulnerable and expendable workers, and yet they are also cast as enemies within the reframing of the War on Drugs in the context of marijuana legalization. Proponents of the latter reference diverting money from criminal drug trafficking organizations, but these rhetorical strategies do not consider the very real material realities of reactive marijuana markets on these low-level marijuana workers. Joker and Adan are examples of the types of violence that Mexicans are increasingly subjected to as participants in the marijuana trade (nonparticipants are increasingly subject to similar levels of violence).

Yet, the "battling cartels" argument for marijuana legalization is complicated by another important facet of Colorado's drug consuming practices. Along with being among the first states to legalize marijuana for adult consumption, the most recent SAMHSA (Substance Abuse and Mental Health Services Administration) surveys from 2010 and 2011, the same period as the marijuana legalization campaign, indicate that Colorado distinguishes itself as a top consumer of cocaine (along with the District of Columbia). This fact, paired with the rhetoric villainizing Mexicans, has had profound effects on Mexican drug smugglers in Colorado. In 2011 and 2012, for example, several DEA operations targeted Mexican cocaine dealers along the I-25 corridor, resulting in several hundred arrests of mostly young, Mexican American males, including one bust that occurred days after the passing of Amendment 64 in 2012. If we recognize the marijuana legalization movement as an effort to rectify the harms of the War on Drugs, then in many ways legalization has resulted in a continuation of differential practices in policing and punishment, which are informed by the same racist attitudes rooted in the marijuana prohibition rhetoric that villainized Mexicans.

The outcomes have extended to the employment of people of color in Colorado's cannabis industry, as many of those who were subject to harsher systems of police profiling and criminal justice inequities are now disqualified from working in the legalized industry.

In Colorado, marijuana legalization supporters also pointed to disruptions in the international drug trade as a key indicator of the success of the state's marijuana policy reform. In 2014, only a few months after legal sales began in Colorado, *Vice News*'s Mary Emily O'Hara reported that legal sales were "crippling" Mexican cartels.[13] This conclusion was given academic grounding and credibility in 2017, when a group of European economists published a study arguing that the introduction of medical marijuana laws had reduced crime in US border states. The study, however, only considered US datasets on crime to draw these conclusions, dismissing Mexico's crime statistics due to the low quality of the data.[14] These conclusions failed to recognize the transnational nature of the border drug trade. A surface evaluation of violent crime in Mexico during the time period of medical marijuana law introduction in the United States—beginning in 1996 with California's Proposition 215—reveals that for the last two decades Mexico has undergone a considerable escalation of drug-related violence. In particular, rates of border violence reached dramatic levels beginning with the presidency of Vicente Fox (2000–2006), continuing to escalate through the Felipe Calderón (2006–2012) and Enrique Peña Nieto (2012–2018) administrations.[15] The reform of marijuana laws in the United States also coincided with the increased border policing and militarization that heavily impacted the border drug trade and morphed into the draconian border enforcement policies of the Trump administration.

After the events of September 11, 2001, the United States began to reevaluate the security of its national borders. The US-Mexico border, specifically, was framed within political discourse as a porous and unsecured boundary where terrorists could enter the nation for future attacks. In an effort to prevent such threats, the federal government provided funds to station more Border Patrol agents along the southern border to help with policing efforts. The increased resources led to greater surveillance, resulting in increased interception of drugs and immigrants. In 2003 the federal government created the Department of Homeland Security (DHS), which now controlled previously independent organizations, such as the Immigration and Naturalization Services (INS) and the US Customs Service.[16] These two organizations were joined in March 2003 to form the largest investigative branch of the DHS: Immigration and Customs

Enforcement (ICE). Paradoxically, however, the increased surveillance of the border and increased interception of drug shipments led to a spike in border violence tied to the drug trade.

As the US-Mexico border experienced this increase in drug policing and the intensification of border militarization, the sphere of drug trafficking was considerably altered by a new development. In the early 2000s, the Gulf Cartel, with its stronghold along the South Texas–Mexico border, began to employ a paramilitary force as hired protection, but also to conduct some trafficking measures. This new force, Los Zetas, was initially composed of "31 deserters from the Mexican Army's Airborne Special Forces Group."[17] However, since its original formation in 1997, "the organization has since grown considerably, now consisting of 100–200 men and women, and is distinguished by its advanced training and proficiency in violence."[18] This paramilitary organization recruits heavily along the South Texas–Mexico border and has established elaborate training camps to train young men in the military tactics and weapons skills necessary to serve as the organization's hitmen. This strategy of employing a paramilitary force, or at least adopting military tactics, was so successful that most drug trafficking organizations began forming their own drug paramilitaries to combat and compete with Los Zetas.

The rapid proliferation of paramilitary drug trafficking practices and organizations sparked significant concern in the United States. For its part, the Mexican government attempted to deal with this growing challenge, when Felipe Calderón assumed the presidency in 2006. Calderón mobilized the Mexican military to combat these new threats, deploying troops to drug trafficking/drug violence hotspots to take the fight to *los delincuentes organizados* (organized crime). The result, however, was a long, bloody, and costly war between drug traffickers and the state. Mexico was at war, but the battling forces on any given day were never certain. The resulting violence was significant along the South Texas–Mexico border, the Gulf Coast, and in southern coastal Mexico, quickly spreading to other border areas, reaching its height in 2008 in Juárez, Chihuahua, Mexico. This moment allowed for the establishment of another US drug policy directed at combating drug trafficking, namely, the Mérida Initiative, which was signed into law by George W. Bush on June 30, 2008. Often referred to as Plan Mexico or Plan Mérida, the $1.4 billion counternarcotics package allocated most of its budget to arming and training Mexican military and local and federal law enforcement forces in an effort to improve their effectiveness against drug trafficking organizations.[19]

The increased violence at the border was a result of competition between drug cartels and the rise of militarized policing in both the United States and Mexico. Furthermore, these changes centralized power within larger transnational criminal organizations that displaced the previous family-operated narco cooperatives. The majority of local smugglers became little more than low-wage, expendable, "contract" laborers for these larger criminal organizations. Within this context, the young smugglers of the border region became the targets of intensified violence from both drug policing agents and drug trafficking operatives, just as they also filled the role of expendable laborers throughout the borderlands and the "outsourcing" of violence into Mexico.[20]

Indeed, the outsourcing of drug violence along the border relies on the cartels enjoying impunity in Mexico as well as the targeting of drug workers through tactical violence. Similar to conventional trade relationships, by outsourcing, I mean the relocation of certain activities to Mexico in order to avoid the regulations or impositions of US legal oversight.[21] In this case, as a result of impunity in Mexico and the exploitability of the US-Mexico border to discipline drug workers through violence, violence is deployed against workers to a greater extent on the Mexican side of the border. Furthermore, drug workers on the American side are removed (or disappeared) to the Mexican side of the border in order to exploit the transnational nature of drug work and the differential punishment systems in the United States and Mexico.

Marijuana on the Border/Cannabis in Colorado

Having provided the context within which the international trafficking and consumption of marijuana occurs, I now turn in this final ethnographic section to a focus on cannabis consumption by Mexicans and the criminalization of Mexican cannabis consumption as a counterpoint to the allegedly responsible consumption of (mostly) white Americans/Coloradoans.

Eleazar Garcia is a nineteen-year-old Mexican American male from the South Texas border. He's lived in one of Starr County's small communities his entire life. Tattoos cover Garza's forearms, and a couple of shiny studs dot his left eyebrow. He drives "a badass truck," as he likes to remind me—a four-door Chevy with twenty-two-inch wheels that sits just a few inches off the ground. During his early teen years Eleazar began consuming marijuana, not unlike most young people who first try marijuana in the United States, who do so between the ages of twelve and sixteen. Eleazar is a type-1 diabetic and argued that cannabis was beneficial for his emotional health, particularly mentally coping with his autoimmune condition. Upon experiencing the negative symptoms of diabetic ketoacidosis, Eleazar was taken by his mother to a nearby emergency room. During the visit, his insulin and blood sugar levels were regulated, but he was also drug tested without his knowledge. As a result of the test coming back positive for marijuana, the State of Texas's Department of Child Protective Services opened up a child-endangerment case against Eleazar's mother. A case officer communicated to her that she would most likely be prosecuted for child endangerment and serve jail time, while Eleazar would be directed into foster care. However, to avoid this fate, she could aid police in charging her son with drug possession, sending him into the juvenile justice system that would include a half-year sentence of detention and drug treatment. She decided to cooperate. As she confessed to me during a conversation, this was the least problematic course of action for her family in this situation. Eleazar completed his six months of detention and was on probation through the county juvenile court system, until he turned eighteen in 2017.

Nowadays, Garza likes to spend his evenings cruising through the small towns that pepper the highway in Starr County, sometimes to visit friends, other times just to be out of the house. Prior to the surge of policing that resulted from Operations Strong Safety and Secure Texas, Garza had minimal problems going on his cruises. The local police and sheriff's deputies knew him and would often just wave as he passed them. When the state troopers arrived in Starr County, the situation changed. Garza was sixteen years old at the time and had recently obtained his driver's license, having completed the necessary requirements after securing his learner's permit a few months earlier. He complained that the state troopers often stopped him, harassing him and telling him that he "fit the description." Eventually, Garza had to limit his cruising to avoid these police encounters, and like many other residents of Starr County, he now actively avoids driving too much. According to John Michael Torres, the spokesperson for a local civil rights organization, "Our members in Starr County have said the 'surge' has changed their lives. You don't go out, they tell us, except when you have to go work or to buy groceries. Anything non-essential—the things that make life more enjoyable and boost the local economy—locals decide not to do, opting to stay home rather than risk traffic fines or immigration checks."[22]

While the drug war on the border has had these disproportionate effects on local residents, the legalization of marijuana in Colorado has resulted in a very different social dynamic for the treatment of young people and adults.

Legalization has resulted in a public health concern aimed at protecting the well-being of young people and warning them about the dangers of cannabis. Though quite flawed, Colorado has made efforts, with childproof packaging and education campaigns, to keep cannabis out of the hands of children. Yet, on Colorado's college campuses, students are now using medical marijuana cards as a source of legal protection, as Patrick O'Brien's work indicates.[23] While Colorado's Amendment 64 guaranties the right for adults twenty-one years of age and older to legally purchase, possess, and grow marijuana, individuals under the age of twenty-one are only able to legally access marijuana through the state's medical marijuana system. My own campus in Colorado has instituted a de facto harm reduction policy that allows for students' drug consumption to be underpoliced unless serious concerns about student health are expressed. And yet the flipside of the children and cannabis discussion has to address the fact that Colorado is known as a haven for medical cannabis for kids. For example, the Stanley brothers are recognized as "some of Colorado's finest cultivators and cannabis breeders," primarily for their development of a high-CBD, low-THC strain of cannabis, which has been used to successfully treat a child with Dravet syndrome as well as other seizure conditions in children.[24] The strain is now known as Charlotte's Web, so named after the child with Dravet syndrome. The notoriety of Realm Oil—the extraction made from the Charlotte's Web strain— brought positive publicity to Colorado's medical marijuana program just as the state was also on track to implement its recreational (or adult-use) marijuana program. Shortly before its full implementation, Dr. Sanjay Gupta debuted a CNN documentary titled simply *Weed*, in which Charlotte's story and her strain were prominently featured. The stories of these primarily upper-middle class, white families coming to Colorado as medical marijuana refugees stands in stark contrast to the experience of Eleazar and his working-class Mexican American family.

Consider now a silenced component of the kids and cannabis discussion. In the case of Latinx youth, legalization of cannabis for adult-use and medical purposes in Colorado has resulted in hyperpolicing and criminalization.[25] The national lifetime marijuana use rate for Latinx youth is 18.1 percent.[26] Indeed, drug use surveys of American youth have shown marijuana use among Latinx youth steadily increasing in comparison to their parents.[27] In the specific case of Colorado, the Colorado Department of Public Health and Environment has begun to closely monitor marijuana use rates among adolescents in the state in order to track and identify health concerns related to marijuana through the implementation of the Healthy Kids Colorado Survey. In the most recent survey, marijuana use among Latinx youth was estimated at 24 percent, six percentage points greater than the national rate. And while legalization advocates are quick to highlight that marijuana arrests are down among adults across all racial groups, in 2016 youth arrests of Latinx and African Americans were in fact steadily climbing, by 29 and 58 percent, respectively.[28] Meanwhile, white youth arrests are down by 8 percent. The increased marijuana usage rates for youth of color, coupled with the increased policing of this demographic, have created the circumstances for a continuation of the drug war. The continued criminalization of youth of color post-legalization is a clear indication that policy changes (though difficult in their own right) are much easier to accomplish than the cultural change necessary to achieve social justice and reparations for the losses incurred by this community in the drug wars. In the wake of ongoing concerns over police violence against communities of color, legalization has done little to change the process of policing or police attitudes. As the police chief of Thornton, Colorado, communicated to law enforcement officers and government officials that have since passed their own legalization programs at the October 2016 Marijuana Management Symposium, "You have to mourn the end of prohibition. It was hard for us, we were sad. We just had to get over it and get to work."

Conclusion

To return to Aaron Smith's opening point concerning legalization, in our efforts to reform marijuana laws, protect consumers, and create a safe and reliable system of sale and production, we are primarily protecting a privileged segment of our drug-consuming and drug-selling society. Yet, within this new "strange" arrangement, we do have the presence of the familiar: with cannabis prohibition, as now with legalization, Mexicans continue to be the criminals, the villains, the enemies . . . and the real victims.

And this is what we must be mindful of as we move forward with cannabis legalization as a platform for social justice. Michelle Alexander's *New Jim Crow* has been instrumental in raising the American public's consciousness about the racial injustices of the drug war, and oddly enough was utilized and referenced by individuals in the marijuana legalization movement.[29] Perhaps most people are less comfortable invoking her criticism of "the unbearable whiteness" of the cannabis industry post-legalization.[30] According to a press platform with the Drug Policy Alliance:

> "When I see images of people using marijuana and images of people who are now trying to run legitimate marijuana businesses, they're almost all white," [Alexander] said, noting she supports legalizing pot. "After 40 years of impoverished black men getting prison time for selling weed, white men are planning to get rich doing the same thing?" she added. "So that's why I think we have to start talking about reparations for the war on drugs. How do we repair the harms caused?"[31]

We are not alone in our critique of the cannabis industries' emphasis on profits over social justice. Reza Rajavi, a serial entrepreneur and a leader in the marijuana legalization movement in Denver for the last decade, expressed his disappointment with the cannabis industry at the Cannabis Sustainability Symposium on October 26, 2016.[32] Reza passionately argued that "the marijuana industry can and should do things differently," emphasizing that the history of the cannabis legalization movement was the history of a social justice reform, rooted in the tenets of harm reduction. He blasted the corporatization and profit-driven turn that the cannabis movement had taken, reminding his audience that the cannabis industry "used to be driven by mom and pops, by bootstrappers." After this impassioned speech, I conducted a short interview with Reza, and he informed me that although he was deeply committed to the social justice capabilities and reparative potential of the cannabis industry, he was opposed to any type of affirmative action or unionizing. In his estimation, the industry could accomplish the same outcomes through internal accountability.

In 2019, just five years after retail marijuana sales began in Colorado, the City of Denver commissioned a study focused on cannabis employment and opportunity. In June 2020 the findings from the study were made publicly available and revealed that workers (68 percent) and owners (nearly 75 percent) were overwhelmingly white.[33] With respect to communities of color, African Americans represented roughly 6 percent of both cannabis business owners and workers, while Latinxs represented approximately 13 percent of owners and just over 12 percent of workers in the cannabis industry.[34] This while African Americans represent 4.6 percent of the state's population and 9.4 percent of Denver's population, with Latinxs representing 21.8 and 30.3 percent respectively.[35] With this in mind, in June 2020 legislators took note of the continued exclusion of Colorado's communities of color from the legal cannabis industry and introduced HB20-1424: Social Equity Licensees in Regulated Marijuana.[36] Sponsored by African American state representative James Coleman and Latina state senator Julie Gonzales, HB20-1424 allows for the governor of Colorado to expedite marijuana possession pardons, allows for the equity license applicants to "use existing cannabis facilities to build their business," and focuses "on restorative justice for communities harmed by enforcement of the war on drugs."[37] On June 29, 2020, Colorado governor Jared Polis signed HB20-1424 into law, paving the way for greater government oversight and accountability for ensuring equitable access to cannabis business employment and ownership opportunities for Colorado's African American and Latinx communities. Given the inability of the industry to maintain its social justice imperative, the best course of action for moving forward is external (government) accountability. It is our responsibility to break down cannabigotry within the industry and invest in communities of color as we abolish the war on marijuana. As the Latinx population has historically been the target of marijuana prohibition and continues to be villainized and criminalized through an association with drug trafficking, it is imperative to spotlight the injustices experienced by the Latinx community through the long history of marijuana prohibition and the current moment and future of marijuana legalization.

Notes

1. "Marijuana Legalization Town Hall Debate," YouTube video, accessed October 1, 2021, https://www.youtube.com/watch?v=wmmkFI_Zl-M.

2. "Yes on 64 TV Ad—'Vote for Colorado,'" YouTube video, October 6, 2012, https://www.youtube.com/watch?v=1KAOq7XX2OY.

3. "Yes on 64 Web/Radio Ad—Melissa Etheridge," YouTube video, October 11, 2012, https://www.youtube.com/watch?v=A4UmVguKe_A.

4. Chavez 2013.

5. Campos 2018; Johnson 2017.

6. Bullington 1977.

7. As a prohibited psychoactive substance, alcohol fits into the trajectory of US drug policy and its effects on Mexico-United States drug smuggling.

8. Gilliland 1968.

9. Gooberman 1974.

10. Translated from Spanish by the author. Direct quote from interview: "Bring that asshole here and if he did steal the weed I'll kill him myself."

11. Translated from Spanish by the author. Direct quote from interview: "If I hadn't been such good friends with your deceased grandfather Blas, I'd kill both of you here and now."

12. Dudley Althaus, "Nearly 50 Bodies Recovered from Latest Mexico Massacre," *Houston Chronicle*, May 13, 2012, https://www.chron.com/communityblogs /atmosphere/article/Nearly-50-bodies-recovered-from-latest-Mexico-3555205 .php.

13. Mary Emily O'Hara, "Legal Pot in the US Is Crippling Mexican Cartels," *Vice News*, May 8, 2014, https://www.vice.com/en/article/d3j55x/legal-pot-in-the -us-is-crippling-mexican-cartels.

14. Gavrilova et al. 2019.

15. Correa-Cabrera 2017.

16. "Department Subcomponents and Agencies," United States Department of Homeland Security, accessed January 7, 2010, http://www.dhs.gov/xabout /structure/.

17. Brands 2009.

18. Ibid.

19. Ibid., 2.

20. Guerra 2015.

21. As an example, many industrial activities were outsourced to Mexico due to environmental policy that permitted greater industrial contamination in Mexico that would not have been permitted in the United States. These activities also benefited from the exploitability and management of workers. See Peña 1997.

22. Steve Taylor, "DPS: We're Going to Triple the Number of Troopers in Starr County," *Rio Grande Guardian*, October 2, 2015, https://riograndeguardian .com/dps-were-going-to-triple-the-number-of-troopers-in-starr-county/.

23. O'Brien 2013.

24. "The Stanley Brothers," accessed September 15, 2021, https://www.charlottesweb .com/frequently-asked-questions.

25. Rios 2011.

26. Lac et al. 2011.

27. "National Survey on Drug Use and Health: Hispanics," US Department of Health and Human Services, accessed September 15, 2021, https://www.samhsa .gov/data/sites/default/files/reports/rpt31101/2019NSDUH-Hispanic/Hispanic %202019%20NSDUH.pdf.

28. "Marijuana Legalization in Colorado: Early Findings of a Report Pursuant to Senate Bill 13–283 March 2016," Colorado Department of Public Safety Division of Criminal Justice Office of Research and Statistics, accessed September 15, 2021, https://cdpsdocs.state.co.us/ors/docs/reports/2016-SB13-283-Rpt.pdf.

29. Alexander 2010.

30. Angela Bacca, "The Unbearable Whiteness of the Marijuana Industry," *AlterNet*, April 1, 2015, https://www.alternet.org/2015/04/incredible-whiteness-colorado -cannabis-business/.

31. "DPA Telephone Town Hall: The New Jim Crow: What's Next with Michelle Alexander," Drug Policy Alliance, March 5, 2014, https://www.drugpolicy.org /resource/dpa-telephone-town-hall-new-jim-crow-whats-next-michelle -alexander.

32. Pseudonym.

33. "Cannabis Business and Employment Opportunity Study Report," Analytic Insight for the Department of Excise and Licenses City and County of Denver, June 2020.

34. Ibid.

35. United States Census Bureau, "Quick Facts: Colorado," accessed February 25, 2019, https://www.census.gov/quickfacts/CO; United States Census Bureau, "Quick Facts: Denver City, Colorado; Denver County, Colorado," accessed February 25, 2019, https://www.census.gov/quickfacts/fact/table/denvercity colorado,denvercountycolorado/PST045219.

36. "HB20–1424 Social Equity Licenses in Regulated Marijuana," Accessed February 25, 2019, https://leg.colorado.gov/bills/hb20–1424.

37. Kyle Jaeger, "Colorado Governor Signs Marijuana Social Equity Bill Letting Him Expedite Possession Pardons," *Marijuana Moment*, June 29, 2020, https:// www.marijuanamoment.net/colorado-governor-signs-marijuana-social-equity -bill-letting-him-expedite-possession-pardons/.

CHAPTER EIGHT

Becoming a Sanctuary People
Latina/o Practices of Accompaniment in Northeast Ohio

GINA M. PÉREZ

Since the 2016 presidential election, discussions about sanctuary seem to be everywhere. Politically progressive efforts supporting sanctuary cities, campuses, states, and streets are just as ubiquitous as efforts to curtail movements enacting various sanctuary policies, criticizing them as dangerous, illegal, and even anti-American. For Latinas/os in Ohio, the notion of sanctuary has particular salience as communities of faith, local activists, and community members mobilize to respond to an increasingly dangerous and uncertain landscape that has come to define their diverse experiences as those of shared precarity. Since 2017, for example, Ohio has indexed some of the highest numbers of public sanctuary cases in the nation. The state has also received significant numbers of Puerto Ricans relocating to cities like Lorain and Cleveland in the wake of the devastating effects of Hurricane Maria in September 2017. In both instances, local responses have been framed in a variety of ways, such as offering sanctuary, refuge, hospitality, and accompaniment to those who are vulnerable and most in need. For the late community activist Manuel Castro, such actions are at the heart of what he referred to as being and becoming sanctuary people. This chapter uses Castro's notion of sanctuary people as a framework for analyzing new ways of being (ontologies) and knowing (epistemologies) that emerge when a diverse range of people engage in an equally diverse set of practices to provide safety, refuge, and enactments of solidarity to Latinas/os in the face of dire circumstances. From indefinitely housing people desperate to remain with their families in the face of deportation to ensuring that new residents displaced by (un)natural disasters receive the services and support they need to rebuild their lives in new and unfamiliar places, sanctuary practices in Ohio exemplify a type of refusal and futurity this anthology seeks to explore ethnographically. Indeed, to be a sanctuary people is to gesture simultaneously toward *a refusal* that opposes and contests the dominant order "in ways unthought or unrecognized" and toward *a future* whereby people "actively struggle for and creatively imagine more just and equitable worlds."[1]

This chapter examines the different ways becoming a sanctuary people has meant the binding up of different individuals in support of Latinas/os in northeast Ohio. For some this move is about new ways of knowing and being, responding to the immediacy of events that have created a context of shared precarity of Ohio's Latina/o communities. But for others, becoming a sanctuary people is grounded in longer histories of faith-based activism, community organizing, and solidarity efforts both locally and transnationally. By foregrounding the role of faith communities in these efforts, my work builds on burgeoning scholarship in Latina/o/x Studies analyzing progressive religious activism and the kinds of solidarities across difference — race, ethnicity, linguistic, class, citizenship, gender, education, for example — such organizing engenders. Such an approach also moves us beyond what some religious studies scholars have identified as "common political binaries (like Right/Left and progress/tradition) and to [rethink] long-accepted theories of religion and social movements as well as the role of faith in democratic politics and civic life."[2] While neither faith-based organizing nor multiethnic collaborations are new, careful analytic attention to sanctuary practices in Ohio reveals the enduring power of place and social location in giving shape to these efforts, which address both the immediate needs of this historical moment as well as the kinds of futures that are being imagined.

Latinas/os in Ohio

According to the 2017 American Community Survey, nearly 437,000 residents in Ohio are Latino, a number that has doubled since 2000.[3] Ohio's Latina/o population is approximately 3.7 percent of the state total, a number than is far lower than the percentage nationally (18 percent). Approximately 21 percent of Ohio Latinos were born outside of the United States, but the majority are US-born. 45 percent are of Mexican ancestry, with three-quarters of these being born in the United States. Not only have Mexican and Mexican American populations in Ohio more than doubled in size since 2000, they account for much of the growth of the state's Latina/o population. Puerto Ricans make up nearly a third of Ohio Latinas/os and, like Mexican Americans, have long roots within Ohio. Finally, approximately 10 percent of Ohio Latinas/os hail from Guatemala, El Salvador, and Honduras, the majority of whom were born abroad.

Ohio Latinas/os are largely urban, with approximately one-third living in the four major cities of Columbus, Cleveland, Lorain, and Toledo. The rural areas in the north and northwest of the state have higher proportions of Latino residents, reflecting local political economies that rely heavily on agricultural laborers in gardening, nursery, and dairy industries. Lorain County and the city of Lorain index the highest percentage of Latinas/os in the state (10 percent and approximately 28 percent, respectively). And as is the case nationally, Ohio Latinas/os are younger than the overall state population, with the median age being 26.2 years (compared to 39.3 overall). With a medium household income of $40,921 compared to $54,000 for all of Ohioans, Latinas/os in Ohio experience higher poverty rates than the population overall. With 7.1 percent of Latinas/os unemployed, approximately 27 percent of Latinos in Ohio live below the poverty line, and a quarter of the eighty-four thousand Latino households lives in poverty. The educational attainment of Latinas/os in Ohio lags behind the state overall as well, with approximately 23 percent of adults not having a high school diploma and 12 percent having less than a high school education (compared to 3 percent statewide). These data provide important context for understanding the material conditions in which the majority of Ohio Latinas/os live and reflect the economic and social realities that have defined the population historically.

As a community that has a long history rooted in migrant labor circuits of Mexican and Mexican American families in the early twentieth century, as well as in postwar Puerto Rican migration to work in expanding industrial sectors of the economy, the settlement experiences of Latinas/os in Northeast Ohio share a great deal with those characterizing other midwestern cities, including Chicago. In the city of Lorain, the recruitment of Puerto Ricans to work for companies like US Steel and the United Tube Company helped plant the seeds for further growth. Oral history accounts of these early years emphasize the important role that a smaller Mexican community played in helping to provide housing and sense of community to Puerto Rican newcomers, who quickly outnumbered Mexican residents in the city and began establishing important civic, religious, and service organizations in the postwar era. In addition to El Hogar Puertorriqueño and Mexican Mutual, organizations like El Centro de Servicios Sociales were established to meet the needs of a community that faced economic, social, and political marginalization. Historian Gene Rivera also notes the important role churches played in the development of Latina/o Lorain, including the founding of La Capilla de Sagrado Corazón in 1952, the first Hispanic church in the state of Ohio, and El Templo Bethel, a Pentecostal

Church, faith communities that still serve a growing and diversifying Latina/o population in Lorain today.[4]

Lorain's Latina/o communities are among many that comprise the International City, as the city is proudly referred to by local residents. Every year the city celebrates its immigrant history with an international festival, complete with multicultural princesses representing immigrants from Hungary, Slovenia, Mexico, Puerto Rico, Poland, and the Czech Republic. Lorain is also home to strong labor unions and organizing that connect the struggles of white, African American, and Latina/o working class residents. The history of Latina/o activism and organizing in Lorain and northeast Ohio include its active involvement with the United Farm Workers (UWF) in the 1960s and 1970s and its support of the grape boycott and organizing efforts to convince local grocery stores to boycott grapes.[5] In 1972 local community activists such as Miguel and Teresita Romero welcomed UFW leader Cesar Chavez and hosted a meeting with him and the community at Sacred Heart Chapel, an event that brought together Mexican, Mexican American, and Puerto Rican residents to hear him speak of the union's efforts to organize farm workers both in California and Ohio.[6] Similarly, Puerto Ricans in Lorain used their work in El Hogar Puertorriqueño to not only challenge urban renewal policies that decimated the once thriving Latina/o commercial area of Vine Avenue but also to address the lack of affordable housing for Puerto Rican and Mexican residents in South Lorain, where the majority of Latinas/os continue to reside. These local efforts operated simultaneously with transnational organizing that included campaigning for the release of Puerto Rican political prisoner Oscar López Rivera and the development of various organizations and conferences to address the needs of Latinas/os in Lorain.[7] Many of these events included inviting Puerto Rican activists and leaders from cities like Chicago as well as Puerto Rico, an approach that affirms a diasporic and transnational approach to understanding the challenges in Lorain.

This history of organizing, activism, and advocacy established a solid foundation for the development of new strategies responding to the changing needs of Latina/o residents in Lorain and throughout northeast Ohio in the twenty-first century. In 2014 community members in Lorain established the Lorain Ohio Immigrant Rights Association (LOIRA), and since that time have been actively involved in developing relationships with local law enforcement, city councils, churches, colleges and universities, and other civic organizations throughout northeast Ohio to create networks of support to respond to increased immigration enforcement, which has made undocumented immigrants increasingly vulnerable. For immigrant rights activist Anabel Barron Sánchez, her work with LOIRA was not something she anticipated doing. In fact, in oral histories, public lectures, and community conversations, she consistently shares the story of how her own detention and deportation order politicized her and led her to immigrant rights activism that now defines much of the work she does in the community. Similarly, recently retired Lorain police chief Celestino Rivera conveys how despite his own political consciousness as a Puerto Rican police officer committed to equity in policing, he was surprised when he was approached by immigrant rights activists, community and religious leaders, to revise his own police department's relationship to ICE and immigration officials. As increased immigrant surveillance and detention impacted local community members, people responded in a variety of ways. And while many of these responses intensified in the wake of the 2016 presidential election, it is important to locate the ability to respond and the variety of tools people drew on as being honed in past struggles that offered opportunities for people to imagine and actively create radically resistive futures.

Sanctuary in Ohio

Since 2016 Ohio has become home to a high proportion of public sanctuary cases in the country. According to a Church World Service report from 2018, with five people housed in different religious communities—Presbyterian, Mennonite, and Lutheran churches, for example—Ohio is one of fifteen states where thirty-six people have sought public and physical sanctuary in houses of worship. This number does not, however, capture the number of people who, in the face of deportation and family separation, have employed other means to remain in the communities where they have often lived and worked for decades. Indeed, religious leaders, immigration activists, and scholars have argued that public and physical sanctuary is one of many strategies faith communities use to resist what some scholars refer to as the "deportation regime."[8] According to Allison Harrington, pastor of Southside Presbyterian Church in Tucson, Arizona, "Sanctuary is a tactic, not the goal." Pastor Pablo Mayorga of Iglesia Presbiteriana Hispana in Oakland, California, emphasized this point when he noted the range of strategies members of his church and the Bay Area Interfaith Movement engage in to provide support, comfort, and refuge for members of his congregation.

Indeed, these sentiments gesturing to the complexity and power of sanctuary are echoed by activists in Ohio whose sustained immigrant advocacy, support, and organizing has led some to declare themselves sanctuary churches and others to actually welcome people into sanctuary for long periods of time. "Sanctuary is one of the only active forms of resistance we have now," explains Manuel Castro. It is a Saturday morning in October 2017, and a small group of us is gathered in a quiet meeting room in the Columbus Mennonite Church on the city's north side to meet Edith Espinal, who recently took sanctuary in the church. As a middle-aged mother of three who has lived in Columbus intermittently for more than twenty years, Edith has struggled to remain in Ohio with her family and decided to seek sanctuary after it became clear to her that she was in danger of being deported. After briefly entering into sanctuary in the Mennonite church on September 5, 2017, the day Attorney General Jeff Sessions announced the end of DACA—a decision informed by her understanding that she could apply for a stay of removal that was later denied on September 25—Edith made the decision to enter into sanctuary once again on October 2, remaining there until February 18, 2021.[9] While Edith is one of only a handful of people seeking sanctuary in Ohio, she is part of broader sanctuary practices and movements that have a long history in churches, faith-based organizations, and broader activism.

Research on recent examples of sanctuary movements in the United States and internationally is quite vast.[10] And while there is debate about the efficacy of sanctuary as a political strategy, there seem to be several important areas of consensus among those who study and work with sanctuary movements. First, as Linda Rabben has argued, "sanctuary has remained a morally and religiously based obligation that often takes place outside or against the law."[11] Second, as many writers have noted, the current movement has deep roots in the Central American solidarity and sanctuary movements of the 1980s, which were bound up with intersectional struggles beyond immigration, including LGBT liberation movements and antimilitarization and anti-imperialist organizing.[12] And finally, and perhaps most importantly, today's sanctuary movement represents a form of what political scientist Amalia Pallares refers to as "family activism," a complex political strategy by immigrant rights activists as they construct, reinforce, challenge, and redefine notions of family to challenge deportation and family separation.[13]

As Edith described her decision to seek sanctuary in the Columbus Mennonite Church, she consistently referred to her family, especially her three children, and how being able to remain near them compelled her to seek sanctuary. These sentiments were echoed in an interview she gave to the *Columbus Dispatch*, in which she explained how much her family needs her and how they rely on each other: "We very much need each other. I'm the one that guides the family and makes sure the kids are doing what they should be, that they're not getting into trouble."[14] Like other undocumented mothers, Edith highlights her importance as a mother in her struggle to remain in Ohio, a familiar strategy whereby mothers make "claims of belonging that are based on or strengthened by their motherhood."[15] The emphasis on preserving family unity, according to Pallares, recognizes the legal basis of family reunification in immigration policy and is mobilized by "community, political and religious leaders" as part of immigration activist and reformist efforts.[16]

For Pastor Joel, family, faith, and seeking refuge provide the spiritual and theological basis for providing sanctuary to Edith. According to the Columbus Mennonite Church website, seeking sanctuary from violence is foundational to the church's American origins. Not only is sanctuary central to how "Mennonites tell our history," it forms the moral and spiritual framework that compels them to respond:

> In light of this calling, we have welcomed Edith Espinal into sanctuary in our church building. Edith is a neighbor. Edith is a mother. Edith is a child of God who fled violence and sought refuge in our country many years ago and wishes to stay united with her family in this city that has become her home. . . . We as a congregation have heard Edith's story. We've been inspired by her courage. We are compelled to offer our church building as a place of safety and support where she can stay united with her three children and her husband.[17]

According to Pastor Joel, both this history of being what he calls "sanctuary people" and the congregation's experiences with the Central American solidarity movement of the 1980s provided fertile ground for inviting Edith into sanctuary. Indeed, in the 1980s, the Columbus Mennonite Church already played a supportive role in the sanctuary movement while not actually providing sanctuary at that time.

This experience with sanctuary is an important part of the congregation's history and was a meaningful invitation to reflection as part of its fifty-five-year anniversary celebration. In August 2017, as Edith was considering going into sanctuary, Manuel Castro reached out to various church leaders in the Columbus area, including Joel, who then brought the idea to his congregation.

According to Pastor Joel, he expected there might be reluctance and that people might respond saying "this is moving way too fast," expressing concerns not just about the legal questions but about the fact that entering into this commitment could last for a very long time. Joel explained that given that his congregation is largely middle- and upper-middle class, money was not an issue; and after conversations about legal questions and the logistics of ensuring there were proper facilities to house Edith (including a shower and a room for her to live) the conversation shifted to how best to *accompany* Edith and her family through house arrest and her restricted movement for the indefinite future. "Sanctuary has been a gift and has transformed us," Pastor Joel observed. The bigger story of all of this, he explained, is how sanctuary is making them reflect on what it means to be a sanctuary people. He described how providing sanctuary has deep roots in Rome and Israel and how this experience is providing them an opportunity to reflect on this meaning for them as a spiritual community. "It has been beautiful," Manuel added. "ICE and others didn't want Edith in sanctuary because there is power in this kind of resistance." Edith concurred: "Según el abogado, sanctuario no es una buena opción. Quería que yo regresará a Mexico y no le gustaba la idea del sanctuario." (According to the lawyer, sanctuary is not a good option. She wanted me to return to Mexico and didn't like the idea of sanctuary.)

Manuel and Edith's observation about the power of sanctuary-as-resistance resonates with the experiences of others who have made similar choices in Ohio. On September 12, 2017, Leonor Garcia entered into sanctuary in Forest Hill Presbyterian Church in Cleveland Heights after an ICE check-in that ended in her receiving a deportation order, ankle monitor, and the reality of being separated from her four children. In a statement from Pastor John Lentz Jr. of Forest Hills Presbyterian Church, he explained the church's decision to invite Leonor into sanctuary:

> We are here today to announce that Forest Hills church has invited Leonor to live here at this church in sanctuary until such time that she is able to return to her home in Akron, to her work, to her community, and most of all to her family. . . . Separating a mother from her children is not what we do as a people of faith. It is not what Americans should do either. Rather, giving women shelter is what we do. Showing hospitality to those in need is what defines us. Standing with all of God's children everywhere is who we are. Being the beloved community is what we will be.[18]

Like Pastor Joel, Pastor John Lentz emphasizes the centrality of preserving families as central to their faith community's deepest beliefs and links these values to those of the nation, holding Americans to a higher moral order by giving "women shelter" and "showing hospitality." Moreover, by emphasizing the religious basis of hospitality, Pastor John draws on ancient traditions of sanctuary that are not only rooted in welcoming the stranger, the biblical basis that was often embraced in the first sanctuary movement of the 1980s, but also guide how one treats one's neighbor and those in need. This embrace of extending hospitality to neighbors rather than strangers is important and represents an important shift in how faith communities frame their sanctuary practices in Ohio and nationally. Both Leonor and Edith have deep roots in Ohio, and their role as neighbors, coworkers, mothers, and long-standing community members is often put forth as a reminder that Latina/o communities have long histories in the state.

This focus on the valued role of these women as mothers, neighbors, and community members was echoed by religious leaders and community activists at a press conference on July 2, 2018, announcing that Miriam Vargas would enter into sanctuary at the First English Lutheran Church in Columbus. As a mother of two US citizen daughters and resident of Columbus for more than thirteen years, Miriam made the decision after conversations with Edith and others involved in the Columbus Sanctuary Collective, explaining that her reason to enter into sanctuary was to remain with her children. "The only thing I'm asking for is to not be separated from my children, my family," she announced at the press conference from the top of the stone church steps.[19] Other speakers affirmed their role in helping to keep Miriam with her family, with one minister noting, "The goal of sanctuary is to get out. We are learning to hold on to hope and what it means to be a sanctuary space. Sanctuary is an identity that you cultivate over time, not just a one-time decision." This notion of sanctuary as an identity is at the heart of Manuel Castro's notion of "sanctuary people" and is central to the work that he and activists and faith communities are involved in throughout Columbus that extends beyond immigration. So while there is an immediacy involved in public sanctuary work that is grounded in making it possible for Miriam, Edith, and Leonor to remain with their families and to return to their homes, these actions are part of broader organizing efforts that use the language of hospitality and safety to address issues of structural violence that include not only immigrant deportation but also limitations in asylum law and police violence in communities of color. By focusing on structural forces that render families vulnerable and fractured, these efforts embody a broader approach to sanctuary work that Naomi Paik refers to as imagining a "abolitionist futures" and involve strategies such as teleconferences, listening sessions, Mother's Day celebrations, public protests of police violence, and political organizing that serve as a reminder of the centrality of mothering and motherhood as a potentially radical act. In the short film *Tres Madres: Three Mothers Fighting for Justice*, three women, Edith Espinal, Adrienne Hood, and Jaqueline Kifuko, "came together this Mother's Day to share their story with the world and ask you to join the fight for the families that cannot be together."[20] The video focuses on their stories and links them up as a struggle to preserve families, the rights of mothers to remain in the United States and protect their children, and the broader policies preventing them from doing so.

Sanctuary struggles, therefore, are deeply gendered strategies of resistance and refusal. Of the dozens of people living in public sanctuary in the United States, the majority are women, a trend reflected in Ohio as well. By emphasizing their roles as mothers to challenge state power, Edith, Leonor, Miriam, Adrienne, and Jaqueline engage in gendered political strategies rooted in histories of struggle that connect them to social movements and freedom struggles in Latin America, Africa, and beyond.

These gendered sanctuary practices address the punitive responses to cities, states, and others who dare to defy the federal government's demand that local entities collaborate and support federal immigration enforcement, especially in Ohio. In addition to the Trump administration's consistent threats to punish sanctuary cities, elected officials in Ohio, such as Treasurer Josh Mandel, have publicly announced support of state legislation that would punish cities and individuals who stand with sanctuary cities by holding them criminally liable for crimes committed by undocumented immigrants.[21] Such attacks have led some immigration activists to consider whether a new language of resistance is needed. After mass at Sacred Heart Chapel in Lorain, Ohio, one Sunday morning, don Miguel shared with me and my family the work he and his wife were doing visiting local prisons and how important it is to have married couples and families involved in this particular kind of pastoral work. Having his wife present to talk with the wives of incarcerated husbands provided invaluable support, he explained. "In the work we are doing here and with immigration, I really think we need to think about this as a kind of hospitality. Maybe we need to talk more about *hospitality* rather than sanctuary," he explained. "Sanctuary," he worried, has become such a loaded word, a sentiment shared by a number of people. Indeed, discussions around developing rhetorical strategies that capture the spirit and values guiding activist and community organizing aimed at supporting Latina/o communities is a recurring theme among many leaders, activists, and community workers. And while some in Ohio continue to embrace and deploy sanctuary practices, arguing for its historical and continued spiritual power, others have considered other framings of this work. A focus on accompaniment, welcoming the stranger, and hospitality, therefore, represents examples of how Latinas/os have tried to capture the ways their work has been stretched and refashioned—and was in stark relief as Puerto Ricans responded to the devastating impact of Hurricane Maria in September 2017.

Refuge and Shelter from the Storm

According to anthropologist Isa Rodríguez Soto, by the time Hurricane Maria hit Puerto Rico on September 20, 2017, "the Puerto Rican people were already amid a disaster, an unnatural disaster created by U.S. imperialism. The economy was in shambles; there is a total lack of political will to ensure transparency and accountability; and most people were struggling to survive."[22] One of the most significant consequences of Hurricane Maria has been a massive exodus that rivals postwar Puerto Rican migration. According to a report by the Center for Puerto Rican Studies on the first anniversary of the hurricane, by 2018 nearly 160,000 Puerto Ricans had relocated throughout cities in the United States: "This exodus represents one of the most significant movements of Puerto Ricans to the U.S. mainland in the island's history in terms of both volume and duration [and] is as high as the net migration flow in the previous two years combined."[23] This new migration was preceded by years of significant Puerto Rican outmigration as a result of Puerto Rico's debt crisis, a stagnant economy, and economic policies at the local and federal governments that have devastated the island's economy. As Vélez-Vélez and Villarrubia-Mendoza noted in interviews with people following the hurricane, "interviewees consistently reiterate that the humanitarian crisis that people are experiencing preexisted the hurricane. . . . Most organizers point out that the conditions of precarity can be traced to a myriad of factors, such as austerity measures imposed by PROMESA, state mismanagement and/or neglect, a stagnant economy driven by foreign incentives and a mediocre policy develop approach that follows a top-down model."[24] These failed economic policies, as well as the (un)natural disaster that followed, have had a significant consequence: they lay bare what some scholars have referred to as "Puerto Rican cultural trauma" and the renewed use of migration as a "form of governance on the island."[25]

Residents in northeast Ohio quickly witnessed the trauma of displacement and migration in the wake of Maria. Service organizations, churches, community leaders, and residents organized food drives, collected clothing, and rented trucks to send pallets of food, medicine, and clothes to Puerto Rico to help with immediate relief efforts on the island. As Puerto Rican families began arriving to Lorain and Cleveland, these same organizations, together with schools, hospitals, social workers, community colleges, and employers, organized and attended multiple fairs focused on helping those relocating to the area, with a primary focus on securing housing and enrolling children in local schools. According to Victor Leandry, executive director of El Centro de Servicios Sociales in Lorain, the impact of Hurricane Maria's devastation was facilitating new Puerto Rican migration to the Ohio region. "When I walk into [El Centro] at nine in the morning, we are already seeing a migration."[26] These sentiments were shared widely throughout northeast Ohio as cities like Cleveland and Lorain prepared and organized to meet the needs of potentially thousands of newly arrived Puerto Ricans, many of whom used kin and extended kin networks for temporary housing. As Edwin Meléndez and Jennifer Hinojosa noted, of the ten largest Puerto Rican communities in the United States, Ohio ranks eighth and consequently was predicted to be a significant settlement community for people leaving the island in the years to come. These diasporic communities, therefore, were not only key in mobilizing to respond to the immediate effects of the hurricane on the island but also draw on what Marisa Alicea and Maura Toro-Morn describe as "existing transnational connections and newly developed networks of aid and support" that connect cities like Chicago, Lorain, and Cleveland to Puerto Rican communities on the island.[27]

As the reality of how long the road to recovery would be continued to set in, local leaders focused their efforts on ensuring the long-term needs of newcomers, including providing adequate housing and ESL classes, providing clothing for the cold weather, enrolling children in schools, and providing them with backpacks, pencils, and other school supplies. In Cleveland a collaboration between Cuyahoga Community College (Tri-C), the Spanish American Committee, the Cleveland Metropolitan School District, and Esperanza Inc. (an organization focused on K–12 education and educational access for Northeast

Ohio Latinas/os) resulted in Bienvenidos a Cleveland, an initiative designed to coordinate services and provide information about housing, job opportunities, childcare, and senior care for new Puerto Rican residents. As part of this initiative, Tri-C offered reduced tuition to students from the island and Cleveland schools "hired nine new staff members to meet the needs of newly-enrolled Puerto Rican students."[28] Similar efforts quickly developed in Lorain, with El Centro helping to coordinate efforts with "Lorain Schools, the county commissioners, Mercy Hospital and the Metropolitan Housing Authority."[29] El Centro also created a Spanish-language pamphlet providing great detail about the range of resources and agencies able to help in the resettlement process, including information about mental health resources given both the trauma many Puerto Ricans experienced during the hurricane and the challenges facing them in their new environment.

These needs pose a particular burden for a community that already struggles economically with regional unemployment rates higher than the national average and with Puerto Rican households in particular indexing a poverty rate of 29 percent compared to 22.7 percent nationally.[30] Despite the marginal economic status of large numbers of Puerto Rican families, leaders like Councilman Arroyo noted that community members actively supported and provided hospitality for those who needed housing and struggled to get their children enrolled in public schools. What was desperately needed, however, were greater resources from local, state, and federal officials in the resettlement process for those who had left the island with few resources. "I fear that the next wave of people coming in from Puerto Rico are those that are in even greater need," Councilman Angel Arroyo soberly observed. Thus, while local leaders and community activists note the critical role local communities play in meeting newcomers' needs, they also recognize the need for and are organizing to demand greater federal investment and resources that are in line with relief efforts in places like Houston. According to Councilman Arroyo, "I went to Houston after the hurricane to help and I saw people getting checks for rebuilding in fewer than eight days. In Puerto Rico, they are past 50 days since the hurricane and only 24 percent of the island has power and they are already talking about pulling FEMA out. Yet FEMA stayed in New Orleans and other places for years. Why is Puerto Rico getting the cold shoulder?"[31]

Local churches also played an important role in the relocation and relief efforts. Sacred Heart Chapel in Lorain, for example, was the drop-off site for donations by community members from across the region, which filled the large community gathering space, or *placita*. Sacred Heart also hosted a fair that brought together a range of agencies, public officials, health professionals, teachers, and social workers to provide information, moral support, and a sense of community. According to Anabel Barron Sánchez, a local caseworker, immigration rights activist, and cofounder of LOIRA, mobilizing support for Puerto Rican newcomers is deeply rooted in Lorain's history as the International City and ongoing examples of Mexican/Puerto Rican solidarity that have been nurtured through years of immigrant rights organizing and advocacy at Sacred Heart Chapel. Embracing solidarity is also deeply personal for Anabel, as someone who benefited from community support when she was detained by immigration officials and put into deportation proceedings in 2013. As Anabel recounts in an oral history interview in spring 2018, she reached out to fellow parishioners at Sacred Heart one Sunday morning, sharing her story at each of the English and Spanish language masses. "So during the three masses on Sunday, the 8 am, 10 am, and noon mass I went to the podium, and I shared my story with the parishioners, and I asked them to support me and I asked them to support my kids." According to Anabel, people were moved to tears, a response that surprised her.

> I didn't think that the church would have that reaction towards me. Because after I finished talking there was a line of people, all the way here [outside the chapel], just to give me a hug. And the following Sunday I came back, and I collected more than a hundred letters to support my stay of removal application. These people saw me volunteering and see me here, but I never thought they were going to take the time. . . . And they were coming to the office and dropping off the letters. I was amazed.[32]

For Anabel, this outpouring of support was significant, not only because Sacred Heart is still largely regarded as a Puerto Rican parish but also because it enabled profound and generative solidarity between Puerto Ricans and undocumented migrants from Mexico, El Salvador, and Guatemala who increasingly attended mass and events at Sacred Heart but who didn't feel particularly visible. LOIRA, for example, was established by Anabel and Miguel Romero, and their meetings take place at Sacred Heart. "Know Your Rights" workshops, legal clinics and informational meetings with immigration lawyers, and fundraisers have been organized and attended by a range of people, including Lorain's chief of police Celestino Rivera, who often invokes his own traumatic experiences growing up in Lorain as a young boy as being an important point of departure for his role in developing clear policies guiding interactions between his police officers and immigration officials to protect undocumented immigrants.

This is the context in which Anabel observes the importance of offering particular support for Puerto Ricans relocating to Lorain, carefully noting that Hurricane Maria was followed by a devastating earthquake in Mexico City that also preoccupied the thoughts and energies of Latinas/os in Lorain.

> How can I not be compassionate to the Puerto Rican community after seeing so many videos that people were, clients were showing me? And I guess, this is not about niceties, this is about being a human. [Pause] I know Mexico suffered a lot of losses, especially those kids, [exhale] but, Puerto Rico was worse. And maybe I'm saying this because I didn't lose anyone in the earthquake, but I know that Puerto Rico, the entire island got wiped out. . . . I would say that the Puerto Rican community supports the fundraiser [for victims of the earthquake in Mexico] and the Mexican community has supported the Maria efforts . . . to welcome this community, these families to our community. So, that's the way that I see it. . . . Now it's like a family, OK? We're all together in this.[33]

Binding oneself up with the struggles of others is what guides the work of people like Anabel Barron Sánchez, Victor Leandry, Celestino Rivera, and Miguel Romero. Faith communities foster these relationships and embrace the values of accompaniment and sanctuary to those in need. In the case of Hurricane Maria, faith communities like Sacred Heart organized locally and operated transnationally to accompany and support those affected by the devastation and to demand resources from the state. In doing so, their actions reflect efforts by organizations like the United States Conference of Catholic Bishops, which admonished Congress to meet the needs of hurricane victims and be accountable for producing the very conditions of precarity that characterized the island long before the hurricane. In a statement posted to the Diocese of Cleveland website on November 2, 2017, Bishop Frank Dewane, chairman of the Committee on Domestic Justice and Human Development of the United States Conference of Catholic Bishops, declared:

> The people of Puerto Rico have been facing serious problems for many years: economic upheaval and scarcity, persistent joblessness, and

other social problems resulting from the financial crisis gripping the Commonwealth's economy. They bear little responsibility for the island's financial situation yet have suffered most of the consequences. Now, the recent devastation has made the circumstances, especially for those in need, unbearable.

As pastors, we share in the suffering borne by our brother bishops and the people they shepherd in Puerto Rico. We stand ready, through legislative advocacy as well as by means of the emergency funds set up in the aftermath of Hurricane Maria, to support with compassion our brothers and sisters in such dire need. We urgently beseech all Catholics in the United States to join with all people of good will in supporting these crucial initiatives at this critical point in time for the people of Puerto Rico.[34]

Standing with displaced Puerto Ricans and undocumented immigrants facing immigrant detention through advocacy, accompaniment, and hospitality is the prevailing framework guiding the efforts of activists and faith communities as they collaborate, organize, and develop creative strategies in the face of grim realities.

Conclusion: Toward a Latina/o/x Anthropology of Accompaniment

On July 8, 2018, Bishop Nelson Perez traveled to Lorain to celebrate a special mass for immigrant families at Sacred Heart Chapel. This was not his first visit to Sacred Heart—indeed, he frequently notes how much he enjoys celebrating mass in the largely Latina/o parish. But in the frenzied and mournful days and weeks following an immigration raid, which included the detention of members of Sacred Heart parish, the presence of Bishop Nelson and his clear articulation of church's position regarding immigrants offered much needed solace to a grieving and fearful community. Since his installation as the first Latino bishop in the Diocese of Cleveland on September 5, 2017, he has been vocal in his support of immigrant families and comprehensive immigration reform and offered his first public articulation of his position on September 7, 2017, in response to President Trump's decision to end DACA. Affirming both his commitment to stand with DACA youth as well as his call for Congress to develop legislation to protect them, he observed that during his installation mass just two days before, he had called on people to "accompany those in difficult situations."[35] Bishop Nelson returned to this notion of accompaniment in his homily at Sacred Heart

Chapel ten months later, proclaiming: "For the church, there are no borders. The church cannot be detained. And the same church that was present in the lives of our brothers and sisters in their countries of origin—that encountered them and accompanied them—well they come here, and they're embraced by the same church."[36]

Accompaniment has been a defining value guiding new initiatives and much of the work in the Diocese of Cleveland under Bishop Nelson. In 2018 the diocese launched its Parish Companion Program, designed to "accompany parishioners who are in the final stages of immigration removal proceedings, or who are at risk of removal."[37] A key element of the program is to provide training to "prepare companions for the different scenarios they may encounter and offer an opportunity to meet people from other church communities who care about similar issues of immigration and the realities facing undocumented sisters and brothers."[38] The training includes a focus on the legal issues and practical matters faced by immigrants in deportation proceedings, and it offers concrete ways to accompany people in this process as well as being clear about the scriptural basis for the church's position regarding immigrants and immigration.

And while the notion of accompaniment has a long history in Catholic social teaching, with its clearest manifestation in liberation theology and faith-based social justice struggles throughout Latin America beginning in the 1960s, its current manifestation takes on a particular resonance when applied to Latina/o communities in the United States. In workshops, casual conversations, and discussions around issues ranging from immigration reform, family separation, family relocation due to natural disasters, and meeting the needs of the poor, the language of accompaniment is embraced and suffuses faith-based advocacy, programming, and pastoral care.

Accompaniment is not exclusive to Catholic social teaching. Indeed, it is what informs many faith communities' embrace of hospitality and "welcoming the stranger" in their work with immigrants and immigrant communities in northeast Ohio and beyond. For some scholars, accompaniment has also emerged as an ontological and epistemological alternative to "the knowledge project of neoliberalism."[39] In their provocative essay, "American Studies as Accompaniment," Barbara Tomlinson and George Lipsitz argue for an approach to engaged scholarly work that both carefully reflects on *"the work we want our work to do,"* and "[takes] responsibility for the world we are creating through our endeavors, for the ways of being in the world that we are modeling and promoting" (emphasis in the original).[40] One way to do so, they offer, is by adopting the framework of accompaniment, which they define as "a disposition, a sensibility, and a pattern of behavior. It is both a commitment and a capacity that can be cultivated." And although Tomlinson and Lipsitz speak specifically to these possibilities within American studies, I believe their insights extend far beyond this interdisciplinary field. Indeed, contributors to this anthology demonstrate the ways Latina/o/x ethnographic engagement can be a form of accompaniment even as we document people's efforts to refuse, resist, accommodate, and develop unconventional (and unruly) responses to the myriad challenges they confront daily.

Heeding Yarimar Bonilla and Jonathan Rosa's call to resist the widely circulated belief that the 2016 presidential election ushered in new and exceptionally grim political and social realities, I also want to honor the ways that for many Latinas/os, working in a range of capacities, it seems that each day brings even more troubling announcements that signal the increasingly hostile political and economic contexts in which we all live. For that reason, careful ethnographic attention to the ways local activists organize and resist can both illuminate what might, in fact, be new and exceptional in this historical moment. And it might also provide many of us much-needed hope. As Ramón Rivera-Servera reminds us, activists play a critical role in what he calls the "circulation of hope, an investment in a political optimism" that is a precondition for mobilization.[41] Latina/o/x activists in Ohio both draw on hopeful histories of past sanctuary and solidary movements as they develop new rhetorics and strategies for the political organizing of today. In their embrace of familiar strategies of sanctuary and their efforts to fashion new ones around the notion of hospitality, we see not only the circulation of hope but also a resilience that can inspire new social movements. As Manuel Castro observed in reflecting on the enduring value of the sanctuary movement and Latina/o/x activism more broadly, "The movement never dies. It just changes."

Notes

1. "Introduction," this volume. Except for public leaders and elected officials, the names in this chapter are pseudonyms.

2. Braunstein, Fuist, and Williams 2017.

3. All of these data are from the 2017 American Community Survey by the US Census Bureau and summarized in the report, "Ohio Hispanic Americans."

4. Rivera 2011.

5. Historian Matt Garcia argues that the grape boycott was "the most successful consumer boycott in United States history" (Garcia 2013, 146) and was part of the grape strike that began September 8, 1965, organized by Cesar Chavez and Larry Itilong and the "multiethnic insurgency that was the farm worker movement" (147). The boycott included consumers refusing to buy grapes during the strike, but the UFW also focused on organizing laborers and supporters in "cities and docks where grapes were unloaded, distributed, sold" both in the United States and globally (146).

6. Jose Mendiola, "A Roller Coaster Life," interview by Emily Belle, Latina/o/x Oral Histories of Northeast Ohio.

7. Oscar López was released in 2016.

8. See De Genova and Pruetz 2010; Golash Boza 2015.

9. Danae King, "Woman Says She Is in Sanctuary at Columbus Church for Her Family," *Columbus Dispatch*, http://www.dispatch.com/news/20171004/woman -says-she-is-in-sanctuary-at-columbus-church-for-her-family, October 3, 2017. See also "Mexican Woman Again Seeks Sanctuary in Columbus Church," *Columbus Dispatch*, http://www.dispatch.com/news/20171003/mexican-woman -again-seeks-sanctuary-in-columbus-church. Edith Espinal remained in sanctuary at the Columbus Mennonite Church for forty months until receiving an order of supervision from Immigration and Customs Enforcement February 18, 2021. She was one of many who left public sanctuary shortly after President Biden assumed office in January 2021.

10. See, for example, Pallares and Flores González 2010; Pallares 2014, Rabben 2016; Lippert and Rehaag 2014; Cunningham 1995.

11. Rabben 2016, 218.

12. Hobson 2016.

13. Pallares 2014, x, 23.

14. King.

15. Pallares 2014, x.

16. Ibid., 23.

17. "Sanctuary for Edith," accessed November 20, 2017, http://www.columbusmen nonite.org/who-we-are/sanctuary-edith.

18. "Leonor, Ohio Mom of Four, Takes Sanctuary in Ohio Church," *America's Voice*, September 12, 2017, https://americasvoice.org/blog/leonor-takes-sanctuary-in -ohio-church/.

19. "East Columbus Church Offers Sanctuary to Local Mother and Children," July 2,

2018, https://www.columbusunderground.com/east-columbus-church-offers
-sanctuary-to-local-mother-and-children-ls1.

20.   "Tres Madres: Three Mothers Fighting for Justice," YouTube video, accessed
      April 2019, https://www.youtube.com/watch?v=UfmXS4fzVSs.

21.   "Ohio Treasurer Josh Mandel Backs Bill Banning Sanctuary Cities in Ohio,"
      February 6, 2017, *Cleveland Plain Dealer*, http://www.cleveland.com/politics
      /index.ssf/2017/02/ohio_treasurer_josh_mandel_bac.html. See also Gina Pérez,
      "In Defense of Ohio's Sanctuary Cities," *Cleveland Plain Dealer*, February 24,
      2017, http://www.cleveland.com/opinion/index.ssf/2017/02
      /in_defense_of_ohios_sanctuary.html.

22.   Isa Rodriguez Soto, "Colonialism's Orchestrated Disasters in Puerto Rico,"
      Anthropology News, November 27, 2017.

23.   Jennifer Hinojosa and Edwin Meléndez, "Puerto Rican Exodus: One Year since
      Hurricane Maria," research brief, Center for Puerto Rican Studies, September
      2018, https://centropr.hunter.cuny.edu/research/data-center/research-briefs
      /puerto-rican-exodus-one-year-hurricane-maria. Estimates of the Puerto Rican
      exodus vary widely and reflect both the difficulty of capturing outflows as well
      as different methodologies used to trace Puerto Ricans relocating throughout
      the diaspora. See Yarimar Bonilla, "How Puerto Ricans Fit into an Increasingly
      Anti-Immigrant U.S.," *Washington Post*, January 20, 2018, https://www.washing
      tonpost.com/news/posteverything/wp/2018/01/19/how-the-u-s-will-replace
      -immigrant-workers-with-puerto-ricans/. See also Llorens 2018. In October
      2017, Meléndez and Hinojosa estimated that the post-Maria exodus could
      be unprecedented: "Puerto Rico will lose the same population in a span of a
      couple of years after Hurricane Maria as the island lost during a prior *decade*
      of economic stagnation" (emphasis mine). "Estimates of Post-Hurricane Maria
      Exodus from Puerto Rico," research brief, Center for Puerto Rican Studies,
      October 2017, https://centropr.hunter.cuny.edu/research/data-center
      /research-briefs/estimates-post-hurricane-maria-exodus-puerto-rico.

24.   Vélez-Vélez and Villarrubia-Mendoza 2018, 542–43.

25.   Lloréns 2018; Bonilla 2020.

26.   "Puerto Rican Exodus Could Boost Small Town USA," *CNN Money*, October 13,
      2017, http://money.cnn.com/2017/10/13/news/economy/puerto-rican-maria
      -migration-small-towns/index.html.

27.   See Alicea and Toro-Morn 2018.

28.   "The Aftermath of Hurricane Maria," *Cleveland Magazine*, April 19, 2018, https://
      clevelandmagazine.com/cleader/business/articles/the-aftermath-of-hurricane
      -maria.

29. "From Puerto Rico to Lorain, Students Lean to Adapt," *Chronicle*, March 4, 2018, http://www.chroniclet.com/Local-News/2018/03/04/From-Puerto-Rico-to-Lorain-Students-learn-to-adapt.html.

30. "Puerto Ricans in Ohio, the United States and Puerto Rico, 2014," Center for Puerto Rican Studies, April 2016, https://centropr.hunter.cuny.edu/research/data-center/data-sheets/puerto-ricans-ohio-united-states-and-puerto-rico.

31. "Northeast Ohio Needs Coordinated Effort to Help Puerto Ricans Fleeing Hurricane," *Cleveland Plain Dealer*, November 13, 2017, http://www.cleveland.com/metro/index.ssf/2017/11/northeast_ohio_needs_coordinat.html.

32. Anabel Barron Sánchez, "A Roller Coaster Life," interview by Caide Jackson, Latina/o/x Oral Histories of Northeast Ohio, March 12, 2018, http://languages.oberlin.edu/blogs/gperez/2018/05/.

33. Ibid.

34. "Statement on the Emerging Crisis in Puerto Rico and the Response by the Catholic Church," Catholic Diocese of Cleveland website, November 2, 2017, https://www.dioceseofcleveland.org/news/2017/11/02/statement-on-the-emerging-crisis-in-puerto-rico-and-the-response-by-the-catholic-church. See also "Letter to Congress," United States Conference of Catholic Bishops, October 12, 2017, http://www.usccb.org/issues-and-action/human-life-and-dignity/global-issues/latin-america-caribbean/letter-to-congress-on-puerto-rico-2017–10–12.cfm.

35. "Statement from Most Reverend Nelson J. Perez, Bishop of Cleveland, on the Administration's Decision to End the Deferred Action for Childhood Arrivals (DACA) Program," Department of Communications, Diocese of Cleveland, September 7, 2017.

36. "Cleveland Bishop Nelson Says, 'Churches Have No Borders'; Prays for Immigration Reform," WKSU, July 9, 2018, https://www.wksu.org/post/cleveland-bishop-nelson-perez-says-churches-have-no-borders-prays-immigration-reform#stream/0.

37. *Parish Companion Program Handbook*, Catholic Diocese of Cleveland, updated November 6, 2018 (see https://www.dioceseofcleveland.org/files/assets/parish-companion-program-handbook.pdf).

38. "Diocese of Cleveland Parish Companionship Program Training Session," in *Parish Companion Program Handbook*, March 24, 2018.

39. Tomlinson and Lipsitz 2019, 204.

40. Tomlinson and Lipsitz 2013, 9, emphasis in the original.

41. Rivera-Servera 2012, 95.

CHAPTER NINE

Witnessing in Brown

On Making Dead to Let Live

GILBERTO ROSAS

Witnessing in brown captures the dilemmas of working with those who lack the privilege of citizenship in the current age, organized by white supremacy and human sacrifice. The concept captures how they must be made dead in order to live or, even more complexly, make themselves dead by experiencing brutal conditions—what I am calling necro-subjection. Necro-subjection sheds light on a neglected history of subjection, its linkages to the politics of death. In contrast to the often-flattening notions of power that interest certain followers of Foucault, necro-subjection as a concept brings flesh to the analysis and analyzes how these kinds of power capture and kill; how they generate and penetrate psychic and somatic effects; and how these effects may birth resistance or, more likely, usher in unrecognized refusals at the level of life itself. Alex E. Chávez writes in his powerful and poetic *Sounds of Crossing: Music, Migration, and the Aural Poetics of Huapango Arribeño*, "Biopolitical production is to be considered as the total integration of all human creative capacities central to a social production—the production of, yes, material life mediated by economic relations, but also the transformative production of new forms of social life, forms of living derived from the body."[1] The nuance is crucial: necro-subjection underscores not the politics of life and death but those of death and life. I have witnessed its birth in the ever-increasing violence of undocumented border crossings, the exposure of the individuated self to deadly environs, the complex demands to depict oneself as a victim in immigration proceedings, and—as recent tragic events in my hometown of El Paso show—resilience in the wake of killer white nationalism.

Elsewhere, I practiced what I now see as witnessing in brown:

The grainy shots of the gray cement drainage ditch capture the sinewy subterranean scatological connection between Nogales, Arizona, and

Nogales, Sonora. The scene is being filmed by an officer of the Nogales, Arizona, police department. . . . The footage shows police officers and Border Patrol agents (most of whom are Hispanic), hands on their holsters, asking the youths what they are doing, telling them to go back to Mexico. . . . The grainy footage then shifts to the flash of a light cutting through the darkness of the sewer tunnel behind the youths. A group of the undocumented materializes on the screen as they make their way toward the bright sunlight of Nogales, Arizona. El Enano (the dwarf, a nickname of one of the youths) wields a metal pipe. He repeatedly strikes one of the migrants in the leg. A child in the group screams. Another of the young men of Barrio Libre seizes a migrant by his lapel. With his other hand, he rips a chain from the neck of the unlucky man, who is wearing a cowboy hat—a telltale sign of a chúntaro. The officers above, once again on the screen, order the youths to stop.[2]

These *chúntaros*, the uninitiated border-crossing hicks in Chicanx drag, make themselves subject to death.[3] Beaten, brutalized, but alive, they escape into the United States. The videotape sits on my bookshelf, further documentation of the complex reverberations of border enforcement practices that speak to profound disruptions and orders of cruelty, which reach back at least to the 1990s.

What of other irregular border crossers? What of the men, women, children, and families who attempt to cross the weaponized environs that the deserts of the Southwestern United States have become? "The border is where thousands of those have died; social violence will increase," predicts the Border Patrol Strategic Action Plan 1994 and Beyond, or what border scholars and the more aware policy makers would eventually term "prevention through deterrence." People risking life and limb in such conditions lack the cultural acumen of long-standing "border people."[4] They end up in the "killing deserts."[5] Or they may suffer other kinds of violence, taken or normalized as natural, such as that which Jason De León describes in his *Land of Open Graves*.[6] Neither random accidents nor natural disasters produce the deaths of noncitizen border-crossers: the United States and its agents designate certain groups within the racialized category of "illegal." They deserve attrition, exhaustion, heat, the burning of their insides, as they make their way ever northward.

I chart these and related modalities, not of life and death but death and life. I assume a politically depressive pessimism of the intellect to this end. Witnessing insists so.[7]

People disappear forever in the killing deserts. Animals, heat, cold, smugglers, "delinquents," Border Patrol agents conspire in the death and degradation of border crossers. Rain and sun cause their corpses to wear away, slowly, deteriorating into the most elemental of human remains. The US-Mexico border kills. Experiences of crossing it without documentation pervade the contemporary social science of the border region.[8] These experiences deepen relations of illegality and deportability, what some aptly term "deportation terror."[9] Many noncitizens succeed in crossing it. They live.

What does it mean to almost die? What does it mean to expose oneself and possibly one's loved ones to death and other cruel fates? What does it mean to be the subject of death and its politics? What does it mean to be disappeared, erased, to be made dead, socially if not politically? What does it mean to be detained or, more accurately, incarcerated and separated from parents and other kin? Those who cross the border irregularly and increasingly those who seek to cross it with appropriate authorization, such as those seeking the international right of asylum, have been rendered surplus, an attribute of the inner solidarity of Western liberalism and the enduring presence of colonialist and white supremacist relations that evince genocidal practices.

Necro-subjection involves representing those who are made—and who make themselves—dead in order to live, those who cannot represent themselves, those who must be represented by the latest Brumaire. Making dead in order to live is part of a project of documenting and expressing contemporary brutalities without exacerbating the obscene suffering of border crossers and demands to revictimize them both in legal proceedings and engaged traditions of scholarship, so that we analyze, recognize, and ultimately struggle against violence and oppression, both spectacular and mundane. This project—a historically and politically derived reflexive analysis of providing expert testimony in immigration proceedings on behalf of people fleeing Mexico's drug war and its methodological and theoretical implications and dilemmas—thus recognizes the complexity of working with groups struggling against systemic oppression and how it infiltrates them and activist-scholars alike.[10]

I made a conscious political choice in my witnessing work to break with protocol. As an expert witness, I am not supposed to discuss the specifics of cases. I have made a point of negotiating with the clients and attorneys and explaining that I want to document what is occurring in my capacity as an expert witness.

To write about these experiences and to draw on the respondents' stories is to commit a kind of betrayal. But ethnography, if one follows certain feminist directions in the discipline, must betray. For Kamala Visweswaran, the assumption of a universal sisterhood between women demands betrayal, and in this she echoes other feminist ethnographers, like Patricia Zavella, who work on "the inside," being of the same race, ethnic, gender, and class background as their interlocutors.[11]

In my case, a "brown" scholar, an anthropologist, steeped in the complex currents of the discipline's antiracism and vexed by the demands of having to make people dead in order to live, must appeal to imperial and downright racist presumptions about Mexico and other parts of Latin America as I testify on behalf of a respondent. I speak for, rather than work with, those seeking asylum, relief from removal, or some other legal status, and tell the court what I see and learn from the stories that I hear.

That is, I follow Cherríe Moraga and "a long a line of vendidas," as well as those, like Asale Angel-Ajani, who caution against peddling the pain of "real life flesh and blood," in her case African immigrant women incarcerated in Italy. Indeed, the act of witnessing in anthropology too often attempts to (re)establish the authority of the ethnographer, although, as Angel-Ajani reminds us, not all ethnographers who evoke the figure of the witness necessarily position themselves as an authority. But the figure of the witness and the act of witnessing create a powerful position from which to legitimate devastating and multivalent histories about the survivors of violence and persecution. Despite the good intentions of anthropologists, witnessing is not always noble; we must wrestle with such ethnographic productions and their adverse if not perverse reverberations. And yet, witnessing in the discipline holds a rich purchase. Ruth Behar argues that "anthropology . . . is the most fascinating, bizarre, disturbing, and necessary form of witnessing left to us at the end of the twentieth century." For Nancy Scheper-Hughes, "the act of witnessing is what lends our work its moral (and at times its almost theological) character."[12]

To be a brown witness in an immigration proceeding is to document necro-subjection in practice. Winning asylum or other relief from deportation increasingly demands accounts of deep victimization on behalf of individuals and collectivities, playing to a deeply ingrained racial paternalism found in present-day Western liberalism. It coincides with the surveillance, policing, and detention of immigrants, echoing the birth of the prison industrial complex and the hyperincarceration of African Americans.[13] This order of subjection occurs among those attempting to irregularly cross the US-Mexico border region, in politically related legal immigration proceedings, and in many other hotspots across the globe, where surplus humanity threatens or appears to threaten the established polarity between us and other, between friends and enemies, where the whiteness of the social contract must be reaffirmed.[14]

Witnessing in brown is far more than the conundrum of testifying from some middling racial ground, or how brownness or Latinidad is too often (mis) recognized. The concept describes a kind of committed testimony, a political positioning born out of a racial politics. It contributes to abolitionist anthropology, part of a larger transdisciplinary work that challenges the state-sanctioned legal or extralegal production of politically organized premature death.[15]

This chapter moves through multiple ethnographic moments, ranging from my ethnography of a population of criminalized youth at the US-Mexico border and their subjugation to undocumented border-crossing life to my contemporary, critical auto-ethnographic research as an expert witness on behalf of others also seeking asylum and related legal remedies in immigration courts. The demands for necro-subjection, which I observe in immigration courts and participate in, speak to the emergence of the living dead, those who can never rest.[16] They are evident as zombies in popular culture, as well as the never-ending drug wars.

Such figures reflect a gradual zombification of rural life in certain parts of Mexico and refuse dominant theorizations of the subject. They resonate with contemporary dystopic imaginaries, these brown figures of zombies. Neither wholly living nor wholly dead, they abandon the everyday, the snuffing out of residual ways of life, and the spectacular terror of privatized and public sovereigns. Although many who flee Mexico, Central America, and other parts of the globe are not Indigenous, they seek to escape the genocidal logic of dispossession. In the process, they may become new kinds of settlers.[17] These zombies-in-the-making are misrecognized as traditional immigrant laborers, given the long-standing imperial relationship between the United States and Mexico.[18] This emergent current of forced migration to the United States refuses the merciless crossings through the killing deserts. They present themselves to the authorities at the US-Mexico border. They request political asylum. And the authorities increasingly deny them haven.

Brute force and the social facts of violence no longer constitute an anomaly of racial liberal rule, if they ever did, for those forming or inhabiting its colonial "dark" side. Violence is unexceptional. These figures are, as Sylvia Wynter puts it, "a category defined at the global level by refugee/economic migrants stranded outside the gates of the rich countries."[19] These postcolonial variants of Fanon's *damnés* reaffirm how, as Aníbal Quijano notes, the idea of race has become the "most efficient instrument of social domination in the last 500 years."[20] No longer content to stay cordoned off in the hinterlands, the new refugees face global structures of white supremacy. They move despite an increasingly globalized nativism, which demands the contortions of life and death.

The new refugees flee. They escape. They refuse the tyrannies of the new normal, as well as a return to the contemporary temporality, where their residual ways of life face an extended, excruciating demise, echoing their own "slow death."[21]

Necro-subjective Witnessing in Immigration Court

Asylum is a protection granted to foreign nationals already in the United States, or at its borders, who meet the international standards of the "refugee." The United Nations 1951 Refugee Convention and 1967 Protocol Relating to the Status of Refugees define a refugee as a person who is unable or unwilling to return to his or her home country and cannot obtain protection in that country. Said person must have suffered persecution or hold a well-founded fear of persecution "on account of race, religion, nationality, membership in a particular social group, or political opinion." Congress incorporated this definition into US immigration law in the Refugee Act of 1980. As a signatory to the 1967 Protocol and through US immigration law, the United States has legal obligations to provide protection and certain rights to those who qualify as refugees. To be awarded asylum involves accounting for membership in one of the protected categories, often taken as innate, such as sex, what the law designates as "color," or kinship ties. Asylum may also be awarded through what is referred to as a "particular social group," based on shared past experiences. It can range in meaning to include land ownership or even small business ownership. Asylum cases often hinge on the government's inability or unwillingness to protect those at risk.

Those who are seeking legal redress from deportation and detention may pursue a similar legal remedy: appealing to the UN Convention against Torture and Other Cruel, Inhuman or Degrading Treatment or Punishment. It includes a provision that prevents expulsion to another state when there are substantial grounds for believing that the expellee would be in danger of torture or the infliction of pain or suffering, whether physical or mental, including punishment or coercion.

New forms of sociality crack open such legal categories. The law chases new subjectivities, as does social theory. Typically, and all too problematically cast as liberal entrepreneurial subjects extraordinaire, bent on the American dream of wealth and consumption, the new immigrants are fleeing the spectacular terror of the drug war in some regions of Mexico. They also escape a less recognized wearing-away of residual ways of life, the kinds of life contemporary settler societies, to adapt Patrick Wolfe, snuff out, grind away, or abandon in far more common ways.[22]

I sit in the witness stand and adjust the mic.[23] The judge; two attorneys representing the Department of Homeland Security; "the respondents," who are a couple and their three children facing imminent deportation; their attorney; and a small audience, including some of their family members, sit in this courtroom in San Antonio, Texas. A middle-aged husband and wife are trying to avoid deportation to their one-time home, now dominated by a ruthless cartel, which they have fled.

Many thousands of others like this couple are being held in detention centers in small towns in the United States. They refused to circumvent border enforcement, presenting themselves to the authorities at ports of entry into Texas and requesting political asylum. An administratively appointed judge wields sovereign power. He decides who can move and who can settle—a core political struggle of the moment—whether to detain the couple, "remove" or deport them, or award them asylum.[24]

The couple from Mexico fled a massacre. It was the horrendous culmination of the kind of private and indirect governance occurring around the globe.[25] Short, quiet, and humble, the male head of household picked melons in a small agricultural village for a transnational agrarian company based in the United States. Several years ago, he and his coworkers began receiving threats to get off the fields where they worked. They were written on little pieces of paper and left on stones in the field, where he and his coworkers would discover them. This man reported that if they "continued to work there they were going to be disappeared."

One day, on which he happened not to make it to work, a group of men armed with assault rifles killed some nine of his coworkers in the fields. He explained in the court that "delinquents" committed the crime, a gloss for those working in organized crime. One of his close friends was killed in this event. He feared that what had happened to his coworkers would happen to him. He also worried that his children would be kidnapped and harmed. Later, a relative of this man was murdered; only his head was found. Strange men began menacing his partner, looking for the man at his home. The couple fled to the United States, seeking asylum.

I must testify as to whether the "removal" of a middle-aged couple, specifically their deportation to Mexico, places them in imminent danger. Immigration attorneys increasingly ask social science experts like me to corroborate immigrant testimony in asylum and related proceedings. This scenario underlines their marginality: their existence demands validation.[26] They have been rendered officially voiceless, effectively rightless in these proceedings.[27]

I consciously summon the demons — "the rapists . . . the murderers . . . the drug lords." I testify: "Mexico is experiencing the devastating effects of its drug war. Most experts agree it began near the end of 2006. The cartels rape and deploy sexual violence. They sever limbs and heads to intimidate law enforcement and civilians alike." I tell of the *fosos clandestinos*, mass graves that appear occasionally in Mexican media, of bodies consumed in acid. Of how human rights organizations describe Mexico as rife with abuses. I explain that I am convinced the level of violence in the country is underreported.

I tell how the North American Free Trade Agreement and its asymmetric terms of trade ravaged Mexico's rural economies, transforming them into zones of undocumented immigration. Some of those who stayed behind soon cultivated marijuana and other drugs — primarily for consumption in the United States. I then rehearse the facts: the 160,000 deaths in Mexico tied to the drug war over the past decade; the 40,000 more who have "disappeared." I explain that Central American women, who are crossing the thickening border that Mexico has become, know to take birth control pills. I spew blood. Stories of corpses, of human bodies thrown into vats of acid, of dismemberment and beheading. I seek that ripe, imperially charged sensibility.

I want to elaborate. I want to tell how US addiction animates the carnage, how it feeds the dead. I want to tell of racisms in this age of human sacrifice, premature death, vile misogyny, and related exclusions of both sides of the US-Mexico divide. I feed the hunger — sated neither by the *carne* nor the carnality of power that cannot be lost — of the social hegemonies about Mexico generally and Mexicans specifically, as well as those from other parts of the globe.[28] I want to suggest that this hunger is tied to US colonialism. I want to chart for the court the genealogies of military training and local machinations of empire. But there is little space for complexity. I hear myself explain, "There is blurring in daily life in large swaths of Mexico among elements of the local, national, and regional government and the cartels." I explain that Ciudad Juárez, a city on the US-Mexico border opposite my hometown of El Paso, Texas, was more lethal than Afghanistan in 2010.

I paint a picture of this ordinary couple struggling in daily life. I describe how they toil; how the stained jeans that the man wears as he testifies are likely his only clothes; how he works, plays, and, yes, testifies in them. I speculate about the paltry government services—such as the underperforming public education system—he finished sixth grade, she did not attend—eviscerated by the promises of a new liberalism that never came. I paint a picture of their home, with a solitary lightbulb that glows at night, cinderblock walls, and dirt floors, homes similar to those I have seen in Nogales, Sonora, and across Mexico. The land itself and their will become subject to further dispossessions by privatized sovereigns.

I make dead to let live.

I affirm imperial and racial, late liberal common sense. White liberalism demands that my serving as a brown witness is rife with the monstrous racist and gendered imperialist projections about Mexicans. Racial liberalism demands that I exercise the pain of "real life flesh and blood," to harken back to Angel-Ajani. It requires that I dance with the devil. Necro-subjection continues a long line of vendidxs.

Violent masculinities and victimized femininities are the heart of the case, the latter echoing Lynn Stephen's notion of "gendered embodied structures of violence."[29] They must be. I must render Mexicans and their situation back in their home country so hopeless, so bleak, so full of imminent danger, and so full of despair that the judge finds in favor of their application. I return to the mass disappearances, the decapitations and dismemberments, the clandestine graves, the tearing asunder of bodies, the menace.

I mobilize the specter of sexual violence and rape, again and again. Liberalism demands that the cartels, officialdom, the courts, and I mobilize weaponized machismo.[30] Liberalism also demand its corollary: victimized femininity.

Necropolitical States

Appreciating "states" as both rich psychic interiorities and objects of deep attachment that lord over life, death, racisms, and various other power relations, always in relation to capital and empire, allows me to further unpack necro-subjection. These individuated or collective experiences capture processes of making dead to let live. They articulate complex histories of anti-Black racism generally and anti-Haitian xenophobia specifically, animating US immigrant detention and deportation practices and their deep linkages to US-Mexico border enforcement.[31] The latest fulfillment of totalitarian fantasies of racial, gendered, and sexual purification concretizes in calls for walls: modalities of prisons, the preeminent institution of contemporary carceral landscapes, as well as borders and other spaces of detention.

A growing body of scholars and policy makers declares that the crisis in Mexico represents the failure of the Mexican state. Other scholars hold that the drug war cloaks more sinister forces, be it clamping down on social mobilization, the latest intensified violent regime of dispossession, or related, long-standing collaborations between Mexico and the United States in the unruly governance of illicit commodities and their Baudrillardian confabulations.[32] Are these simply monstrous fables?

The established social myths about Mexicans' immigration to the United States—their widespread rendering as "cheap," "disposable," "deportable," and increasingly "detainable," such awkward neologisms aside, labor—obscure those whose are forced to immigrate as an effect of organized state and state-like terror in Mexico, where hunger and related forms of deprivation are normalized. These regimes of impoverishment are the unremarkable, inert violence of late liberalism rooted in histories of colonialism, enslavement, and other dispossessions.[33] The polarity between politically versus economically motivated alienage found in US immigration law cuts too neatly. It lends itself to unfolding liberal rationalities.

My witnessing does not document "the criminal capture of the Mexican state," a certain technocratic discourse circulating among governing elites about Mexico, other parts of the globe, and increasingly the contemporary United States. It is not that narco-traffickers or gangsters in other parts of the globe, secure in their wealth, have undertaken or are in the process of completing a coup d'état, albeit from the side or above.[34] Imperial states, long about slavery and increasingly eviscerated of their better logics, frequently exercise terror and torture as legitimation, not as the rule, but as their rule.

Spectacular terror is instrumental in a kind of capitalist accumulation that has reconstituted itself since the 1970s, akin to what Karl Marx termed "primitive accumulation" in chapter 26 of *Das Kapital*. It is based in dispossession, fraud, and violence. It involves privatizing or cordoning off the commons, including Indigenous lands and related strategic resources. Rosa Luxembourg, David

Harvey, and others hold that such forms of accumulation must constantly be revitalized;[35] consequently, so is the *longue durée* of "slavery, colonization, apartheid, capitalist alienation, immigration and asylum politics, postcolonial liberal multiculturalism, gender and sexual normativity, securitarian governmentality, and humanitarian reason," as well as related modes of anti-human-making and modes of dispossession.[36] They demand an analysis of "life itself" at the level of power and the subject, which normative accountings of the subject misrecognize and misapprehend.

Foucault's influential *"Society Must Be Defended"* underlines the inextricable ties among racism, state formation, life, and death. In this never finished genealogy, modern racism was first articulated as a discourse of social war in the eighteenth century. It developed during the second half of the nineteenth century, absorbing important impulses from psychiatry as a means to protect society against the abnormal. Racism, in this formulation, "constitutes the necessary precondition that makes killing permissible." It essentially introduces "a break between what must live and what must die."[37] The social construction of race articulates a caesura between worthy and unworthy life and resonates with the formulations mentioned above of contemporary racism as inextricably lethal—placing bodies closer and closer to death—rather than the constructivist emphasis of racism strangling the contemporary liberal academy.[38] Although Foucault's lectures lack any substantial discussion of European colonialism or the history of the idea of race, they deserve appreciation and invite analysis of modes of making life and death as modes of biopolitical government, which impinges on individuals in their most basic relationship to themselves and others, as it does on collectivities. The integration of sovereign power (the "right of the sword," the right to take life or give death) was complemented by a new right that did not erase the old right, but which did penetrate it, permeate it. This is the *power to "make" live and "let" die*. A certain death power animates this governance of others, and racism "constitutes the necessary precondition that makes killing permissible."[39]

Contemporary projects of existence exert pressure on those competing analytics of the subject and subjection. They demand an epistemic rupture, a reversal of the modes of subjection articulated by Foucault and his army of followers in his profound and influential "The Subject and Power," which seem well-suited to more harmonious political moments, but not to moments rife with crisis in which hierarchies and inequalities break through normativities and challenge instrumentalist reckonings with violence. Just as the Black slave and white supremacist foundations of capitalism scandalize all too orthodox projects of working-class unity found in certain readings of Antonio Gramsci, Achille Mbembe's fierce engagement with Foucault's concept of biopower from the contemporary postcolony and his demand for an analytics of necropolitics provokes its own scandal.[40]

Mbembe is concerned with figures of sovereignty. Central to his project of conceptualization is "the generalized instrumentalization of human existence and the material destruction of human bodies and populations." He presents a reading of politics as the work of death starting from Hegel's account: "The human being truly becomes a subject—that is, separated from the animal—in the struggle and the work through which he or she confronts death."[41] Necro-politics captures how certain lives in dark realms of jeopardy have increasingly become normalized in parts of Mexico, Latin America, Europe and its one-time colonies, the United States, and other parts of the globe. The ultimate expression of sovereignty is to have the power and capacity to dictate who may live and who may die, and biopower is the domain of life over which power has taken control. Mbembe's essay draws on the concept of biopower and explores its relation to notions of sovereignty and the state of exception in order to answer many questions about the politics of death, specifically "the generalized instrumentalization of human existence and the material destruction of human bodies and populations." Necropolitics and necropower help account for the various ways in which, in our contemporary world, war machines and states of exception are deployed in the interest of maximum destruction of persons and the creation of death-worlds, new and unique forms of social existence in which vast populations are subjected to conditions of life conferring upon them the status of living dead.

Mbembe argues that biopolitics fails to explain how the threat of violence, human destruction, and death prevails as a technique of governance in many contemporary settings, challenging Foucault's reliance on Western European examples. The Cameroonian philosopher instead draws on examples from the more politically volatile states of postcolonial Africa and the Near East. These provide insights through which we can understand politics as a form of war in which the sovereign emerges through the determination of who dies or does not die and, therefore, lives. The meaning of death in necropolitics appears in interpretations of corpses, killers, and those subject to them.

My concept of necro-subjection extends this project. It speaks to the demands of both suffering and violence that contemporary US-Mexico border crossings have become. Making dead to let live also echoes practices of brown witnessing. Nevertheless, necro-subjection refuses analytical closures of this and related schools of thought, thus following calls to "theorize with horror."[42] To wrestle with the actually existing, multiple orders of oppression infiltrating this different kind of subjection demands decentering. The demand—foisted upon me by immigration courts—is to center on the margins and peripheries, as illustrated by those who live on the jagged, illegal edges of societies. While Foucault's insight into biopolitical power's production and management of life remains crucial, the right to decide life and death is never completely excised from certain kinds of sovereign power, be it authoritarian or liberal democratic and its deep ties to empire. A politics of life must commit "the subjugation of life to the power of death," or it lends itself to a politics and an analysis of the privileged.[43] Necro-subjection moves to the center of analysis the subject forged in discourses and related micropolitical processes of a once robust liberalism that is increasingly dystopic. It emerges when "the right to punish" shifts "from the vengeance of the sovereign to the defense of society."[44] It captures those subjects who regularly face the horror of death, of being made—or even making themselves—dead in order to live. From a hail of bullets raining down from the sky in imperial executions in the Middle East to the almost banal slaughter of youth in public schools in the United States, what were once promises of liberal statehood now seem increasingly to secure against but also generate terror, amplifying contemporary government's deep linkages to slavery, racism, misogyny, capital, and the refusal to treat such oppressions as ancillary or superstructural.[45]

Necropolitics brings the politics of life and death to an analysis of never-ending warfare, the uneven distribution of disease, and other forms of social and discursive exclusions in modernity. Private armies, so-called war machines, states of exceptions, and related phenomena perversely birth death-worlds. Under terms of necropower, the lines between resistance and suicide, redemption and sacrifice, freedom and martyrdom are blurred.[46] The suicide bomber becomes recognized as a subject through her death, echoing "revolutionary suicide" in African American thought and suggestive of the influence of the Black Panthers on Foucault's oeuvre.[47] The corpses, both discovered and not, may be emblematic of revolutionary suicide.

Imperial sovereignty-making violence and its reverberations devastate. They multiply. They proliferate. Nevertheless, necropolitics understates concurrent everyday dispossessions and the structural violence prefiguring these killer relations. Necro-subjection emphasizes the level of the subject, those who are birthed in and experience killer politics, as well as their kin, in drug war–governed frontier zones of Mexico and Central America, the aforementioned "killing deserts," Palestine, the Dakota pipeline, and elsewhere in the occupied Americas and related settler societies. Necro-subjection accounts for those subjectivities from which societies must be defended.

The concept also wrestles with people and their extraordinary affects that push beyond such ends of life, those who are dying to live, contending with brutal dispossession, and challenging official and privatized hetero-masculine sovereigns who dictate and subjugate. Making dead to let live registers how the contemporary moment demands a theory of the subject engulfed in an extraordinarily other politics of death and life, not exceptions that become the rule, not situated in the naturalization of camplike spaces of liberal democracies, but in the daily workings of state and the law. The concept chases subjectivities along axes of otherness, more precisely racism and its intersecting exclusions, and also, more pertinently, the material subjections—the subject effects—of threats over life, including the horrendous regime of violence against women termed *femicidio*, or femicide, mass graves, and mass disappearances. The concept demands a reckoning with life at the margins, life subjected as illegal, criminal, queer or life cast as too Black, too brown, too Muslim. Necro-subjection is not a liberal analytic of resilience or survival. It is the contemporary subjection of the other, often individuated through violence, entangled in the death struggle of modern capital and the terrifying, often perverse, private and indirect government of difference. Making dead to let live, moreover, grapples with the rich interiorities of necropolitics. The concept deepens questions of the subject and power, the birth of subjectivities wracked in actual and structural relations of violence and its psychic effects, and the extraordinary affects that these processes produce.[48]

The concept invites certain politically useful caveats regarding these operations. Race and its intersections still signify; they may remain positive social identities, a position that subaltern genealogies have long recognized and pointed to as limitations of certain traditions that see race and racism only as negative trajectories. In this respect, necro-subjection in the case of immigration courts or undocumented border crossings demands recognition of long-standing or contemporary practices of escape as disruptive or potentially constituent of new potentialities.[49] It follows notions of refusal, the refusing of life itself. Necro-subjection thus pushes at possibilities beyond traditional binaries of resistance and accommodation, which may or may not infiltrate larger assemblages of culture and politics, those oppositional forces, affects, and practices found outside traditional notions of politics.[50]

Necro-subjectivities haunt. They flag the anomic zones of death and life struggles. They materialize in popular culture if one looks critically. In the television series *Breaking Bad*, mindless, ruthless young men, almost always phenotypically brown, wander through Albuquerque, bent on revenge against Walter White. There are the zombies on dystopic TV shows, always mindless, inevitably brown. These "walkers" in the parlance of television — and a term that appears increasingly in Latina/o/x studies — flit across our screens to co-emerge with the anti-citizens of nowhere, yet everywhere, immigrant others, the homeless denizens, damned to near dead existence.[51] They are the Joaquín Dead: grotesque, dismembered flesh, perhaps the most fundamental of "our" resources. These ravenous subhumans devour white majoritarian flesh, ripping it from bodies with their teeth. As with most zombie nightmares, they quickly become fodder for the larger-than-life struggles, grist for the all-too-"real" human struggles among nonzombies. Protagonists practice killing for a semblance of the way things once were. Zombie fantasies mark a return of sorts, echoing Leo Chavez's assertion that representations themselves are forms of power, rather than mere reflections of power residing in the real.

A reckoning with the Joaquín Dead demands a return to those wretched borders of death and life evident in asylum or related immigration proceedings or at the international boundary, which others must cross irregularly. They all too often bring only the soiled clothes on their back, in either case. They have cultivated the land, lost everything to the narco-governors, only to face detention, deportation, and other punishment upon entering the United States. They speak nonstandard or indigenously marked Spanish, if they speak the dominant language at all, as I sometimes must explain to the courts. They speak in short sentences. They evoke impoverishment, their need for work, unaware that everything they say can be used against them. They live a carceral regime of sovereignty beyond the walls of detention centers and prisons that bleed into daily life, as well as borders.[52] Such differences become instrumental both in their caging and in their lines of flight.

What necro-subjection and its derivatives crystallize are the continuities between liberalism and totalitarianism. They are felt first among the marginals, the Black and brown, the queer, the gender nonconforming, and always other. The promises of liberal citizenship and of modernities, always already illusory for those on the margins, shatter into piercing hierarchies. Resurgent totalitarian logics in the Western democracies, evident in Brexit and among Donald Trump and other rulers, manifest first in cruel dealings with different life.

Conclusion

To be a pessimist of the intellect, but perhaps not the will, is to recognize that those who make themselves dead in asylum proceedings, or risk their lives in irregular border crossings or in other deadly ways, experience their violent instantiation as the other subject so that they can live. Necro-subjection is not the imposition of false consciousness or mystification of social relations. It is the material subjugation of particular lives that are situated socially, materially, discursively, and ideologically closer and closer to death.

To become a subject in difference today all too often demands a reckoning with orders of violence that are intractable, normative, and normalized. These regimes are inextricably tied to race, or more precisely racism(s), and intersecting exclusions, recognitions, and related dynamics. Necro-subjection traces these dynamics, as in the near-death experiences of those vying to cross the desert border of the Southwestern United States. Predatory capitalism and its intersecting prohibitions haunt immigration proceedings, in which practices of expert testimony, affidavit writing, or other kinds of analysis around current questions of asylum from Mexico and elsewhere around the globe must underscore the horrendous. That other life must be characterized as full of pain, despair, brutality, and violence—making people dead—so that they might be freed from detention and deportation to crime-ridden homelands—letting them live—reaffirms paternal liberal social hegemonies.

This discordance reverberates in how Black lives can only be made to matter in the wake of police violence and related banalities of evil so that Indigenous peoples, Black people, Muslims, immigrants, and those frequently racialized as immigrants, among other exclusions that others experience, are birthed into relations of normative liberal politics. It crystallizes how specific lives must be represented as exposed, vulnerable, precarious—a characterization evident in much contemporary ethnography, which some have characterized as "dark."[53] Necro-subjection shows how discourses about Mexican rapists and other bad hombres infiltrate immigration court, setting the stage for critical, strategic redeployments, subversions, and betrayals, following a long line of *vendidas*, *vendidx*-capturing instantiations that feed my insurgent optimism of the will.

Those who experience making dead to let live move through sewers, under borders, beyond the law, from war-torn homelands to hyperghettoes. Necro-subjects may utter and enact refusals that infiltrate larger assemblages of culture and politics or live in the shadows and refuse the contemporary. Or those who are dying to live may march in the streets of Chicago, Los Angeles, and New York or demand a new order of asylum in US immigration courts.

The killer pulse of "imperial sovereignty," to return to the words of Mbembe, races through the concept of necro-subjection. It also captures a new current of immigration to the United States from Mexico, refugees, those typically thought of as coming from other countries, who confront a deeply held sense in the law and civil society that Mexicans constitute a labor force.

Again, they cannot represent themselves; they must be represented. Their lives and homelands must be represented as full of despair, pain, and hopelessness; mired in relations of precarity and dispossession; replete with graft and corruption. Their representations affirm imperial racisms and liberal presumptions of the racial, cultural, and civilizational exceptionalism of the United States. They must make themselves—or they must be made—dead, like many others who cross the US-Mexico border without documentation, as well as many other kinds of border crossers around the globe.

Notes

1. Chávez 2017, 251.

2. See Rosas 2012, which draws on Dunn 1996; Inda 2006 and Nevins 2002.

3. Rosas 2010.

4. See Paredes 1958; Lugo 2008.

5. Rosas 2012.

6. De León 2015.

7. See Berlant 2006; Viego 2007; Muñoz 2014.

8. Rosas 2016; idem., 2006; Inda 2011.

9. See De Genova 2004; Buff 2018.

10. Hale 2001.

11. Visweswaran 1994; Zavella 1996.

12. Behar 1996; Scheper-Hughes 1992.

13. Murakawa 2014.

14. Mills 2008.

15. See Shange's genealogy of abolitionist anthropology in her recent work (2019). And Ruth Wilson's Gilmore's (2007) prescient and abolitionist inspired definition of racism as "the state sanctioned or extralegal production and exploitation of group-differentiated vulnerability to premature death."

16. I echo other anthropologists who follow legal proceedings, such as Lynn Stephen (2019) and her development of the concept of "gendered embodied structures of violence" to document the complex, multiple realms legal and extralegal realms of violence that Mam women from Guatemala experience.

17. See Nájera and Maldonado 2017; Byrd 2011; Morgensen 2011.

18. See Gonzalez and Fernandez 2003.

19. Bauman 1998; Wynter 2003.

20. Fanon 2004; Quijano 1999.

21. Berlant 2007.

22. Wolfe 2006.

23. I discussed the practices of testimony in immigration proceedings as one example of "fugitive" work (2018). Indeed, Maya Berry et al. (2017) hold that a decolonizing and what they call "fugitive anthropology" likely demands breaking with their "intellectual home."

24. See Achille Mbembe, "The Idea of a Borderless World," Africa Is a Country, accessed November 21, 2018, https://africasacountry.com/2018/11/the-idea-of-a-borderless-world?fbclid=IwARocyScyyMMPqSMSSqMLdoyaVJmV17UiBhTQUPMGdoBGYt9X-ocmFKNMLGQ.

25. See Mbembe 2001.

26. Paik 2016.

27. Ibid.

28. See Limón 1994; Mbembe 1992.

29. Stephen 2019.

30. See Triana 2011.

31. Loyd and Mountz 2018.

32. Zavala 2018; Wright 2017.

33. Farmer et al. 2004.

34. Cf. Simon 1991.

35. West 2016.

36. Marx 1978; Fazio 2016.

37. Foucault 2003.

38. Gilmore 2002.

39. Foucault 2003, 254.

40. Wilderson 2003.

41. Mbembe 2003.

42. Debrix 2017.

43. Mbembe 2003, 39.

44. Foucault 1995, 90.

45. See Robinson 2008.

46. Mbembe 2003, 40.

47. See Newton, Cleaver, and Black Panther Party 1970; Heiner 2007.

48. See Foucault 1982, 208–26.

49. See Visweswaran 2010; Federici 2004.

50. For literature on refusal and related concepts, see Simpson 2014; Cohen 2004.

51. See Vega 2015.

52. See Balaguera 2018.

53. Ortner 2016.

CHAPTER TEN

Anthropolocura *as Homeplace Ethnography*

AIMEE VILLARREAL

As a Chicana anthropologist who works in my hometown of Santa Fe, New Mexico, my refusal of the faraway field is a political and ethical stance, a variety of feminist homework.[1] Anthropology privileges relations of travel over relations of dwelling and therefore values research abroad above research conducted at home.[2] "The field" in anthropology is a place of knowledge production where information about the other (and the self) is gathered, documented, dissected, and ultimately translated into a genre of reality storytelling called ethnography. The field has been construed in many ways, both heady and ethically dicey. It is a physical location, a site of enunciation, and an epistemological space of investigation rooted in European and US imperialism and colonialism and other asymmetries of power.[3] The intricacies of power that underpin encounters between self and other, the observer and the observed—as well as the spatial, analytical, and temporal distinction between "home" and "the field"—mimic colonial legacies and logics, knowledges from elsewhere gathered up and carried home to be rendered as ethnography and reconstituted as social theory.[4] Yet, "field" and "home" are inherently relational and dialogical terms. Therefore, the lines between fieldwork and homework are not transparent or definitive.

As ethnographers of American settler states we acknowledge that home is a wounded place with a troubled history. Home is built on stolen and occupied Indigenous land. Therefore, our homework is a spiritual and decolonial project of tearing down oppressive structures, methodologies, and mentalities and re-making them on different grounds. Chicana feminist scholars remind us that the revolution begins at home—in our own families, in our communities, with our embodied and everyday experiences of oppression and violence.[5] As I am writing this chapter in quarantine amid a global pandemic in 2020, homework has taken on a different valence. Governors and mayors issued shelter-in-place orders to prevent the spread of COVID-19 and the slogan "Stay safe, stay home" became a meme and a byline as the death toll climbed into the hundreds of thousands. Meanwhile, furious protests erupted across the nation and the world in reaction to the public murder of George Floyd at the hands of Minneapolis police. Cities smoldered with outrage and exasperation with Donald Trump's negligence, the escalation of the crisis of capitalism, and the *longue durée* of the settler state's racist subjugation of Black people and other racialized minorities. Those who are dehumanized are never at home.[6] Moreover, not everyone has a home, can afford to stay home, or can endure isolation and confinement. The experience of being homebound is akin to sanctuary, an interval between safety and violence.

Native anthropologists who refuse the faraway field to instead do research in their homeplaces and tribes once stood at the margins of a discipline that privileges research abroad. However, the global pandemic has most anthropologists grounded, confined to their homeplaces, unable to travel. This situation presents an interesting reversal of fortune for homeplace ethnographers like me and the contributors of this volume, with special skills and investment in doing anthropology at home. In the spirit of our ancestors who lent their creativity and cultural resources to anthropologists and helped shape the discipline, this chapter brings this volume home and full circle. We call for a decolonial practice of hometown ethnography grounded in an anthropology in reverse, or what Dabi García, Gregorio Gonzales, and I have termed *anthropolocura*—a curative and restorative practice of coalitional knowledge production.

This chapter is a meditation on anthropolocura. What does it mean to do homework/fieldwork in a fragile postcolonial world where citizenship or the very possibility of securing a homeplace or claiming a homeland is structured within what Nandita Sharma names the Postcolonial New World Order, a world in which national membership and the distinction between natives and migrants determines our conditions of life?[7] What insights can the homeplace ethnographer who has long refused research excursions abroad offer to the newly homebound anthropologist or a discipline premised on peering into the homes of others?[8]

Many researchers of color desire to stay home so that they can use their academic knowledge and anthropological training to participate in grassroots activism and movements for social and political change. Positioned at the margins of the discipline, our research agendas have often been considered provincial, muddled in cultural bias, overly political, applied rather than theoretical. Nevertheless, we have endeavored to do our homework, research that matters to our communities of origin, centered on dialogue, collaboration, and building coalitions to confront racist power and the multiple ways that oppression and marginalization interpolate our bodies and shape our daily lives. To use a place-based metaphor that my colleague and partner in anthropolocura Dabi García shared with me, homework is our collective *tarea* of cleaning out the *acequia* to remove barriers so that ideas can flow, the seeds of change can grow, and we can cultivate our fields. Homework is about all the relations that compose a shared homeplace.

Homeplace ethnographers are skeptical of the discipline's "epistemic frame-work of going out to collect and coming home to render," because we have heard it all before.[9] Going away is the product of racialized mechanisms of power that position the places we live as delinquent and expendable. Many of us grew up in small towns, reservations, or urban barrios where we were taught to devalue home. Our teachers and school counselors (sometimes our own family mem-bers) told us that leaving was essential to becoming an educated person. This idea rests on long-standing racist notion that white, middle-class lives are more respectable and valuable than ours. We are told that our degraded state of being is redeemable through colonial educational systems and cultural assimilation, adopting the dominant culture's ways of living, acting, and thinking. Our ances-tors were fed this same racist poison. People were forced to leave their families and sent away to boarding schools designed to make them white, to kill their Indigenous souls.

Following this line of assimilationist violence, we are made to believe that home is a "deficit to overcome," that staying leads to repetition of harmful cycles, unhappy lives, dead ends, or tragic endings.[10] Why linger in a place that global capitalism has ransacked or left behind? On the other hand, sometimes home is not a safe or nurturing place, which makes leaving necessary for survival. Today, staying home or making a livable life in the place you were born can be consid-ered a privilege and a matter of human rights in a world that demands mobility while also inducing migrancy. We are currently witnessing a global refugee crisis in which millions of people have been displaced due to war, state violence, eco-nomic recession, political unrest, or natural disasters. People are forced to flee their homelands and seek asylum in wealthier and more politically stable places as states globally become increasingly inhospitable to migrants and refugees.

Let us not forget that home is also the neoliberal institutions where we make our living and produce and disseminate knowledge, often under conditions of extreme stress and low pay (contingent faculty make up more than 70 per-cent of the workforce in higher education).[11] Homework involves transforming higher education by making it more affordable, accessible, and hospitable to students, staff, and faculty of color. Hometown scholars Patricia Trujillo and Tobe Bott-Lyons point out that "academics who come from communities of color, working class communities, rural communities or from the intersections of these and other vulnerable places are motivated by their experiences of and connections to home."[12] Trujillo laments that "the academy pushes graduates out and away." We are advised to leave in order to come back because the institutions where we earned our degrees do not value or hire homegrown scholars. Full-time tenured positions are scarcer now than ever; therefore, we have to be mobile and willing to be uprooted from our homeplaces in order to enter the game. "When we come home," write Trujillo and Bott-Lyons, "we may find our relationships to our homeplaces frayed, complicated, and ambiguous."[13]

The decision to stay is also scrutinized. Trujillo, who defines herself as a "rural Chicana scholar" and works in a small college in her hometown, says that her decision to stay is often viewed as a type of failure or as settling for less. She has been told that staying home would ruin her academic career. Indeed, anthropologists of color who prefer to do homework within their own communities or in those that are culturally similar to their homeplaces have difficulty finding an academic home in anthropology departments. Instead, we get jobs in ethnic studies and other interdisciplinary programs that are innovative and beneficial to students (particularly those from marginalized communities) but have less resources and institutional support.

In sum, home is never as comfortable or settled as it seems. The 1950s celluloid ideal of white, middle-class domesticity could not contain the feminist revolution brewing in the kitchen and knocking down its doors. Home embodies multiple tensions, desires, disaffections, and dislocations. Homeplaces can be uprooted and remade elsewhere or exist in multiple places simultaneously. Home can mold into resemblances so that it becomes not a definable location or protective space but a structure of feeling, a state of being-at-home in the world.[14] When the intricacies of home are central to the investigation, fieldwork is more akin to homework. This blended or dialectical home/field demands higher levels of accountability for our actions and long-term obligations to our research partners who have extended us their trust and hospitality.

The fraught relationships between the field and home, the local and the global, the particular and the universal are ongoing conversations in anthropology (and other disciplines) because they question the colonial legacies and epistemological foundations of the discipline. Decolonizing anthropology is a project that did not end with the "crisis of representation" that transpired in the 1980s and '90s. It requires more than acknowledgment or rectification of past wrongs. Rewriting culture was a move toward innocence that allowed anthropology to continue to evade its settler colonial legacies and epistemologies. Decolonization demands rupture, restoration, and reparation.[15] In *Fictions of Feminist Ethnography*, Kamala Visweswaran argues that "the experimental or reflexive turn toward the problem of representation did not go far enough to resolve the problem of voicing."[16] In other words, adding Native and minority perspectives from the United States and the Global South did not create a substantial shake-up of anthropological practice. Anthropology in reverse, she suggests, means "speaking from the place one is located, to specify our sites of enunciation as 'home' directs the gaze homeward rather than away."[17] It forces us to interrogate what constitutes home not only for ourselves but for our collaborators and seriously confront the more unsettling question of whose homeland is this? Whose territories have we invaded and claimed as our field site? Homework unsettles home.

Turning homeward is not a remedy for all of our *males*. As a physical, temporal, spatial, and metaphorical site, home is never as stable or dependable as the term implies or feigns to be. Home can engender safety, protection, and familiarity, but it can also be a site of exclusion, anguish, and uncertainty.[18] The struggle for a third space, to create a home in exile, to craft a utopic homeland that affirms feminist principals of solidarity and inclusivity are central concepts in Chicana feminist thought. Gloria Anzaldúa, for example, uses the metaphor of *nepantla* as a constant state of displacement, a liminal space between worlds always unfolding, in transition, and lacking clear boundaries.[19]

This borderlandia is queer space. It invites us to step across the threshold into unfamiliar territories where the outcasts, exiles, and misfits find sanctuary.[20] T. Jackie Cuevas argues that borderlands has become an uncritical "default way of seeing," a catchall alternative that consumes all differences but ignores the subjugated identities, nonnormative sexualities, and gender variances that refuse amalgamation, that dis-identify and displace.[21] Instead, Cuevas urges us to investigate the fissures where borderlands theory does not quite hold, to take an interest in the shifting fault lines of power and agency where the "Chicanx subject becomes racialized, sexualized, gendered, and otherized in a U.S. context."[22] Given this queer/feminist understanding of home as a post-borderlandia that pushes beyond its own boundaries, homeplace ethnography is not provincial or limited because home enfolds multiple sites and dislocations, yearnings, experiences, and sensibilities. Home holds histories and memories, but it is an unruly placeholder. Home emplaces people and things but never fully or completely.

In whatever fashion we choose to define it or fill it with metaphors, home holds us accountable to its failures and possibilities—a place of healing, a place to be nurtured, cultivated, and revitalized through homework. The boundaries between the local and the global are thin and porous not solely because the greedy hands of capitalism draw us closer or force us apart but because the mechanisms of power and domination that we experience in our homeplaces are writ large on a global scale. However, turning homeward resists defining the local as an instance of the everywhere or the nowhere in particular. What does it mean to practice hometown ethnography? What methodologies does it generate or demand of the researcher/resident? How can we bridge ethnic studies and anthropology to mobilize "reverse anthropologies" that lead us homeward instead of forcing us away? I do not claim to have easy or definitive answers to these questions. My intention is to start a conversation and invite participation in the dialogue.

I begin by reorienting the origin story of American anthropology because this is our disciplinary home, whether we choose to claim it or not. Through the metaphor of the laboratory of anthropology, I recast a dialogue between homeplace scholars about reclaiming the laboratory for ourselves. To create a revisionist origin story for the practice of anthropolocura as a methodology (one we can be proud of), I outline how it can shift our perspectives and the rules of engagement.[23] My discussion touches upon the contentious relationship between ethnic studies and anthropology, our attempts to bridge the disciplinary and epistemological cleavages between them and ultimately, find a home in the fault lines. I round out the chapter with some concise examples of homeplace ethnography to illustrate the creative, disorderly, and often maddening productions of anthropolocura in theory and practice.

Our Laboratory of Anthropolocura

New Mexico was designated a laboratory for anthropology as the discipline was gaining public recognition and an institutional foothold in the early twentieth century. Some of the most notable forebears of the American anthropological tradition, such as Frank Hamilton Cushing (1857–1900), Alfred Louis Krober

(1876–1960), Ruth Benedict (1887–1948), and Elsie Clews Parsons (1875–1941), among others, *pasaron por aquí* to pick our proverbial savage minds, observe our doings, and collect our things to generate theories of culture and society, write ethnography, and procure collections for museums and laboratories. The raw materials that living and ancestral Native Americans and internally colonized Mexicans provided them included our lifeways, languages, sacred objects, stories, ceremonies, social and family arrangements, dwellings, our ancestral remains, down to our very flesh and bones. "Many of the early anthropologists," writes Native anthropologist Margaret Bruchac, "imagined themselves to be heroes engaged in dangerous search and rescue missions."[24] The attitude of salvage anthropology, she offers in her groundbreaking book, *Savage Kin: Native Anthropologists and Indigenous Informants*, "was to put white men and women in the role of saviors, willing to step far beyond their comfort zones (to penetrate cultures that their own had not prepared them to enter) to preserve what they believed was destined to disappear." In this sense, Indigenous peoples were never intended to survive. We were, as Gilberto Rosas proposes in his chapter on witnessing, the walking dead.

These vicious motivations and assemblages produced the loot that endowed American anthropology with an archive of knowledge and body of work that positioned us in ways that we have not fully escaped.[25] Our intellectual and material contributions are part of this archive, but this story is rarely brought to light. Following Bruchac's lead, I envision these hidden voices, dusty memories, broken bodies, and sacred beings as ancestors waiting to be released. These materials are brimming with coded messages and beckoning to be restored and rematriated. Our intellectual forebears are the Indigenous gatekeepers, interpreters and guides, the cultural brokers who helped anthropologists collect materials to weave their strange, distorted patterns of culture.

The first wave of homeplace ethnographers comprised community-based scholars. Ella Deloria, Zora Neale Hurston, Jovita González, Sterling Brown, Aurelio Espinosa, Arthur Campa, Edward Dozier, Joe Sando, and Alfonso Ortiz, to name a few, wrote innovative ethnographies using customized methodologies and social theories. They also negotiated competing obligations and pressures (including the need to make a living as writers and community-based scholars). María Eugenia Cotera observes that native ethnographers "drifted in the borderlands between multiple discourses, ideologies, and allegiances."[26] Deloria, González, and Hurston in particular used experimental methods, broke with disciplinary boundaries, and blended genres of writing in ways that we would now call postmodern. Finding elements of Chicana feminism in their works, Cotera suggests that their texts "reveal the decolonizing mechanics of a feminist consciousness located at the crossroads."[27] These scholars were ahead of their time and, perhaps for this reason, did not make much of a dent in the closed anthropological minds of their day. Native speakers, to borrow María Eugenia Cotera's insightful term, are more likely to be read in ethnic studies than in introductory anthropology courses. Nor are they included in the grand origin story of American anthropology, even though native speakers. Doing homework in the early twentieth century often used normative anthropological methods and modes of writing in their early works.[28]

Examples of decolonizing methodologies from this period do exist. This begs the question, why do anthropology students read (or at least know of) Ruth Benedict's *Patterns of Culture* (1934), but only specialists read Ella Deloria's *Waterlily* (1947)? Arthur Campa was working in New Mexico at the same time as Benedict, but *Spanish Religious Folktheatre in the Southwest* (1934) is incognito by comparison to Benedict's work. Into the latter half of the century, *The Hopi-Tewa of Arizona* (1954) by Edward Dozier is an exemplar of community-based historical ethnography. Alfonso Ortiz sparked controversy among some of his relatives and tribal elders when he published *The Tewa World: Space, Time, Being and Becoming in a Pueblo Society* (1969), which applied structuralist theories to explain Tewa moieties. Reading Ortiz's book could spark critical conversations about the relationship between Native Americans and anthropologists and the ethical dilemmas that Native researchers face when attempting to balance the demands of the discipline while respecting the customs of the tribal community. Alternatives do exist but ethnographies written by white scholars about Native Americans are generally part of the anthropological canon. This literature is considered antiquated by today's standards but remains foundational to New Mexico studies. The uninvited guests continue to haunt us.[29]

Genízaro scholar and Native speaker Gregorio Gonzales urges me to see the errors of my interpretation. He says that "recounting how our intellectual predecessors made *males* among our relatives" is unproductive and negates our agency. Counterstories can lead us down troubled paths, ones that cast our living presences as dead or disappearing absences. Native Americans and *nuevomexicanas*/os, as informants, interpreters, guides, and hosts, were not passive victims of the anthropological enterprise. They engaged in verbal art, filtered information, lent their creativity, and unbeknown to most helped shape the discipline. This invisible labor is hidden away in fieldnotes, archives, or museum collections. Some of this material became ethnographies, books about the Native inhabitants of the Southwest borderlands largely written for white university students and academics. While early anthropologists believed that they were documenting and collecting cultures at an objective distance and with some scientific precision, they had limited knowledge of the deep histories and complex epistemologies of the communities of study.[30]

What the purveyors of the laboratory of anthropology collected was "Indian given" and therefore, never as straightforward or transparent as the ethnographer may have assumed.[31] Bruchac suggests that "if we recognize these Indigenous interlocutors as major contributors to the discipline (much as we do long-dead anthropologists), we might better understand the logic of their engagement, and the ferocity of their determination to preserve something of themselves in the written record." This idea inspires me because it demands recognition of the informants' motivations and intellectual resources. It reverses the colonial encounter and its erasures. It springs back like an Aboriginal boomerang and hands us a more empowering origin story from which to speak and ground our practices of anthropolocura.

In the summer of 2018, homeplace anthropologist, activist, and community musician Dabi F. García and I wrote a column in *Anthropology News* for the Association of Latina/o and Latinx Anthropologists Section, in which we pondered the futurity of what was designated a laboratory of anthropology at the dawn of the discipline.[32] The laboratory was a cultural petri dish and methodological training ground where students of the new science of culture could collect specimens and test their theories. But it was also a field of diverse homeplaces where our ancestors were born and are buried and where our families continue to live. It is our shared homeland and the place where we do our tarea, or home/field work. We wrote about how New Mexico has long been a prime location for pondering the future given its association with the atomic bomb, alien crash-landings, science-fiction fantasies, and privatized space travel.

However, this so-called Land of Enchantment belies many disenchanting realties. Besides being a playground for tourists, New Mexico houses the nation's post–Cold War nuclear complex, Los Alamos National Laboratories. The state was declared a national sacrifice zone at the height of World War II to create and test nuclear bombs (and spew radioactive waste) without responsibility or accountability to the people or environments near nuclear test sites and dumping grounds.[33] Environmental colonialism continues to contaminate the land, water, and air. Uranium mining and toxic chemical spills in Navajo Country, hydraulic fracking in Mora County, and petroleum extraction in the southeastern corridor pollute and scar the sacred earth. Meanwhile, rural communities have come to rely on extractive industries, which are both a source of environmental ruination and a source of stable income in a state that does not have enough jobs to ensure that young people will be able to stay in their ancestral homeland.

Correlations can be drawn between the region's settler colonial history and its neocolonial present (marginality/expendability in relation to national economic and security interests) and the emergence of the laboratory of anthropology. Its original purpose was to serve as a repository—to extract, record, and catalogue the cultural material of living and ancestral Native American and nuevo-mexicana/o communities before they were tarnished by modernity. Within the salvage ethnography paradigm that guided early anthropological methods and motives, the Indigenous inhabitants of New Mexico were on the road to extinction. As victims of modernity, we were not expected to exist into the future, at least not with our cultural memories intact. Granted, the laboratory of anthropology made immeasurable contributions to the discipline, including forming ethnographic practice, molding theories of culture and society, and blazing a path for women to enter the field. However, this laboratory was not created to be a material or intellectual space for homeplace scholars to conduct our own investigations, recover the coded messages of our ancestors, or to determine our own futures. Instead, it was intended to enclose us within a particular imaginary of the past that has incredible staying power and has proven difficult to dislodge.

García and I proposed that before we can begin a conversation about anthropological futures, we must reckon with its colonial past (i.e., racialized-sexualized-gendered violence) because these legacies cast long shadows. Anthropologists working in "the field" become part of the political, social, and economic situation that they study, and this interaction has real impacts on communities, both positive and negative. Salvage anthropology set out to capture an authentic past but ignored the present realities of Native American and nuevomexicana/o communities.[34] It buried the Indigenous intellectuals and artisans who helped shape the discipline deep in the archive and composed a past-oriented concept of culture that spawned an entire culture industry, from heritage preservation to museum exhibits and collections. It also gave rise to volumes of literature on tradition and traditionalization, which birthed (and authorized) problematic cultural revitalization movements that promote settler colonial narratives, ideologies, and symbolism.

A recent example is the heated controversy over the Entrada pageant, a dramatic reenactment performed during the annual Santa Fe Fiesta that replays and celebrates the return of Spanish authority to New Mexico twelve years after the 1680 Pueblo Revolt. The pageant is a ritual event organized by Los Caballeros de Vargas, a religious confraternity dedicated to Santa Fe's patroness, Our Lady of the Rosary, also known as La Conquistadora because of her associations with the 1692 reconquest campaign lead by Diego de Vargas. The pageant casts locals in the roles of historical persons such as de Vargas and his Tewa adversary, Cacique Naranjo. The drama narrates the basis of the fiesta and a particular version of Hispano identity and salvation history that has been cultivated by cultural preservation groups since the 1950s.[35] The Entrada pageant is a conquest and conversion drama of sorts. It has elements of the colonial folk dances that are performed in Mexico and other regions of the North American Southwest, such as Los Matachines and Moros y Cristianos, which reenact conflicts between Spaniards and cultural and religious others. For all that, the Entrada is a modern performance that tells a story about the second wave of imperialism and the arrival of Anglo-Protestant modernity.

To be clear, the Entrada pageant is an Anglo invention. In the 1920s Edgar Hewett of the Museum of New Mexico organized "La Fiesta de Santa Fe," a pageant of three cultures with Anglos, Hispanos, and Indians receiving separate recognition.[36] The project was also sponsored by the School of American Research (now called the School for Advanced Research, or SAR). The goal was to attract tourism to northern New Mexico by highlighting the unique history of the region. This Anglo-directed fiesta celebration included a reenactment of General Kearney's military occupation of Santa Fe "without a single shot fired." This narrative recalls de Vargas's "bloodless reconquest," which is the central storyline of the modern-day Entrada pageant's moves toward innocence. This is no coincidence. The original cast comprised Anglos and a few members of the Hispano gentry (some of whom played the roles of Indians). The historical pageantry was a flop. Anglo tourists have always found Indian dances much more appealing.

Nuevomexicanas/os did not appropriate and reinvent the Entrada until the 1950s, which coincided with post–World War II movements to revitalize Hispano-Catholic organizations and establish cultural preservation groups. During World War II, many native New Mexicans left the region to join the military or work in wartime industries. When they returned to the homeland, they wanted to be fully included in US society as Americans. But they also wanted to preserve their culture and traditions, which they believed were diminishing as a result of displacement, assimilation, and Anglo emigration. They revived religious confraternities, took leadership positions in the Fiesta Council, and established clubs such as La Sociedad Folklórica and Los Caballeros de Vargas, groups dedicated to preserving "Spanish culture" on their own terms.[37] Salvage anthropology and its disappearing natives was back with a vengeance. Now the natives were convinced that their culture was under threat of extinction and it was their job to preserve it.

Native American and Chicanx activists have protested the Entrada pageant periodically since the 1970s in both small and dramatic ways. In 1999 Lee Moquino from Santa Clara Pueblo played the role of Cacique Naranjo because he wanted control over Pueblo representation in the performance. The performance is staged and scripted but there is always space for resistance. Moquino added his own emphasis to the line, "Don Diego de Vargas, the return of the Spanish was inevitable even though WE HOPED YOU'D NEVER COME BACK!" In 2003 the men playing the roles of de Vargas and Cacique Naranjo went rogue and refused to perform the prepared script. Instead, they went on stage, shook hands, and waved to the audience. In 2015 national and local political sensibilities aligned to reenergize and also vocalize the silent protest against the Entrada that had occurred the previous year. All across the nation, the icons of colonialism and slavery were coming under scrutiny. Confederate flags and statues were torn down or silently removed in the night. These actions sparked a wildfire of debates, protests, and counterprotests. Icons and celebrations of Spanish colonialism, which are common in New Mexico, were next on the proverbial chopping block.[38]

Protests against the Entrada pageant escalated in 2017. A SWAT team lined the rooftops of the historic Palace of the Governor in the heart of the Downtown Plaza, with rifles pointed down at the protestors. Time seemed to collapse as collective memories of past colonial terror merged with the present. The protestors evoked the leader of the 1680 Pueblo Revolt as they shouted, "Slay, slay like Po'pay!" Counterprotestors also entered the fray. Some of these individuals were members of the Fiesta Council, Los Caballeros de Vargas, and affiliated Hispano-cultural preservation groups. At one point during the Entrada performance one of the actors scolded the protestors, telling them to "respect our religion." Police harassed and intimidated the protestors and arrested activist Jennifer Marely, one of the leaders of Red Nation, the group that escalated the movement to end the Entrada.

In the wake of the turmoil city officials, Pueblo leaders, and clergy (all of them men) came together to find a peaceful resolution to the issue of the Entrada pageant. It was decided that the pageant needed to end or be replaced with a more inclusive celebration of Santa Fe's history and cultural heritage, but some local Hispanics thought the decision was an affront to their religious and cultural traditions. In one instance, a supporter of the performance said, "I don't want to be decolonized!" Her statement was rather shocking, but it also brings us back to anthropolocura. We may live in the same hometown, we may even be family, but this does not guarantee that we share the same cultural identity, vision of inclusion, or political goals.

The Entrada pageant may seem strange, even horrifying to the outsider. So, following Lee Moquino's tactics, I will repeat my lines with dramatic emphasis: The pageant was originally created by Anglo emissaries of the Museum of New Mexico in the 1920s as a tourist attraction. Nuevomexicanas/os took control of the event in the 1950s as part of a broader middle-class-oriented cultural revitalization project. In northern New Mexico, the drive to salvage vanishing cultures is deeply entrenched within the logic of cultural institutions, legal frameworks, ethnic art markets, and even the popular imagination. Hispanic heritage preservation societies are compelled to rescue local culture and religious traditions from disappearing and thus, from changing. Struggles over natural resources, claims to place and space, and notions of local citizenship (the politics of autochthony) get couched in preservationist rhetoric to get heard and often become mired in authenticity testing. This remnant of salvage anthropology can hinder collective movements for social change because the legitimacy of our claims, our voices, and our aspirations for a better future so often hinge on our ability to prove cultural continuity.

On the other hand, knowing how to throw the boomerang just right can bring fortunate returns. I like to think that our animated documentary, *Frontera! Revolt and Rebellion on the Rio Grande* (2014), played a role in the demise of the Entrada pageant. Artist and professor of social documentation at the University of California at Santa Cruz John Jota Leaños invited me to help him produce the film in 2011. As a Xicano from California, Leaños needed a native guide. He understood that "there are many ways to get this story wrong." I spent the next two years recruiting local talent—artists, voice-over actors, and musicians—to make the animation come to life with cultural precision. I also spent many hours researching the Pueblo Revolt and its aftermath using historical accounts, archaeological evidence, and interviews with community members from Acoma, Cochiti, Jemez, San Ildefonso, Santa Clara, and Zuni Pueblos. The goal was to tell a multivocal public history of what Jemez scholar Joe Sando called the "First American Revolution" from Native American and Chicanx perspectives. Collectively, our goal was to tell a colloquial story of the Pueblo Revolt showcasing local voices and aesthetics. We also wanted to understand how this spectacular pan-Indigenous uprising against the Spanish empire that expelled Spanish/Mexican settlers and their Indigenous allies for twelve years was orchestrated through collective action and coalition building. We wanted to highlight its continued relevance today as a source of inspiration for *rebeldía* in New Mexico and beyond.

Anthropologies in Reverse

In her innovative essay, *"El desorden*, Nationalism, and Chicana/o Aesthetics," Laura Elisa Pérez argues that Chicanas/os and other marginalized communities produce sites of disorder within dominated spaces. They create other knowledges "whose ragged discursive edges scrape the delicate shins of the dominating cultures' claims to normality, authority and universalism."[39] Critical of nationalism of all kinds, Pérez has an appreciation for the idea of Aztlán as uncolonized space within the US nation-state, a homeland that shimmers in and out of existence through "willful acts of a collective Chicana/o imagination." Paradoxically, this conjectural homeland cannot be mapped, bordered, or settled but is unfolding in the contingent and everyday practices of living and working in the margins, in the borderlands, in nepantla, in the day-to-day acts of resistance that are "disordering to the dominant culture's *migra*."[40] As a Chicana anthropologist, my ability to navigate multiple worlds given my professional and political identities is an opportunity to embrace collective *desorden* to create spaces for anthropolocura.

Chicanx cultural practices, social movements, and aesthetics have often operated in disordering and profoundly disturbing ways with respect to the dominant social order. Chicana feminism (and its nonconformist Chicanx queer variances) adheres to divergent thinking and thrives on disruption of categories, gender bending, spiritual politics, multiple identities, and personal and social transformation. At the heart of this aspirational project is decolonization through individual and collective acts of rebeldía—Chicana *movidas* both large and small, visible and stealthy, real or imaginary.[41] For instance, resistance to the Santa Fe Entrada pageant ranged from impromptu script disruptions and refusals to silent protests and vociferous collective rebeldía that finally put the hundred-year-old drama to rest.

Gregorio Gonzales's mal-crianza methodologies offer another version of disorderly conduct that bends and upends normative ways of acting, knowing, and living.[42] Leaning into his renegade Genízaridad and outcast positionality across nonrecognized Indigenous communities and federally recognized tribal nations in New Mexico, Gonzales slides in and out of his trickster role and serious *anthropolocote* in his ethnographic practice and writing. What he calls "respectful shit talking" is his modus operandi and oppositional stance. He writes experimental ethnography overlaid and remixed with intentionally coded and convoluted Genízaro storytelling. The same ethnographic scene is told multiple times in circuitous but radically different ways. Sometimes he is a picaresque character named Pedro Urdemalas who is constantly challenging authority and getting himself in trouble with his elders, God, Jesus, and the saints. In other instances, he describes a ride in the back of a truck to gather firewood in *el monte* with his uncles and then the scene shifts into metaphysical conversations with friends over a few beers. Gonzales, who is Comanche, infuses ethnography with poetic musings on "rez dogs" and other subjects that seem curiously out of sync with the rest of the narrative. Indigenous metaphysics in dialogue with critical theory and subaltern philosophy is how Gonzales describes his disorderly "mal-crianza methodologies." His work is disorienting and exhilarating; an ethnography in reverse that confounds expectations and disciplinary conventions.

Any discussion of reverse ethnography must give credit to native anthropologists for opening new dialogues and carving a brilliant path for us to follow. Bruchac defines reverse ethnography as "microhistories embedded within the longue durée of the anthropological project."[43] These microhistories can be material objects or correspondence between Indigenous collaborators and anthropologists that are buried in the archive, but they can also be the innovative, multivocal ethnographies that homeplace researchers produced that did not gain the recognition that they deserved. The now classic works of Zora Neale Hurston, Ella Deloria, and Jovita González and others opened space for native voices in anthropology even though their hybrid and genre-bending novels and ethnographies as well as their methodological innovations went largely unrecognized within the discipline until recently. According to Cotera, "Their storytelling carves out a space for a new form of gendered and racialized consciousness that stands both apart from and within multiple imagined communities."[44] Second-wave native speakers (I prefer to call them homeplace ethnographers rather than native anthropologists) such as Américo Paredes, Delmos Jones, Kirin Narayan, Lila Abu-Lughod, Sylvia Rodriguez, Patricia Zavella, Olga Nájera-Ramírez, Alejandro Lugo, and Carlos G. Vélez-Ibáñez (and many others) illustrate the broad diversity of ways that homeplace ethnographers have made critical interventions in the field (and at home) through community-based research, transnational dialogue, and activism.

Homeworking in the Sanctuary City

While working on the animated documentary about the 1680 Pueblo Revolt, I was conducting homework for my dissertation on the sanctuary movement of the 1980s in New Mexico and how it seeded Somos Un Pueblo Unido, a statewide immigrant rights organization based in Santa Fe. Founded in 1995, Somos is an immigrant-led organization with membership teams across the state who organize for worker and racial justice through grassroots campaigns aimed at political power and policy-making. I began working with Somos in August of 2010 on a bias-based policing study and on municipal policies that aim to protect undocumented residents from deportation and include them in the civic community. I had many conversations with my colleagues, all fiercely intelligent and politically astute Latinas, about what constitutes a sanctuary city. In our many office conversations and long Friday lunches I recounted what I had learned about the 1980s sanctuary movement in the state archives and from my interviews with participants. Somos had drafted and helped pass a resolution prohibiting the use of city resources for immigration enforcement in 1999, which essentially revived Santa Fe's sanctuary city status. Santa Fe was one of the first cities in the nation to declare itself a "city of refuge" in 1985 for Central Americans seeking asylum from devastating civil wars and horrendous acts of state violence and genocide. Governor Toney Anaya issued a proclamation in 1986 establishing New Mexico as the nation's first "state for sanctuary." The newer staff members were unaware of this historical connection.

My research on the Pueblo Revolt revealed an even deeper history of sanctuary in New Mexico. I learned from archaeologists Bob Preucel, Matt Liebmann, and Joseph Aguilar, who study the postrevolt period, that the landscape was flooded with migrants and refugees.[45] Some remained in mission villages founded before the uprising while others occupied Spanish colonial settlements.

Pueblos from diverse tribes abandoned their mission villages and following the sacred migration stories passed down to them from their ancestors, they built new communities atop high mesas.[46] Archaeologists have identified six Pueblo cities of refuge: Dowa Yalanne (Corn Mountain) near Zuni, Tunyo (Black Mesa) at San Ildefonso, Koyiti southwest of Cochiti, and three villages in the vicinity of Jemez: Astialakwa, Potokwa, and Bolestsakwa.[47] These sanctuary cities displayed innovations in art and architecture and incorporated diverse Puebloan refugees who spoke different languages and welcomed Nadé (Apache) and Diné (Navajo) allies.[48]

My colleagues and friends at Somos were fascinated and moved by the idea that New Mexico had a long tradition of sanctuary place-making. Sanctuary, we assessed, is much older than the nation-state and its exclusionary institution of citizenship. We were members of different Pueblo, Apache, Comanche, and Navajo tribal communities long before we were under any settler colonial state formation. We were also nuevomexicanas/os long before we became US citizens by conquest in 1848 (New Mexico did not become a state until 1912). Although we understand that there is no historical continuity between today's secular sanctuary city resolutions and the ancient Pueblo cities of refuge, the idea of a homegrown practice of radical hospitality was compelling and inspiring. We began to build a new narrative of the sanctuary city, organically at first, then more intentionally to advance our campaigns to further sanctuary-like policies in Santa Fe and across the state and to hold elected officials accountable to them. The notion that New Mexico was uniquely positioned within the sanctuary city debates because of its enduring tradition of sanctuary place-making began to gain momentum. I did a few radio interviews about the sanctuary movement in New Mexico, in which I made a convincing case for the state's long-standing tradition of sanctuary, drawing connections to today's immigrant rights movement.

After the election of Donald Trump in 2016, sanctuary cities—municipalities that provide protections for undocumented residents—came under intense scrutiny for ostensibly harboring so-called criminals or potential terrorists in defiance of federal immigration law. In response, schools and universities declared themselves sanctuaries for undocumented students, Muslims, and other likely targets. Cities such as San Francisco, California, and of course, Santa Fe, New Mexico, reasserted their long-standing sanctuary status. In contrast, Texas lawmakers passed SB4, legislation that aimed to prohibit cities and counties from passing immigrant-friendly policies and punish those who refuse to comply.[49] This partisan action incited protest from cities along the US-Mexico border and those with large immigrant populations such as Houston, Dallas, and San Antonio. It also reignited immigrant rights activism and faith-based sanctuary movements. With the eye of the political storm on sanctuary cities, the historicity and sanctity of sanctuary fell to the wayside. While the anti-sanctuary movement was in motion, Santa Fe was preparing its defense, a progressive Welcoming City Resolution and a homespun story of sanctuary rooted in tradition.

In December 2016, immigrant families, faith leaders, labor unions, civil rights organizations, and elected officials packed City Hall in Santa Fe. The community had come together to register their support for the Welcoming City Resolution, one of the most progressive sanctuary city policies in the nation. It passed unanimously in open defiance to the Trump administration's hateful executive orders. The resolution reconfirmed and also expanded the protections for undocumented residents previously established in 1999 when the City of Santa Fe revived its sanctuary status. This history of defiance against unjust laws was not lost on those who gathered to testify in support of the Welcoming City Resolution. A prominent theme in the testimony given that day was that sanctuary is a uniquely New Mexican tradition. Individuals referenced different examples to evidence this claim depending on their personal histories and their relationship to immigration. City Councilor Renee Villarreal, one of the representatives who introduced the proposal, asserted that "New Mexico has a long tradition of providing sanctuary to those fleeing harm, from the Pueblo Revolt to those fleeing persecution in Central America during the 1980s. We won't turn our back on our traditions now. Instead we must strengthen those policies." This historically informed public servant also happens to be my sister. I did not put these beautiful words in her mouth. She worked closely with Somos to draft the Welcoming City Resolution and we have had many deep conversations about my research. In fact, when I was struggling to decide on my dissertation topic, Renee suggested that I write about sanctuary cities and told me about Toney Anaya's 1986 declaration. I took her advice.

In July 2017, *Yes!* magazine published an article titled "The Defiant, Refugee-Loving History of New Mexico: How the State's Unique and Open Relationship with Mexico Is Overshadowing Trump's Immigration Policies." The article celebrated New Mexico's immigrant-friendly policies and noted the state's long tradition of offering sanctuary to refugees and incorporating immigrants into the civic community. The boomerang's trajectory was again bending time and space back into our hands. What I have described in these last few paragraphs exemplifies homeworking and the seemingly magical interworkings of anthropolocura. My family members, coworkers, and research partners all played an important part in how the narrative of sanctuary changed in Santa Fe. Granted, it is a small town and information (and *chisme*) travels fast, but the story of New Mexico's unique sanctuary tradition also circulated well beyond the boundaries of the state. Yes, it may be true that the language of tradition is an aftereffect of salvage anthropology's stranglehold on our homeland. Tradition is a contested and contentious idea that becomes embedded into cultural preservation projects and social movements. However, in this case it bolstered the campaign for the Welcoming City Resolution and brought national attention to New Mexico's progressive local immigration policies. It also helped generate an empowering narrative of belonging, a story of shared histories and futures, a story that we could believe in.[50]

The future can be defined as the collective capacity to aspire and work for a more just borderless world.[51] The ability to imagine a different future and improved conditions of living must be cultivated in marginalized communities who are often left out of future-making projects (or incorporated in problematic ways). Cultural preservation should be defined in terms of continuance, the ability to continue to live and thrive in our homeplaces, to continue producing culture. Native anthropologists, hometown anthropologists, anthropolocotes, however we choose to define ourselves and our community work, are engaged in aspirational practices of activism and coalitional research within our homeplaces. We are reclaiming the laboratory for ourselves to create an aspirational praxis that is unapologetically political, decolonial, and intersectional. Our preference for homework—a collaborative learning process that challenges anthropology's preference for the faraway field—is a natural outgrowth of our abiding investment in documenting and participating in acts of resistance and movements for social change in our communities and in our hometowns. It also stems from our discomfort with and rejection of the colonial legacies of the laboratory of anthropology. The native anthropologist is duplicitous partly because all researchers, writers, and artists are suspect in Indian Country and nativeness is a matter of degree. In a region saturated with anthropological residue, everyone is caught up in anthropolocura, sizing up the cultural landscape and finding their place within it.

Anthropolocura could be considered a type of street therapy or survival strategy that everyone does to some extent.[52] It is a combination of critical discovery (scientific, collective, and personal) and madness. It thrives on the stuff your professors warned you about—personal enmeshment, family ties, durable commitments, challenging emotional work, and unsettling ethical dilemmas. Anthropolocura is insurgent and unruly, adhering to alternate realities and radical forms of dialogue and codes of respect. It is a borderlandia steeped in interdisciplinarity, incarnate (as opposed to abstract), genre-bending, queering, and experimental. Its *locuras* (or theories) emerge from homework and methodologies found at the fault lines of anthropology, ethnic studies, and subjugated other/othered knowledges. At its heart is decolonial *sanación*, an anthropolocura *que cura*.

In conclusion, this chapter sought to outline some of the theoretical and political threads and sources of inspiration that hometown anthropologists and other New Mexico scholars are pulling together to cast off the colonial residue of the laboratory of anthropology. In conversation with my colleagues who are doing research with their tribes or homeplace communities, this chapter claims space for homeplace ethnography and validates anthropolocura—our home-spun "fugitive anthropology" in reverse.[53] As a borderlandia, anthropolocura can take many forms and draws from deep wells of knowledge from Indigenous storytelling and reverse ethnography to ethnic studies and many other subjugated other/othered knowledges. The goal of this project is to turn homeward in order to build a restorative and reparative practice of ethnography whose power lies in the possibility of decolonial sanación, healing ourselves and our communities. We do not claim to have a definitive remedy for all our dilemmas or to have a solution that will resolve all the maddening contradictions that cohere around home and homeworking. What we do know is that hometown ethnography is work that matters to our communities. Kamala Visweswaran reminds us that home, once interrogated, is a place we have never been.[54] Her *consejo* can be taken as a warning, or as mantra of the transformative potential of a homeplace anthropology.

Notes

1. Visweswaran 1994.

2. Clifford 1977, 198.

3. Berry et al. 2017, 537.

4. Gupta and Ferguson 2010, 12–13.

5. Moraga and Anzaldúa 1981, xxiii–xxvi.

6. Manuel 2018, 3

7. Sharma 2020, 14–15.

8. I prefer to identify as a homeplace ethnographer and use this term instead of Native anthropologist. First, nativeness is a fraught term couched in the settler state's enforced separation of natives and migrants. Also, not all scholars trained as anthropologists cheer for team anthropology. Many scholars of color (myself included) have had traumatic experiences in anthropology programs and therefore, dis-identify with the discipline. I'm more interested in the concept of home and doing research that examines the relationships that produce homeplaces. People can have multiple homeplaces, so autochthony is not a prerequisite, only the commitment to homework.

9. Visweswaran 1994, 103.

10. Trujillo and Bott-Lyons 2020, 1–2.

11. Colleen Flaherty, "The Gig Academy," *Inside Higher Ed*, October 10, 2019, https://www.insidehighered.com/news/2019/10/10/what-about-gig-academy.

12. Trujillo and Bott-Lyons 2020, 1–2.

13. Ibid.

14. Chawla 2014, 25.

15. Tuck and Yang 2012, 3–4.

16. Visweswaran 1994, 75.

17. Ibid., 104.

18. Facio 2014, 60–61.

19. Anzaldúa 2009b, 243.

20. Anzaldúa 2009a, 195–96.

21. Cuevas 2018, 11–13.

22. Ibid., 13.

23. Cotera 2008, 10.

24. Bruchac 2018, 8.

25. Ibid., 178.

26. Cotera 2008, 17.

27. Ibid., 17.

28. Ibid., 15–17.

29. In his now classic article, "Anthropologists at Zuni" (1972), Triloki N. Panday recounts stories about early anthropologists that Zuni community members recalled when he was working there in the 1960s. He notes that when strangers came to Zuni they were often asked, "Are you an anthropologist?" (321).

30. Bruchac 2018, 10.

31. Saldaña-Portillo 2016, 11–12. The author argues that "Indians and indios are the condition of possibility for the emergence of the United States as well as Mexico." She uses the term "Indian given" as a reversal of the derogatory term "Indian giver."

32. Villarreal and García 2018.

33. Masco 2006, 35.

34. Panday 1972, 327.

35. For a fuller discussion of Hispano cultural preservation and religious groups and the Entrada pageant, see Horton 2010.

36. Montgomery 2002, 24.

37. Los Caballeros de Vargas is an ethno-religious confraternity founded in 1955.

38. Icons of Spanish colonialism were banished in June 2020. The bronze equestrian statue of Oñate that once stood in front of the Oñate Monument and Resource Center outside Española was removed. Protests erupted around a different Oñate statue in Albuquerque and a protestor was shot. The City of Albuquerque took the statue down shortly thereafter. The small statue of Diego de Vargas in Santa Fe was quietly removed during the night.

39. Pérez 2002, 39.

40. Anzaldúa 2007, 100–101; Pérez 2002, 19–20.

41. Cotera, Blackwell, and Espinosa 2017, 2–3.

42. Gonzales adapts the concept of mal-crianza methodologies from mentor Estevan Rael-Gálvéz.

43. Bruchac 2018, 19.

44. See Cotera 2008.

45. Joseph Aguilar, a Tewa archaeologist from San Ildefonso Pueblo, defines his research at Tunyo, one of the cities of refuge that Pueblo people built in the aftermath of the Pueblo Revolt of 1680, as a "community history project." He trains community members in noninvasive archaeological methods and involves them in the interpretation of the data they gather using drones that take aerial images of the site and GIS sensing technologies.

46. Liebmann et al. 2017, 145.

47. Liebmann 2012.

48. See Villarreal 2019 for a fuller discussion on Indigenous practices of sanctuary.

49. On August 30, 2017, a federal court granted an injunction blocking the key provisions of SB4: (1) Texas cities and counties can direct their officers not to serve in the role of immigration officers; (2) local jails are not required to hold individuals based only on a request by ICE; and (3) local officials and employees can criticize SB4 and speak in favor of changes in immigration enforcement without fear of punishment under SB4 (MALDEF SB4 Fact Sheet, 2017). However, part of this ruling was overturned on appeal, allowing some provisions to remain.

50. The *New York Times* published an article in September 2020 about how some Pueblo people continue to draw inspiration from the Pueblo Revolt in art, activism, and movements for social justice today.

51. Appadurai 2013, 59–60.

52. See Ramos-Zayas 2012.

53. Berry et al. 2017, 535.

54. Visweswann 1997.

Uncertain Future(s)

Latinidad, Anthropology, Institutions

VANESSA DÍAZ, SERGIO LEMUS, AND RYAN MANN-HAMILTON

We write this afterword amid the global COVID-19 pandemic and in the United States, where—perhaps more than ever—the dire and deadly effects of income, health, and racial inequities that have always plagued this nation have been laid bare. We write at a time in which African American, Native American, and Latinx communities have disproportionately contracted and died of COVID-19, a time in which we have witnessed a series of high-profile state-sanctioned (George Floyd, Breonna Taylor) and citizen killings (Ahmaud Arbery) of Black people.[1] The collision of the pandemic with these violent incidents has incited a national movement to address racial justice and the continued attacks on Black life, including Afro-Latinxs. We write at a time when police and law enforcement attacks on Latinxs more broadly have escalated—Joel Acevedo, Sean Monterrosa, Erik Salgado, and Andrés Guardado were all recently killed by police.

Prominent African American activists, such as attorney Ben Crump, have been vocal about underscoring the importance of addressing these attacks on nonwhite life collectively and collaboratively. Historically, collaborative coalition building between groups and movements like the Black Panthers, Young Lords, Brown Berets, the American Indian Movement, the Asian American Movement, and the Gay Liberation Movement is what led to both the progress of and subsequent backlash and US government targeting against these movements. It is important to look back and reflect on this history and these precursors, for it was their coalitional work that embraced intersectional identities as central to Latinidad, particularly Afro and Queer Latinidades. And the present moment—more powerfully than ever—demonstrates the importance of coalitional work in building social movements for change.

Ethnographic Refusals, Unruly Latinidades was compiled amid these crises, which have expanded public conversation around racism, white supremacy, and racist institutions such as law enforcement. As national debates around the abolition and defunding of police grow, for instance, they are converging with increasing calls to abolish Immigration and Customs Enforcement (ICE).[2] Calls for the abolition of these institutions highlight the importance of the kinds of collaborative activism referenced here: while various actors held unique community-based goals, the broader agenda was the same—to end white (hetero) supremacy and US imperialism and colonialism. Today, the #BlackLivesMatter Movement—founded by Queer Black women—is an orienting force in the recent wave of racial justice activism. In the 1960s, it was the Black Power Movement, led by the Black Panther Party. And the parallel Latinx movements were not just *similar* to the Black Panther Party, they were modeled on it—both the Young Lords' and Brown Berets' thirteen-point programs were built on the Black Panthers' ten-point program.

In addition to this history and the current political context, we also write in the wake of the passing of Miriam Jiménez Román and the ten-year anniversary of the *Afro-Latin@Reader*, edited by her and her partner, Juan Flores. Through her groundbreaking efforts to center Afro-Latinidades, Jiménez Román embodied and paved the way for the future of Latinidad that we hope for. As one of the first edited volumes to speak to the AfroLatina/o/x experience across geographies and disciplines, that collection and its collaborators continue to push for the need to address the silences and unequal nature of our home and diasporic societies. *Ethnographic Refusals, Unruly Latinidades* builds on these critical perspectives in an effort to imagine a more intersectional Latinidad, as several of the authors engage with alternative conceptualizations that reject hierarchical orientations toward Spanishness, Americanness, and whiteness and attempt to center Blackness and Indigeneity.

While we acknowledge the significance of this collection as the first of its kind for Latinx anthropology and anthropologists, we are intentionally centering our closing reflections on Latinidad and Latinx studies, rather than anthropology. In the foreword to this volume, Arlene Dávila opens with a pointed critique of anthropology, noting that while the "tired" discipline is "unbearable," its colonial past continues to shape its scholarship. And while each of us coauthors of this afterword have different relationships to anthropology, we collectively understand the ways anthropology has denied the validity of our diverse forms of knowledge production. Ultimately, this volume represents an important shift—and perhaps hope—for anthropology, while also recognizing that some of us also believe that it may be time to simply "let anthropology burn," as Ryan Cecil Jobson has aptly suggested.[3] Thus, in these concluding pages, we purposefully turn to (1) reflections on inclusivity and Latinidad; (2) the future of interdisciplinary studies of Latinxs—including the potential for Latinx anthropology; and (3) Latinx futures more broadly. These thoughts are undergirded by a deep engagement with *refusal*, as we problematize the limitations and white supremacist groundings of dominant conceptualizations of both Latinidad and anthropology.

As we recognize the unique role this volume plays in Latinx anthropological futures, we note Savannah Shange's call for an "abolitionist anthropology" that will move the discipline toward a "genre of Black study."[4] What does this mean for Latinx anthropology? For one, we must acknowledge that framing Latinidad and Blackness as mutually exclusive is Black erasure. And this reckoning begins with disturbing the commonly held notion that all Latinxs are mixed, an origin story that sidesteps issues of colorism and racism within the Latinx community through the lens of "mestilegio" (*el privilegio del mestizaje* [the privilege of mestizaje]) and "requires a critical examination of 'brownness' as a stereotypical reference point for Latinidad that simultaneously stakes a claim to racial marginalization and proximity to whiteness through troublesome ideologies of mestizaje."[5] Though Latinxs readily claim mixture, for some that mixture is more pronounced while being barely present for others. The Association of Latina/o & Latinx Anthropologists (ALLA) 2020 "Statement against Anti-Black Racism" speaks to the work that lies ahead for Latinx anthropology, interdisciplinary Latinx studies, and Latinidad more broadly:

> The universal framing of Latinxs as people of color erases the hegemony of whiteness and white supremacy in our communities, preventing us from addressing endemic Latinx anti-Blackness and the systematic marginalization and erasure of Black Latinxs. In the context of these power relations, the slogan "Latinxs for Black Lives" erases Blackness from Latinidad rather than joining long-standing Afro-Latinx and Black movements throughout the Americas and the world in affirming that Black Lives Matter/Las Vidas Negras Importan."

As education scholar Blanca Vega urges, it's "time to make Latinxs uncomfortable for their antiBlack comments, jokes, values, beliefs, and practices. It's NOT time to protect Latinidad. It's time to disrupt it."[6] Given that mainstream (including academic) representations of Latinxs are often whitewashed,[7] our students are often shocked to learn that, of the millions of peoples forcefully taken from Africa to the Americas, over 90 percent arrived in Latin America and the Caribbean.[8] In many cases, before taking our classes, students of all races are not even familiar with the idea of Afro-Latinidad. After the Cuban rap group Obsesión came to Díaz's class, for instance, she was struck by the emotional reaction from an African American student who wrote that the visit was transformational and helped him understand that "although we were separated by distance and culture, our histories were the same." For Mann-Hamilton, teaching at Laguardia College has provided a vital space to think about Latinidad and engage with multiple conceptions of the category as they emerge from students and local communities. Many Latinx youth are connecting to differing visions of Latinidad and seeking connections across spaces and generations. Many of Mann-Hamilton's students in New York City use Latinx as a racial category and are confused by the distinction between ethnicity and race. Others have embraced the AfroLatinx category, as it speaks more clearly to their family histories and lived experience. Disrupting existing whitewashed representations must be at the center of what it means to engage with *unruly Latinidades*, or perhaps to be unruly Latinxs. This reimagining is necessary, and thus the study of Latinxs demands fluidity rather than a solidification of terms. In the same way that we must actively shift these white supremacist framings—and in this way *refuse* certain Latinidades—we must also refuse particular (and similarly white supremacist) narratives about what anthropology is and is not.

The future of Latinx anthropology—and Latinx studies for that matter—requires a reckoning with and reevaluation of the construction of Latinidad itself. If we are to imagine Latinidad as a site of refusal and representation, we should be more expansive in our storytelling and include not only Indigenous and African legacies and histories but also the journey of Asian, Middle East, and other ethnicities to Latin America and thus delve into other equally complex histories across the Americas and in the United States. And yet, while we may be moving toward an inclusive Latinidad, there exist silences, restrictions, and hierarchies that will continue to exclude and place some at the margins. For some of us, it is difficult to embrace Latinidad, having been left outside of it, having to prove that our race, our name, our history ought to be included. For Mann-Hamilton, it is from those margins and in delving into the multiple episodes of movement and migration in his own family history that he has constructed a more expansive vision and understanding. He was born—to a Black Dominican mother—and raised in Puerto Rico; his family hails from Cuba, Nevis, and various African American communities on the Eastern Seaboard of the United States who migrated to the Republic of Haiti and subsequently became Dominicans. There are many like him who refuse to let their own Latinx reality be left out of the broader narratives of Latinidad.

Regional conceptualizations of Latinidad also played a distinct role in Díaz's life. As a Puerto Rican raised in southern California—where less than 1 percent of the population is Puerto Rican—her Latinidad was often illegible to the predominantly Mexican Latinxs in California.[9] She became the first non-Chicanx officer of her high school's MEChA, but not without controversy. As a child, her father's forced migration from Puerto Rico during Operation Bootstrap landed him in East Harlem, where he was part of a large Caribbean migrant community. After moves back and forth between Puerto Rico and New York, he moved to southern California as a young adult, where he was derogatorily racialized as both Mexican and African American. As a member of the Young Socialist Alliance (YSA) and the Young Lords in New York and a writer for the Socialist Worker Party's newspaper the *Militant*, he established himself as an activist in California. Building community through local work with the YSA and the *Militant*, he eventually became one of the few Puerto Ricans to play a key organizing role in the Chicano Moratorium. His activism and inclusion in the Chicano movement not only represented the beginnings of a more inclusive Latinidad—his writings about and speeches at the Moratorium also underscored the kind of collaboration and anticolonial, anti-imperial coalition building previously mentioned.[10] These family histories are not merely anecdotal. Rather, they demonstrate the embodied knowledge and intergenerational struggles we all carry with us. These are the stories that led us to this work, that led to this book, as we all continue the work of our ancestors in our distinct refusals of the status quo.

Ethnographic Refusals, Unruly Latinidades addresses two pressing and interwoven concerns, which have intellectual, communal, and individual consequences: the erasures of Latinidad and of anthropology. In the case of the latter, while the discipline is constantly undergoing critique and reevaluation of its racist and colonial roots, we have yet to see a systematic overhaul of anthropological practice (as the foreword and many of the chapters in this volume make clear). In their work on institutional racism and white supremacy, Jonathan Rosa and Vanessa Díaz take anthropological empiricism and ethnographic exceptionalism to task, noting that "the privileging of anthropological empiricism, too often prevents scholars of color—particularly those writing about communities close to home—from being viewed as legitimate theorists or even legitimate anthropologists and instead consistently relegates their conceptualizations to the 'savage slot' (Trouillot 2003)."[11] Indeed, the authors' ethnographic refusal is itself a refusal of dominant anthropological orders in favor of "intersectional feminist conceptions of theory in the flesh" as methodological approach and theoretical framing, otherwise.[12]

As Latinx anthropologists, we have historically felt a need and responsibility to critically address the effects of power on our communities. Thus, turning our ethnographic lens toward our friends, families, communities, and our daily lives necessitates a refusal of status quo approaches to fieldwork and the white supremacist canon of anthropological "theory." As this collection demonstrates, it requires a remaking of social analyses to recall the work of anthropologist Renato Rosaldo. It requires serious listening in solidarity and an ethical grappling with our role as "outsiders within."[13] To illustrate this point, for instance, Lemus came of age in a small rural community in the state of Jalisco, Mexico. Before Lemus was born, his father, Don Luis, had traveled as a farm worker in the mid-1970s to Riverside, California, to pick oranges and to Idaho to pick potatoes. He later worked at a ranch in Idaho before moving to Chicago in the late 1980s. In 1995 Don Luis brought his family north of the Rio Grande and settled in Chicago. Now living and working in the border state of Texas years later, Lemus's personal history has shaped how he writes about borders and working-class life and his perspective that we cannot understand society at large without grappling with its border-making and ordering process. Indeed, his early experiences of crossing borders inform his approach to the discipline, for his perspectives on the relationship between culture, power, the state, and capitalism center around how that very nexus produces disciplinary borders and the disciplining of anthropology as a whole.[14] Given the complexity of our—the authors of this afterword—experiences and histories, the question remains: how will these connections be accounted for, expressed, and incorporated not only within the conceptual framings of Latinidad but also within the institutions that promote its study?

The *longue durée* of racial and ethnic uniformity in scholarship and research in American anthropology is also a question of exclusion—not only at the level of scholarship but also in hiring practices. While an increase in BIPOC faculty at predominately white institutions (PWI) came in the wake of the movements for ethnic studies in the 1960s and 1970s, there still exists an extreme lack of underrepresented minority faculty members in the ranks of academia.[15] This lack of representation is structurally driven by "gatekeepers" operating within disciplinary "decision-making" rooms—spaces that impede the democratization of higher education.[16] As a result, very few of us have had the privilege of being trained as anthropologists by someone who looked like us or shared our background. To transform the predominantly white institutional space of the academy, we need to ask: where will the next generations of Latinx anthropologists come from? And who will be there to train and work with them?[17] Addressing the fundamental problem of a lack of diverse Latinx faculty in anthropology is one of the many steps to achieve greater accountability and equity—thus a demand for the inclusion of Afro-Latinx, Indigenous Latinx, and Queer Latinx faculty and students should be a priority.[18]

Beyond the uncertain future(s) of anthropology also lies the uncertain future of academia more broadly. Many—if not most—colleges and universities are unclear about what lies ahead in a post-COVID pandemic world. While disciplines and institutions may cease to exist or radically transform their practices in the production of knowledge, we will still be here, our communities will still be here, our scholarship will still be here—irrespective of academic approval. And so, as our present context pushes us to imagine the ends of disciplines and academia, we must also imagine potential futures, however uncertain. For in the face of long-standing histories of exclusion, oppression, criminalization, and of coercing opposition into submission, equally long-standing projects and movements for justice and freedom have persisted. This volume attests to all of this in rich ethnographic detail and reminds us to claim our rightful space at the anthropological table by refusing to let Latinx anthropology be left out of contemporary conversations about American anthropology or to let colonial disciplines validate or confine us.

Notes

1. We have also seen an escalation of forms of harassment of Black people (Amy Cooper to Christian Cooper).

2. Cullors-Brignac 2020.

3. Jobson 2020.

4. Shange 2019, 9.

5. Mann-Hamilton 2018; ALLA 2020.

6. Blanca E. Vega, "Hey 'woke' Latinxs who are comfortable making White people uncomfortable: it might be time to make Latinxs uncomfortable for

their antiBlack comments, jokes, values, beliefs, and practices. It's NOT time to protect Latinidad. It's time to disrupt it. Besitos," August 2, 2020, 6:40 a.m., https://twitter.com/blancavnyc/status/1289919125934940160?s=1.

7. Dávila 2008.

8. Gates 2012, 2.

9. US Census Bureau 2010.

10. Díaz 2012, 129,

11. Rosa and Díaz 2019, 127.

12. Ibid.

13. Rosaldo 1989; Harrison 2008.

14. Lemus 2015.

15. Zambrana 2018, 57.

16. Rosaldo 1989, xi.

17. See Lugo 2010.

18. Yet, given the unwelcoming environment at PWI, the successful recruitment of underrepresented minority faculty member must also be coupled with retention efforts, mentoring plans, attention to community building, and access to academic and professional development. Perhaps most importantly, these faculty should not be expected to shoulder the diversity work alone.

Acosta, Katie L. 2014. *Amiga y Amantes: Sexually Nonconforming Latinas Negotiate Family*. New Brunswick, NJ: Rutgers University Press.

Ainsworth, Tiffiny A., and Jeffrey H. Spiegel. 2010. "Quality of Life of Individuals with and without Facial Feminization Surgery or Gender Reassignment Surgery." *Quality of Life Research* 19 (7): 1019–24.

Alvord, Daniel R., Cecilia Menjívar, and Andrea Gómez Cervantes. 2018. "The Legal Violence in the 2017 Executive Orders: The Expansion of Immigrant Criminalization in Kansas." *Social Currents* 5 (5): 411–20.

Alexander, M. Jacqui. 2005. *Pedagogies of Crossing: Meditations on Feminism, Sexual Politics, Memory, and the Sacred*. Durham, NC: Duke University Press.

Alexander, Michelle. 2010. *The New Jim Crow: Mass Incarceration in the Age of Colorblindness*. New York City: New Press.

Alicea, Marisa, and Marua Toro-Morn. 2018. "Puerto Rican Chicago *Dice Presente*: Preliminary Reflections on Community Responses to Hurricanes Irma and Maria." *Latino Studies* 16 (4): 548–58.

Amezcua, Michael. Forthcoming. *The Second City Anew: Mexicans, Urban Culture, and Migration in the Transformation of Chicago, 1940–1986*. Chicago: University of Chicago Press.

Anzaldúa, Gloria. 2007. *Borderlands/La Frontera: The New Mestiza*, 3rd ed. San Francisco: Aunt Lute Books.

———. 2009a. "El Mundo Zurdo" In *The Gloria Anzaldúa Reader*, edited by Gloria Anzaldúa and AnaLouise Keating, 195–96. Durham: Duke University Press.

———. 2009b. "(Un)natural Bridges, (Un)safe Spaces." Anzaldúa and Keating, *Gloria Anzaldúa Reader*, 242–43.

———. 2015. *Light in the Dark/Luz en lo Oscuro: Rewriting Identity, Spirituality, Reality*. Edited by AnaLouise Keating. Durham, NC: Duke University Press.

Aparicio, Ana. 2018. "The Politics of Gender in Suburban Public Space." In *Gender: Space*, edited by Aimee Cox. Farmington Hills: Macmillan.

Aparicio, Frances R., and Susana Chávez-Silverman. 1997. *Tropicalizations: Transcultural Representations of Latinidad*. Hanover, NH: University Press of New England.

Appadurai, Arjun. 2013. *The Future as Cultural Fact: Essays on the Global Condition*. London: Verso Books.

Arnason, Arnar. 2012. *Landscapes beyond Land: Routes, Aesthetics, Narratives*. New York: Berghahn.

Arndt, Grant. 2014. "The Emergence of Indigeneity and the Politics of Race and Culture in Native North America." *Reviews in Anthropology* 43 (1): 79–105.

Arvizu, Steven F., James Diego Vigil, Juan Castañon García, Sam Rios, Senon Valadez, Carlos H. Arce, Margarita B. Melville, and Esteban Villa. 1978. "Decolonizing Anthropology." *Grito del Sol* 3 (2).

Asian Communities for Reproductive Justice and SisterSong. 2005. "A New Vision for Advancing Our Movement for Reproductive Health, Reproductive Rights and Reproductive Justice." Oakland: Asian Communities for Reproductive Justice.

Association of Latina/o & Latinx Anthropologists. 2020. "Statement against Anti-Black Racism." http://alla.americananthro.org/.

Ayala, César, and Rafael Bernabe. 2007. *Puerto Rico in the American Century: A History since 1898*. Chapel Hill: University of North Carolina Press.

Balaguera, Martha. 2018. "Trans-Migrations: Agency and Confinement at the Limits of Sovereignty." In "Displacement," edited by Denise Horne and Serena Parekh. Special issue, *Signs: Journal of Women in Culture and Society* 43 (3): 641–64.

Balcázar, Héctor, Matilde Alvarado, Mary Luna Hollen, Yanira Gonzalez-Cruz, and Verónica Pedregón. 2005. "Evaluation of Salud para Su Corazón (Health for Your Heart)—National Council of La Raza Promotora Outreach Program." *Preventing Chronic Disease: Public Health Research, Practice, and Policy* 2 (3): A09.

Barry, Kathleen. 1996. *The Prostitution of Sexuality: The Global Exploitation of Women*. New York: New York University Press.

Batalova, Jeanne, Michael Fix, and Mark Greenberg. 2019. "Millions Will Feel Chilling Effects of U.S. Public-Charge Rule That Is Also Likely to Reshape Legal Immigration." Migration Policy Institute, Washington, DC. https://www.migra tionpolicy.org/news/chilling-effects-us-public-charge-rule-commentary #:~:text=August%202019-,Millions%20Will%20Feel%20Chilling%20Effects %20of%20U.S.%20Public%2DCharge%20Rule,Likely%20to%20Reshape %20Legal%20Immigration&text=The%20rule%20will%20foreseeably%20 have,admissions%20and%20adjustments%20of%20status.

Bauman, Zygmunt. 1998. *Globalization: The Human Consequences*. New York: Columbia University Press.

Bearak, Jonathan, Rachel K. Jones, Elizabeth Nash, and Megan K. Donovan. 2020. "COVID-19 Abortion Bans Would Greatly Increase Driving Distances for Those Seeking Care." Guttmacher Institute. https://www.guttmacher.org /article/2020/04/covid-19-abortion-bans-would-greatly-increase-driving -distances-those-seeking-care.

Behar, Ruth. 1996. *The Vulnerable Observer: Anthropology That Breaks Your Heart*. Boston: Beacon Press.

Behar, Ruth, and Deborah A. Gordon, eds. 1995. *Women Writing Culture*. Berkeley: University of California Press.

Beliso-De Jesús. 2015. *Electric Santería: Racial and Sexual Assemblages of Transnational Religion*. New York: Columbia University Press.

Bennet, Larry, Bennett, Roberta Garner, and Euan Hague, eds. 2017. *Neoliberal Chicago*. Urbana: University of Illinois Press.

Berlant, Lauren. 2006. "'Cruel Optimism.' Differences: A Journal of Feminist." *Cultural Studies* 17 (3): 20–36.

———. 2007. "Slow Death (Sovereignty, Obesity, Lateral Agency)." *Critical Inquiry* 33 (4): 754–80.

Berry, Maya J., Claudia Chávez Argüelles, Shanya Cordis, Sarah Ihmoud, and Elizabeth Velásquez Estrada. 2017. "Toward a Fugitive Anthropology: Gender, Race, and Violence in the Field." *Cultural Anthropology* 32 (4): 537–65.

Betancur, John J., and Janet L. Smith. 2016. *Claiming Neighborhood: New Ways of Understanding Urban Change*. Urbana: University of Illinois Press.

Blackwell, Maylei, Floridalma Boj Lopez, and Luis Urrieta. 2017. "Special Issue: Critical Latinx Indigeneities." In "Critical Latinx Indigeneities," special issue, *Latino Studies* 15 (2): 126–37.

Bloemraad, Irene, and Christine Trost. "It's a Family Affair: Intergenerational Mobilization in the Spring 2006 Protests." 2008. *American Behavioral Scientist* 52 (4): 507–32.

Boas, Franz. *Race, Language, and Culture*. 1982. Chicago: University of Chicago Press.

Bonilla, Yarimar. 2020. "The Coloniality of Disaster." *Political Geography* 78:102181.

Bookman, Ann, and Sandra Morgen, eds. 1988. *Women and the Politics of Empowerment*. Philadelphia: Temple University Press.

Brands, Hal. 2009. *Mexico's Narco-Insurgency and U.S. Counterdrug Policy*. Carlisle, PA: Strategic Studies Institute, US Army War College.

Braunstein, Ruth, Todd Nicholas Fuist, and Rhys H. Williams. 2017. *Religion and Progressive Activism: New Stories about Faith and Politics*. New York: New York University Press.

Breitbart, Myrna. 1998. "'Dana's Mystical Tunnel': Young People's Designs for Survival and Change in the City." In *Cool Places: Geographies of Youth Cultures*, edited by Tracey Skelton and Gill Valentine, 305–28. New York: Routledge.

Brennan, Denise. 2004. *What's Love Got to Do with It?: Transnational Desires and Sex Tourism in the Dominican Republic*. Durham, NC: Duke University Press.

Briggs, Laura. 2017. *How All Politics Became Reproductive Politics: From Welfare Reform to Foreclosure to Trump*. Berkeley: University of California Press.

Brodkin, Karen. 1998. *How Jews Became White Folks and What That Says about Race in America*. New Brunswick: Rutgers University Press.

Bruce, Caitlin Frances. 2016. "Challenging National Borders and Local Genre Forms: Declaration of Immigration as Volatile Cultural Text." *Public Art Dialogue* 6 (2): 206–27.

Bruchac, Margaret M. 2018. *Savage Kin: Indigenous Informants and American Anthropologists*. Native Peoples of the Americas Series. Tucson: University of Arizona Press.

Buff, Rachel. 2018. *Against the Deportation Terror: Organizing for Immigrant Rights in the Twentieth Century*. Philadelphia: Temple University Press.

Bullington, Bruce. 1977. *Heroin Use in the Barrio*. Lexington, MA: Lexington Books.

Butler, Judith. 2004. *Undoing Gender*. New York: Routledge.

Byrd, Jodi A. 2011. *The Transit of Empire: Indigenous Critiques of Colonialism*. Minneapolis: University of Minnesota Press.

Cabezas, Amalia L. 2009. Economies of Desire: *Sex and Tourism in Cuba and the Dominican Republic*. Philadelphia: Temple University Press.

Cacho, Lisa. 2012. *Social Death: Racialized Rightlessness and the Criminalization of the Unprotected*. New York: New York University Press.

Caldwell, Kia Lilly, Kathleen Coll, Tracy Fisher, Renya K. Ramirez, and Lok Siu, eds. 2009. *Gendered Citizenships: Transnational Perspectives on Knowledge Production, Political Activism, and Culture*. New York: Palgrave Macmillan.

Campos, Isaac. 2018. "Mexicans and the Origins of Marijuana Prohibition in the United States: A Reassessment." *Social History of Alcohol and Drugs* 32:6–37.

Carney, Megan A., and Keegan C. Krause. 2020. "Immigration/Migration and Healthy Publics: The Threat of Food Insecurity." *Palgrave Communications* 6 (93): 1–12.

Castañeda, Quetzil E. 1996. *In the Museum of Maya Culture: Touring Chichén Itzá*. Minneapolis: University of Minnesota Press.

Castanha, Anthony. 2011. *The Myth of Indigenous Caribbean Extinction: Continuity and Reclamation in Borikén (Puerto Rico)*. New York: Palgrave Macmillan.

Center for Reproductive Rights, and National Latina Institute for Reproductive Health. 2013. "Nuestra Voz, Nuestra Salud, Nuestro Texas: The Fight for Women's Reproductive Health in the Rio Grande Valley." New York: Center for Reproductive Rights and National Latina Institute for Reproductive Health.

———. 2015a. "Nuestro Texas: A Reproductive Justice Agenda for Latinas." New York: Center for Reproductive Rights and National Latina Institute for Reproductive Health.

———. 2015b. "Somos Poderosas! A Human Rights Hearing in the Rio Grande

Valley." New York: Center for Reproductive Rights and National Latina Institute for Reproductive Health.

Center for Reproductive Rights, National Latina Institute for Reproductive Health, and SisterSong Women of Color Reproductive Justice Collective. 2014. "Reproductive Injustice: Racial and Gender Discrimination in U.S. Health Care, a Shadow Report for the UN Committee on the Elimination of Racial Discrimination." New York: Center for Reproductive Rights.

Chávez, Alex E. 2017. *Sounds of Crossing: Music, Migration, and the Aural Poetics of Huapango Arribeño*. Durham, NC: Duke University Press.

Chavez, Leo. 1998. *Shadowed Lives: Undocumented Immigrants in American Society*. Boston: Wadworth.

———. 2008. *The Latino Threat: Constructing Immigrants, Citizens, and the Nation*. Stanford, CA: Stanford University Press.

———. 2013. The Latino Threat: Constructing Immigrants, Citizens, and the Nation. 2nd ed. Stanford: Stanford University Press.

Chawla, Devika. 2014. *Home, Uprooted: Stories of India's Partition*. New York: Fordham University Press.

Cheng, Wendy. 2013. *The Changs Next Door to the Diazes: Remapping Race in Suburban California*. Minneapolis: University of Minnesota Press.

Chilton, Mariana, Maureen M. Black, Carol Berkowitz, Patrick H. Casey, John Cook, Diana Cutts, Ruth Rose Jacobs, Timothy Heeren, Stephanie Ettinger de Cuba, Sharon Coleman, Alan Meyers, and Deborah A. Frank. 2009. "Food Insecurity and Risk of Poor Health among US-Born Children of Immigrants." *American Journal of Public Health* 99 (3): 556–62.

Cintron, Ralph. 2007. *Angel's Town: Chero Ways, Gang Life, and Rhetorics of the Everyday*. Boston: Beacon.

Clark, D. Anthony Tyeeme, and Malea Powell. 2008. "Resisting Exile in the 'Land of the Free': Indigenous Groundwork at Colonial Intersections." *American Indian Quarterly* 32 (1): 1–15.

Clifford, James. 1977. "Spatial Practices: Fieldwork, Travel, and the Disciplining of Anthropology" In Gupta and Ferguson, *Anthropological Locations*, 185–222.

Clifford, James, and George Marcus, eds. 1986. *Writing Culture: The Poetics and Politics of Ethnography*. Berkeley: University of California Press.

Cohen, Cathy J. 2004. "Deviance as Resistance: A New Research Agenda for the Study of Black Politics." *Du Bois Review: Social Science Research on Race* 1 (1): 27–45.

Collins, Patricia Hill, and Sirma Bilge. 2016. *Intersectionality*. Malden, MA: Polity.

Committee on Minorities and Anthropology. 1973. "The Minority Experience in

Anthropology." American Anthropological Association. https://www.ameri
cananthro.org/ParticipateAndAdvocate/Content.aspx?ItemNumber=1514.

Correa-Cabrera, Guadalupe. 2017. *Los Zetas: Criminal Corporations, Energy, and Civil War in Mexico*. Austin: University of Texas Press.

Cotera, María Eugenia. 2008. *Native Speakers: Ella Deloria, Zora Neale Hurston, Jovita González, and the Poetics of Culture*. Austin: University of Texas Press, 2008.

Coulthard, Glen S. 2014. *Red Skin, White Masks: Rejecting the Colonial Politics of Recognition*. Minneapolis: University of Minnesota Press.

Craven, Christa, and Dána-Ain Davis, eds. 2013. *Feminist Activist Ethnography: Counterpoints to Neoliberalism in North America*. Lanham, MD: Lexington.

Crenshaw, Kimberlé. 1991. "Mapping the Margins: Intersectionality, Identity Politics and Violence against Women of Color." *Stanford Law Review* 43:1241–99.

Cuevas, T. Jackqueline. 2018. *Post-Borderlandia: Chicana Literature and Gender Variant Critique*. New Brunswick, NJ: Rutgers University Press.

Cunningham, Hilary. 1995. *God and Caesar at the Rio Grande: Sanctuary and the Politics of Religion*. Minneapolis: University of Minnesota Press.

Daughtry, J. Martin. 2015. "Acoustic Palimpsests and the Politics of Listening." *Music & Politics* 7 (1): 1–34.

Dávila, Arlene. 1997. *Sponsored Identities: Cultural Politics in Puerto Rico*. Philadelphia: Temple University Press.

———. 2001. "Local/Diasporic Taínos: Towards a Cultural Politics of Memory, Reality, and Imagery." In *Taíno Revival: Critical Perspectives on Puerto Rican Identity and Cultural Politics*, edited by Gabriel Haslip-Viera, 33–55. Princeton, NJ: Markus Wiener.

———. 2004. *Barrio Dreams: Puerto Ricans, Latinos, and the Neoliberal City*. Berkeley: University of California Press.

———. 2008. *Latino Spin: Public Image and the Whitewashing of Race*. New York: New York University Press.

———. 2012. *Culture Works: Space, Value, and Mobility across the Neoliberal Americas*. New York: New York University Press.

———. 2020. *Latinx Art: Artists, Markets, Politics*. Durham, NC: Duke University Press.

Davis, Dana-Ain. 2007. "Narrating the Mute: Racializing and Racism in a Neoliberal Moment." *Souls* 9 (4): 346–60.

Dawson, Ruth, and Adam Sonfield. 2020. "Conservatives Are Using the Intersection of Immigration, Health Care and Reproductive Rights Policy to Undermine Them All." *Guttmacher Policy Review* 23:19–25.

Day, R. Sue. 2004. *Nourishing the Future: The Case for Community-Based Nutrition Research in the Lower Rio Grande Valley*. Houston: University of Texas School of Public Health at Houston.

Debrix, François. 2017. *Global Powers of Horror: Security, Politics, and the Body in Pieces*. London: Taylor and Francis.

De Genova, Nicholas. 2004. "The Legal Production of Mexican/Migrant 'Illegality.'" *Latino Studies* 2 (2): 160–85.

———. 2005. *Working the Boundaries: Race, Space, and "Illegality" in Mexican Chicago*. Durham, NC: Duke University Press.

De Genova, Nicholas, and Ana Y. Ramos-Zayas. 2003. *Latino Crossings: Mexicans, Puerto Ricans, and the Politics of Race and Citizenship*. New York: Routledge.

De Genova, Nicholas and Nathalie Peutz, eds. (with William Walters and Galina Cornelisse). 2010. *The Deportation Regime: Sovereignty, Space, and the Freedom of Movement*. Durham: Duke University Press.

De Lara, Juan D. 2018. *Inland Shift: Race, Space, and Capital in Inland Southern California*. Berkeley: University of California Press.

Del Castillo, Adelaida R. 2007. "Illegal Status and Social Citizenship: Thoughts on Mexican Immigrants in a Postnational World." In *Women and Migration in the U.S.-Mexico Borderlands: A Reader*, edited by Denise A. Segura and Patricia Zavella, 92–103. Durham, NC: Duke University Press.

De León, Jason. 2015. *The Land of Open Graves: Living and Dying on the Migrant Trail*. Berkeley: University of California Press.

Delgado, Melvin, and Keva Barton. 1998. "Murals in Latino Communities: Social Indicators of Community Strengths." *Social Work* 43 (4): 346–56.

Della Penna, Craig. 1997. *Holyoke*. Charleston, SC: Arcadia.

Den Ouden, Amy E. 2005. *Beyond Conquest: Native Peoples and the Struggle for History in New England*. Lincoln: University of Nebraska Press.

de Onís, Catalina. 2017. "What's in an 'X'? An Exchange about the Politics of 'Latinx.'" *Chiricú Journal: Latina/o Literatures, Arts, and Cultures* 1 (2): 78–91.

Desai, Manisha. 2013. "The Possibilities and Perils for Scholar-Activists and Activist-Scholars: Reflections on the Feminist Dialogues." In *Insurgent Encounters: Transnational Activism, Ethnography, and the Political*, edited by Jeffrey S. Juris and Alex Khasnabish, 89–107. Durham, NC: Duke University Press.

Diaz, David, and Rodolfo Torres. 2012. *Latino Urbanism: The Politics of Planning, Policy, and Redevelopment*. New York: New York University Press.

Díaz, Vanessa. 2017. "'De Puerto Rico a Nueva York, de Puerto Rico a California': A Micro-History of Puerto Rican Activism and Pan-Ethnic Alliance in Southern California." In "The Legacies of Puerto Rican Social, Cultural, and

Political Activism in the United States," special issue, *Latino(a) Research Review*.

Díaz-Barriga, Miguel, and Margaret E. Dorsey. 2020. *Fencing in Democracy: Border Walls, Necrocitizenship, and the Security State*. Durham, NC: Duke University Press.

Duggan, Lisa, and José Esteban Munoz. 2009. "Hope and Hopelessness: A Dialogue." *Women and Performance: A Journal of Feminist Theory* 19 (2): 276–83.

Dunn, Timothy J. 1996. *The Militarization of the US-Mexico Border, 1978–1992: Low-Intensity Conflict Doctrine Comes Home*. Austin: University of Texas at Austin Center for Mexican American Studies, 1996.

Ellison, Treva, Kai M. Green, Matt Richardson, and C. Riley Snorton. 2016. "We Got Issues: Toward a Black Trans*/Studies." *TSQ: Transgender Studies Quarterly* 4 (2): 162–69.

Erlmann, Veit, ed. 2004. *Hearing Cultures: Essays on Sound, Listening and Modernity*. Oxford: Berg.

Facio, Elisa. 2014. "Spirit Journey: 'Home' as a Site for Healing and Transformation." In *Fleshing the Spirit: Spirituality and Activism in Chicana, Latina, and Indigenous Women's Lives*, edited by Elisa Facio and Irene Lara, 60–67. Tucson: University of Arizona Press.

Fanon, Frantz. (1961) 2004. *The Wretched of the Earth*. Translated by Richard Philcox. New York: Grove Press.

Farmer, Paul, Philippe Bourgois, Didier Fassin, Linda Green, H. K. Heggenhougen, Laurence Kirmayer, and Loc Wacquant. 2004. "An Anthropology of Structural Violence." *Current Anthropology* 45 (3): 305–25.

Farr, Marcia. 2004. *Ethnolinguistic Chicago: Language and Literacy in the City's Neighborhoods*. Mahwah, NJ: Lawrence Erlbaum.

———. 2006. *Rancheros in Chicagoacán: Language and Identity in a Transnational Community*. Austin: University of Texas Press.

Fassin, Didier, ed. 2017. *If Truth Be Told: The Politics of Public Ethnography*. Durham, NC: Duke University Press.

Fazio, Carlos. 2016. *Estado de emergencia: De la guerra de Calderón a la guerra de Peña Nieto*. Mexico City: Penguin Random House Grupo Editorial Mexico.

Federici, Silvia. 2004. *Caliban and the Witch*. New York: Autonomedia.

Feld, Steve, and Keith Basso. 1996. *Senses of Place*. Santa Fe: School for Advanced Research Press.

Feliciano, Zadia M., and Andrew Green. 2017. "US Multinationals in Puerto Rico and the Repeal of Section 936 Tax Exemption for U.S. Corporations." Working paper, National Bureau of Economic Research.

Ficek, Rosa E. 2018. "Infrastructure and Colonial Difference in Puerto Rico after Hurricane María." *Transforming Anthropology* 26 (2): 102–17.

Flores, Juan. 2000. *From Bomba to Hip-Hop: Puerto Rican Culture and Latino Identity.* New York: Columbia University Press.

———. 2009. *The Diaspora Strikes Back: Caribeño Tales of Learning and Turning.* New York: Taylor and Francis.

Flores, William V., and Rina Benmayor, eds. 1997. *Latino Cultural Citizenship: Claiming Identity, Space and Rights.* Boston: Beacon.

Forster-Cox, Susan, Thenral Mangadu, Benjamín Jacquez, and Adriana Corona. 2007. "The Effectiveness of the Promotora (Community Health Worker) Model of Intervention for Improving Pesticide Safety in US/Mexico Border Homes." *Californian Journal of Health Promotion* 5 (1): 62–75.

Foucault, Michel. 1982. "The Subject and Power." *Critical Inquiry* 8 (4): 777–95.

———. 1995. *Discipline and Punish: The Birth of the Prison.* Translated by Alan Sheridan. New York: Vintage.

Foucault, Michel, and François Ewald. 2003. *"Society Must Be Defended": Lectures at the Collège de France, 1975–1976.* Vol. 1. New York: Macmillan.

Galarte, Francisco. 2014. "On Trans* Chican@: Amor, Justicia, y Dignidad." *Aztlán: A Journal of Chicano Studies* 39 (1): 229–36.

Gálvez, Alyshia. 2013. "Immigrant Citizenship: Neoliberalism, Immobility and the Vernacular Meaning of Citizenship." *Identities: Global Studies in Culture and Power* 20 (6): 720–37.

Garcia, Lorena. 2012. *Respect Yourself, Protect Yourself: Latina Girls and Sexual Identity.* New York: New York University Press.

Garcia, Maria Elena. 2000. "Ethnographic Responsibility and the Anthropological Endeavor: Beyond Identity Discourse." *Anthropological Quarterly* 73 (2): 89–101.

Garcia, Matt. 2013. "A Moveable Feast: The UFW Grape Boycott and Farm Worker Justice." In "Strikes and Social Conflicts," special issue, *International Labor and Working-Class History* 83:146–53.

Gates, Henry Louis, Jr. 2012. *Black in Latin America.* New York: NYU Press.

Gavrilova, Evelina, Takuma Makada, and Floris Zoutman. 2019. "Is Legal Pot Crippling Mexican Drug Trafficking Organisations? The Effect of Medical Marijuana Laws on US Crime." *Economic Journal* 129 (617): 375–407.

Gilliland, Maude T. 1968. *Horsebackers of the Brush Country: A Story of Texas Rangers and Mexican Smugglers.* Brownsville, TX: Springman-King Lithograph.

Gilmore, Ruth Wilson. 2002. "Fatal Couplings of Power and Difference: Notes on Racism and Geography." *Professional Geographer* 54 (1): 15–24.

———. 2007. *Golden Gulag: Prisons, Surplus, Crisis, and Opposition in Globalizing California.* Berkeley: University of California Press.

———. 2008. "Forgotten Places and the Seeds of Grassroots Planning." In *Engaging Contradictions: Theory, Politics, and Methods of Activist Scholarship*, edited by Charles R. Hale, 31–61. Berkeley: University of California Press, 2008.

Glenn, Evelyn Nakano. 2015. "Settler Colonialism as Structure: A Framework for Comparative Studies of US Race and Gender Formation." *Sociology of Race and Ethnicity* 1 (1): 52–72.

Golash Boza, Tanya. 2015. *Deported: Immigrant Policing, Disposable Labor, and Global Capitalism.* New York: New York University Press.

Gold, Rachel Benson, and Adam Sonfield. 2019. "Title X Family Planning Services: Impactful but at Severe Risk." Guttmacher Institute. https://www.guttmacher .org/article/2019/10/title-x-family-planning-services-impactful-severe-risk.

Gold, Rachel Benson, and Kinsey Hasstedt. 2016. "Lessons from Texas: Widespread Consequences of Assaults on Abortion Access." *American Journal of Public Health* 106 (6): 970–71.

Goldstein, Alyosha. 2016. "Promises Are Over: Puerto Rico and the Ends of Decolonization." *Theory & Event* 19 (4). Available at muse.jhu.edu/article/633271.

Gomberg-Muñoz, R. 2010. *Labor and Legality: An Ethnography of a Mexican Immigrant Network.* Issues of Globalization: Case Studies in Contemporary Anthropology. Oxford: Oxford University Press.

Gonzalez, Gilbert G., and Raul A. Fernandez. 2003. *A Century of Chicano History: Empire, Nations, and Migration.* New York: Routledge.

Gonzales, Roberto G., and Leo R. Chavez. 2012. "'Awakening to a Nightmare': Abjectivity and Illegality in the Lives of Undocumented 1.5-Generation Latino Immigrants in the United States." *Current Anthropology* 53 (3): 255–81.

Gooberman, Lawrence A. 1974. *Operation Intercept: The Multiple Consequences of Public Policy.* Elmsford, NY: Pergamon.

Góralska, Magdalena. 2020. "Anthropology from Home: Advice on Digital Ethnography for the Pandemic Times." *Anthropology in Action* 27 (1): 46–52.

Green, Kai M. 2017. "Trans* Movement/Trans* Moment: An Afterword." *International Journal of Qualitative Studies in Education* 30 (3): 320–21.

Gregory, Steven. 1998. *Black Corona: Race and the Politics of Place in an Urban Community.* Princeton, NJ: Princeton University Press.

Griffin, Michael, and Jennie Weiss Block, eds. 2013. *In the Company of the Poor: Conversations with Dr. Paul Farmer and Fr. Gustavo Gutiérrez.* New York: Orbis.

Grosfoguel, Ramón. 2003. *Colonial Subjects: Puerto Ricans in a Global Perspective.* Berkeley: University of California Press.

Grossman, Daniel, Kari White, Kristine Hopkins, and Joseph E. Potter. 2014. "The Public Health Threat of Anti-Abortion Legislation." *Contraception* 89: 73–74.

Guerra, Santiago. 2015. "*La Chota y Los Mafiosos*: Mexican American Casualties of the Border Drug War." *Latino Studies* 13 (2): 227–44.

Gupta, Akhil, and James Ferguson. 2010. "Discipline and Practice." In *Anthropological Locations: Boundaries and Grounds of a Field Science*, edited by Gupta and Ferguson, 12–15. Berkeley: University of California Press.

Gutiérrez, Elena R. 2008. *Fertile Matters: The Politics of Mexican-Origin Women's Reproduction*. Austin: University of Texas Press.

Guttmacher Institute. 2014. "More State Abortion Restrictions Were Enacted in 2011–2013 Than in the Entire Previous Decade." Guttmacher Institute. https://www.guttmacher.org/article/2014/01/more-state-abortion-restrictions-were-enacted-2011-2013-entire-previous-decade.

Gwaltney, John Langston. 1980. *Drylongso: A Self Portrait of Black America*. New York: Random House.

Hale, Charles R. 2001. "What Is Activist Research?" *Social Science Research Council* 2 (1–2): 13–15.

Hale, Charles R., ed. 2008. *Engaging Contradictions: Theory, Politics, and Methods of Activist Scholarship*. Berkeley: University of California Press.

Hale, Charles R., and Lynn Stephen, eds. 2013. *Otros Saberes: Collaborative Research on Indigenous and Afro-Descendant Cultural Politics*. Santa Fe: School for Advanced Research Press.

Hanlon, Bernadette, and Thomas J. Vicino. 2007. "The Decline of the Inner Suburbs: The New Suburban Gothic in the United States." *Geography Compass* 1 (3): 641–56.

Harney, Stefano, and Fred Moten. 2013. *The Undercommons: Fugitive Planning and Black Study*. Brooklyn, NY: Minor Compositions.

Harrison, Faye Venetia. 1997. *Decolonizing Anthropology: Moving Further toward an Anthropology of Liberation*. Arlington, VA: Association of Black Anthropologists, American Anthropological Association.

———. 2008. *Outsider Within: Reworking Anthropology in the Global Age*. Urbana: University of Illinois Press.

Heiner, Brady Thomas. 2007. "Foucault and the Black Panthers." *Cityscape* 11 (3): 313–56.

Henry K. Kaiser Foundation, The. 2018. "Key Facts About the Uninsured Population." Menlo Park, CA: Henry K. Kaiser Foundation.

Hill, Sarah. 2003. "Metaphoric Enrichment and Material Poverty: The Making of

'Colonias.'" In *Ethnography at the Border*, edited by Pablo Vila, 141–65. Minneapolis: University of Minnesota Press.

Hobson, Emily. 2016. *Lavender and Red: Liberation and Solidarity in the Gay and Lesbian Left*. Berkeley: University of California Press.

Holloway, John. 2002. *Change the World without Taking Power*. London: Pluto.

Horton, Sarah Bronwen. 2010. *The Santa Fe Fiesta, Reinvented: Staking Ethno-Nationalist Claims to a Disappearing Homeland*. Santa Fe, NM: School for Advanced Research.

Howes, David. 2005. "Introduction: Empire of the Senses." In *Empire of the Senses: The Sensual Culture Reader*, edited by David Howes, 1–20. Oxford: Berg.

Human Impact Partners and La Unión del Pueblo Entero. 2018. "The Effects of Forced Family Separation in the Rio Grande Valley: A Family Unity, Family Health Research Update." Oakland, CA: Human Impact Partners and La Unión Del Pueblo Entero.

Hurston, Zora Neale. 1990. *Tell My Horse: Voodoo and Life in Haiti and Jamaica*. New York: Harper and Row.

———. 1999. *Their Eyes Were Watching God: A Novel*. New York: HarperCollins.

Hurston, Zora Neale, and Carla Kaplan. 2001. *Every Tongue Got to Confess: Negro Folk-Tales from the Gulf States*. New York: HarperCollins.

Hurston, Zora Neale, and Cheryl A. Wall. 1995. *Folklore, Memoirs, and Other Writings*. New York: Library of the Americas.

Ignatiev, Noel. 1995. *How the Irish Became White*. New York: Routledge, 1995.

Inda, Jonathan Xavier. 2006. *Targeting Immigrants: Government, Technology, and Ethics*. Malden, MA: Wiley-Blackwell.

———. 2010. "Borderzones of Enforcement: Criminalization, Workplace Raids, and Migrant Counterconducts." In *The Contested Politics of Mobility: Borderzones and Irregularity*, edited by Vicki Squire, 74–90. London: Routledge.

Innis-Jiménez, Michael. 2013. *Steel Barrio: The Great Mexican Migration to South Chicago, 1915–1940*. New York: New York University Press.

Jackson, John L. 2005. "Race and the Social Science of Sincerity." *contexts* 4 (4): 38-42.

Jackson, Shona N. 2012. *Creole Indigeneity: Between Myth and Nation in the Caribbean*. Minneapolis: University of Minnesota Press.

Jobson, Ryan Cecil. 2020. "The Case for Letting Anthropology Burn: Sociocultural Anthropology in 2019." *American Anthropologist* 122: 259–71.

Johnson, Gaye Theresa. 2013. *Space of Conflict, Sounds of Solidarity: Music, Race, and Spatial Entitlement in Los Angeles*. Berkeley: University of California Press.

Johnson, Nick. 2017. *Grass Roots: A History of Cannabis in the American West*. Corvallis: Oregon State University Press.

Jones, Delmos. 1970. "Towards a Native Anthropology." *Human Organization* 29 (4): 251–59.

Kertzer, David. 1988. *Ritual, Politics, and Power*. New Haven, CT: Yale University Press.

Klopotek, Brian. 2011. *Recognition Odysseys*. Durham, NC: Duke University Press.

LaBelle, Brandon. 2010. *Acoustic Territories: Sound Culture and Everyday Life*. New York: Bloomsbury.

Lac, A., J. B. Bunger, T. Basáñez, A. Ritt-Olson, D. W. Soto, and L. Baezconde-Garbanati. 2011. "Marijuana Use among Latino Adolescents: Gender Differences in Protective Familial Factors." *Substance Use and Misuse* 46 (5): 644–55.

Lake Research Partners. "Poll: Latino Voters Hold Compassionate Views on Abortion." 2011. Washington, DC: Lake Research Partners.

Lamphere, Louise. 2018. "The Transformation of Ethnography: From Malinowski's Tent to the Practice of Collaborative/Activist Anthropology." *Human Organization* 77 (1): 64–76.

Langhout, Regina Day. 2014. "Photovoice as a Methodology." In *Migration and Health: Research Methods Handbook*, edited by Xóchitl Castañeda, Lainz Rodríguez, and Marc Schenker, 327–42. Berkeley: University of California Press.

Latina Feminist Group. 2001. *Telling to Live: Latina Feminist Testimonios*. Durham, NC: Duke University Press.

Lees, Loretta, Tom Slater, and Elvin Wyly. 2008. *Gentrification*. New York: Routledge.

Lefebvre, Henri. 1991. *The Production of Space*. Malden, MA: Blackwell.

Lemus, Sergio. 2015. "Class, Labor, and Color Hierarchies: An Ethnographic Study of Mexican Yarderos/as in South Chicago." PhD diss., University of Illinois at Urbana-Champaign.

Lewis, Oscar. 1969. "Culture of Poverty." In *On Understanding Poverty: Perspectives from the Social Sciences*, edited by Daniel P. Moynihan, 187–220. New York: Basic Books.

Liebmann, Matthew. 2012. *Revolt: An Archaeological History of Pueblo Resistance and Revitalization in Seventeenth-Century New Mexico*. Tucson: University of Arizona Press.

Liebmann, Mathew, Robert Preucel, and Joseph Aguilar. 2017. "The Pueblo World Transformed: Alliances, Factionalism, and Animosities in the Northern Rio Grande." In *New Mexico and the Primería Alta: The Colonial Period in the American Southwest*, edited by John G. Douglass and William M. Graves, 143–46. Boulder: University Press of Colorado.

Limón, José Eduardo. *Dancing with the Devil: Society and Cultural Poetics in Mexican-American South Texas*. Madison: University of Wisconsin Press, 1994.

Lippard, Lucy. "Trojan Horses: Activist Art and Power." In *Modern Art Culture: A Reader*, edited by Francis Fraschina, 195–209. New York: Routledge, 2009.

Lippert, Randy K., and Sean Rehaag, eds. 2013. *Sanctuary Practices in International Perspectives: Migration, Citizenship, and Social Movements*. New York: Routledge.

Lipsitz, George. 2006. *The Possessive Investment in Whiteness: How White People Profit from Identity Politics*. Philadelphia: Temple University Press, 2006.

———. 2007. *Footsteps in the Dark: The Hidden Histories of Popular Music*. Minneapolis: University of Minnesota Press.

Llorens, Hilda. 2018. "'Imagining Disaster:' Puerto Rico through the Eye of Hurricane Maria," *Transforming Anthropology* 26 (2): 136–56.

Londoño, Johana. 2010. "Latino Design in an Age of Neoliberal Multiculturalism: Contemporary Changes in Latin/o American Urban Cultural Representation." *Identities: Global Studies in Culture and Power* 17 (5): 487–509.

Lonetree, Amy. 2012. *Decolonizing Museums: Representing Native America in National and Tribal Museums*. Chapel Hill: University of North Carolina Press.

Loperena, Christopher A. 2017. "Settler Violence?: Race and Emergent Frontiers of Progress in Honduras." *American Quarterly* 69 (4): 801–7.

López Oro, Paul Joseph. 2016. "'Ni de aquí, ni de allá': Garífuna Subjectivities and the Politics of Diasporic Belonging." In *Afro-Latin@s in Movement*, edited by Petra R. Rivera-Rideau, Jennifer A. Jones, and Tianna S. Paschel, 61–83. New York: Palgrave Macmillan.

López, Iris Ofelia. 2008. *Matters of Choice: Puerto Rican Women's Struggle for Reproductive Freedom*. New Brunswick, NJ: Rutgers University Press.

Loyd, Jenna M., and Alison Mountz. 2018. *Boats, Borders, and Bases: Race, the Cold War, and the Rise of Migration Detention in the United States*. Oakland: University of California Press.

Lugo, Alejandro. 2008. *Fragmented Lives, Assembled Parts: Culture, Capitalism, and Conquest at the US-Mexico Border*. Austin: University of Texas Press, 2008.

———. 2010. "Comments/Reflections." Presented at the "ALLA Book Award Winners Roundtable: Latina and Latino Anthropology for the Next Decade." American Anthropological Association Meetings in New Orleans, November 18, 2010.

Luna, Zakiya, and Kristin Luker. 2013. "Reproductive Justice." *Annual Review of Law and Social Science* 9:327–52.

MacKinnon, Catherine. 1991. "Pornography as Defamation and Discrimination." *Boston University Law Review* 71 (5): 973–818.

Mann-Hamilton, Ryan. 2018. "What Privilege? Mestilegio, Blackness and the Contours of Solidarity." In *White Latino Privilege: Caribbean Latino Perspectives in the Second Decade of the 21st Century*. Edited by Gabriel Haslip-Viera. Bronx, NY: Latino Studies Press.

Manuel, Zenju Earthlyn. 2018. *Sanctuary: A Meditation on Home, Homelessness, and Belonging*. Somerville, MA: Wisdom.

Marable, Manning. 2006. *Living Black History: How Reimagining the African-American Past Can Remake America's Racial Future*. New York: Basic Books.

Martínez-San Miguel, Yolanda. 2011. "Taíno Warriors?: Strategies for Recovering Indigenous Voices in Colonial and Contemporary Hispanic Caribbean Discourses." *Centro Journal* 23 (1).

Marx, Karl. *Capital*. Vol. 1. London: Penguin, 1978.

Masco, Joseph. 2006. *Nuclear Borderlands: The Manhattan Project in Post-Cold War New Mexico*. Princeton, NJ: Princeton University Press.

Maurrasse, David J. 2006. *Listening to Harlem: Gentrification, Community, and Business*. London: Routledge.

May, Vivian M. 2015. *Pursuing Intersectionality, Unsettling Dominant Imaginaries*. New York: Routledge.

Mbembe, Achille. 1992. "The Banality of Power and the Aesthetics of Vulgarity in the Postcolony." *Public Culture* 4 (2): 1–30.

———. 2003. "Necropolitics." *Public Culture* 15 (1): 11–40.

———. 2018. "The Idea of a Borderless World." *Africa's a Country*. https://africasa country.com/2018/11/the-idea-of-a-borderless-world.

Meléndez, Edwin, and Jennifer Hinojosa. 2017. "Estimates of Post-Hurricane Maria Exodus from Puerto Rico." Center for Puerto Rican Studies, Hunter College, https://centropr.hunter.cuny.edu/research/data-center/research-briefs/estimates-post-hurricane-maria-exodus-puerto-rico.

Menjívar, Cecilia, and Leisy Abrego. 2012. "Legal Violence: Immigration Law and the Lives of Central American Immigrants." *American Journal of Sociology* 117 (5): 1380–421.

Merry, Sally Engle. 2006. "Transnational Human Rights and Local Activism: Mapping the Middle." *American Anthropologist* 108 (1): 38–51.

Mier, Nelda, Marcia G. Ory, Dongling Zhan, Martha Conkling, Joseph R. Sharkey, and James N. Burdine. 2008. "Health-Related Quality of Life among Mexican Americans Living in Colonias at the Texas-Mexico Border." *Social Science & Medicine* 66:1760–71.

Miles, Tiya. 2015. *Ties That Bind: The Story of an Afro-Cherokee Family in Slavery and Freedom*. Berkeley: University of California Press.

Mills, Charles W. 2008. "Racial Liberalism." *PMLA* 123 (5): 1380–97.

Montejano, David. 1987. *Anglos and Mexicans in the Making of Texas, 1936–1986.* Austin: University of Texas Press.

Montgomery, Charles H. 2002. *The Spanish Redemption: Heritage, Power, and Loss on New Mexico's Upper Rio Grande.* Berkeley: University of California Press.

Moore, Mignon R. 2011. *Invisible Families: Gay Identities, Relationships, and Motherhood among Black Women.* Berkeley: University of California Press.

Moraga, Cherrie. 1983. *Loving in the War Years: Lo Que Nunca Pasó por Sus Labios.* Boston: South End Press.

Moraga, Cherríe, and Gloria Anzaldúa, eds. 1981. *This Bridge Called My Back: Writings by Radical Women of Color.* Watertown, MA: Persephone Press.

Morgan, Lynn M., and Elizabeth F. S. Roberts. 2012. "Reproductive Governance in Latin America." *Anthropology & Medicine* 19 (2): 241–54.

Morgensen, Scott Lauria. 2011. "The Biopolitics of Settler Colonialism: Right Here, Right Now." *Settler Colonial Studies* 1 (1): 52–76.

Muñoz, José Esteban. 2006. "Feeling Brown, Feeling Down: Latina Affect, the Performativity of Race, and the Depressive Position." *Signs: Journal of Women in Culture and Society* 31 (3): 675–88.

———. 2009. *Disidentifications: Queers of Color and the Performance of Politics. Cruising Utopia: The Then and There of Queer Futurity.* New York: New York University Press.

Murakawa, N. 2014. *The First Civil Right: How Liberals Built Prison America.* New York: Oxford University Press.

Nájera, Lourdes Gutiérrez, and Korinta Maldonado. 2017. "Transnational Settler Colonial Formations and Global Capital: A Consideration of Indigenous Mexican Migrants." *American Quarterly* 69 (4): 809–21.

National Latina Institute for Reproductive Health. 2013a. "Latinas and Cervical Cancer in Texas: A Public Health Crisis." New York: National Latina Institute for Reproductive Health.

———. 2013b. "NLIRH Strategic Plan, 2013–2018." New York: National Latina Institute for Reproductive Health.

National Latina Institute for Reproductive Health, National Asian Pacific American Women's Forum, and In Our Own Voice. 2018. "Proposed Change, Expansion of the Definition of Public Charge: A Threat to Women of Color." New York: National Latina Institute for Reproductive Health, National Asian Pacific American Women's Forum, In Our Own Voice.

Neumaier, Diane. 1990. "Judy Baca: Our People Are the Internal Exiles." In *Making Face, Making Soul: Haciendo Caras: Creative and Critical Perspectives by*

Women of Color, edited by Gloria Anzaldúa, 256–70. San Francisco: Aunt Lute.

Nevins, Joseph. 2002. *Operation Gatekeeper: The Rise of the "Illegal Alien" and the Making of the U.S.-Mexico Boundary*. New York: Routledge.

Newton, Huey P. 1970. *The Genius of Huey P. Newton: Minister of Defense, Black Panther Party*. N.p.: Ministry of Information, Black Panther Party.

Niedt, Christopher. 2013. *Social Justice in Diverse Suburbs: History, Politics, and Prospects*. Philadelphia: Temple University Press.

Novak, David, and Matt Sakakeeny. 2015. *Keywords in Sound*. Durham, NC: Duke University Press.

Núñez-Mchiri, Guillermina Gina. 2012. "Housing, Colonias, and Social Justice in the U.S.-Mexico Border Region." In *Social Justice in the U.S.-Mexico Border Region*, edited by Mark Lusk, Kathleen Staudt, and Eva Moya, 109–26. New York: Springer.

O'Brien, Patrick K. 2013. "Medical Marijuana and Social Control: Escaping Criminalization and Embracing Medicalization." *Deviant Behavior* 34 (6): 423–43.

Ochoa Gautier, Ana María. 2006. "Sonic Transculturation, Epistemologies of Purification and the Aural Public Sphere in Latin America." *Social Identities* 12 (6): 803–25.

Odland, Bruce, and Sam Auinger. 2009. "Reflections on the Sonic Commons." *Leonardo Music Journal* 19:63–68.

"Ohio Hispanic Americans." 2017. Ohio Development Services Agency. https://development.ohio.gov/files/research/P7002.pdf.

Ong, Aihwa. 1999. *Flexible Citizenship: The Cultural Logics of Transnationality*. Durham, NC: Duke University Press.

———. 2006. *Neoliberalism as Exception: Mutations in Citizenship and Sovereignty*. Durham, NC: Duke University Press, 2006.

Ortiz, Alfonso. 1969. *The Tewa World: Space, Time, Being & Becoming in a Pueblo Society*. Chicago: University of Chicago Press.

Ortner, Sherry B. 2016. "Dark Anthropology and Its Others: Theory since the Eighties." *HAU: Journal of Ethnographic Theory* 6 (1): 47–73.

Paik, A. Naomi. 2016. *Rightlessness: Testimony and Redress in US Prison Camps since World War II*. Chapel Hill: University of North Carolina Press.

Pallares, Amalia. 2014. *Family Activism: Immigrant Struggles and the Politics of Noncitizenship*. New Brunswick, NJ: Rutgers University Press, 2014.

Pallares, Amalia, and Nilda Flores-González. 2010. *¡Marcha!: Latino Chicago and the Immigrant Rights Movement*. Urbana: University of Illinois Press.

Panday, Triloki N. 1972. "Anthropologists at Zuni." *Proceedings of the American Philosophical Society* 116 (4): 321–37.

Paredes, Américo. 1958. *With a Pistol in His Hand: A Border Ballad and Its Hero.* Austin: University of Texas Press, 1958.

———. 1993. "On Ethnographic Work among Minority Groups: A Folklorist's Perspective." In *Folklore and Culture on the Texas-Mexican Border by Américo Paredes*, edited by Richard Bauman, 73–110. Austin: Center for Mexican American Studies.

Passel, Jeffrey S., D'Vera Cohn, and Molly Rohal. 2014. "Unauthorized Immigrant Totals Rise in 7 States, Fall in 14: Decline in Those from Mexico Fuels Most State Decreases." Washington, DC: Pew Research Center's Hispanic Trends Project.

Pateman, Carole. 1988. *The Sexual Contract.* Stanford, CA: Stanford University Press.

Peña, Devon. 1997. *The Terror of the Machine: Technology, Work, Gender and Ecology on the U.S.-Mexico Border.* Austin: University of Texas Press.

Pérez, Elisa. 2002. "*El desorden*, Nationalism, and Chicana/o Aesthetics." In *Gender, Race, and Nation: A Global Perspective*, edited by Vanaja Dhruvarajan and Jill Vickers, 19–39. Toronto: University of Toronto Press.

Pérez, Gina. 2004. *The Near Northwest Side Story: Migration, Displacement, and Puerto Rican Families.* Berkeley: University of California Press.

———. 2015. *Citizen, Student, Soldier: Latina/o Youth, JROTC, and the American Dream.* New York: New York University Press.

Pérez, Gina, Frank A. Guridy, and Adrian Burgos Jr., eds. 2010. *Beyond El Barrio: Everyday Life in Latina/o America.* New York: New York University Press.

Perrino, S., and S. Wortham. 2017. "Discursive Struggles over Migration," special issue, *Language and Communication* 59.

Pew Research Center. 2014. "The Shifting Religious Identity of Latinos in the United States." Washington, DC: Pew Research Center.

Philis-Tsimikas, Athena, Adelaide Fortmann, Leticia Lleva-Ocana, Chris Walker, and Linda C. Gallo. 2011. "Peer-Led Diabetes Education Programs in High-Risk Mexican Americans Improve Glycemic Control Compared with Standard Approaches." *Diabetes Care* 34 (9): 1926–31.

Pineda, Baron. 2017. "Indigenous Pan-Americanism: Contesting Settler Colonialism and the Doctrine of Discovery at the UN Permanent Forum on Indigenous Issues." *American Quarterly* 69 (4): 823–32.

Povinelli, Elizabeth A. 2002. *The Cunning of Recognition: Indigenous Alterities and the Making of Australian Multiculturalism.* Durham, NC: Duke University Press.

———. 2011. *Economies of Abandonment: Social Belonging and Endurance in Late Liberalism.* Durham, NC: Duke University Press.

Price, Kimala. 2010. "What Is Reproductive Justice? How Women of Color Activists Are Redefining the Pro-Choice Paradigm." *Meridians: Feminism, Race, Transnationalism* 10 (2): 42–65.

———. 2017. "Queering Reproductive Justice: Toward a Theory and Praxis for Building Intersectional Political Alliances." In *LGBTQ Politics: A Critical Reader*, edited by Marla Brettschneider, Susan Burgess, and Cricket Keating, 72–88. New York: NYU Press.

Pyles, Loretta. 2018. *Healing Justice: Holistic Self-Care for Change Makers*. New York: Oxford University Press.

Quijada, David Alberto Cerecer, Caitlin Cahill, and Matt Bradley. 2013. "Toward a Critical Youth Policy Praxis: Critical Youth Studies and Participatory Action Research." *Theory into Practice* 52 (3): 216–23.

Quijano, Aníbal. 1999. "¡Qué tal raza!" *Ecuador Debate* 48:141–52.

Rabben, Linda. 2016. *Sanctuary and Asylum: A Social and Political History*. Seattle: University of Washington Press.

Ramírez, Leonard G., and Yenelli Flores. 2011. *Chicanas of 18th Street: Narrative of a Movement from Latino Chicago*. Urbana: University of Illinois Press.

Ramos-Zayas, Ana Y. 2003. *National Performances: The Politics of Class, Race, and Space in Puerto Rican Chicago*. Chicago: Chicago University Press.

———. 2012. *Street Therapists: Race, Affect, and Neoliberal Personhood in Latino Newark*. Chicago: University of Chicago Press, 2012.

Ranco, Darren J. 2006. "Toward a Native Anthropology: Hermeneutics, Hunting Stories, and Theorizing from Within." *Wicazo Sa Review* 21 (2): 61–78.

Rice, Tom. "Listening." 2015. In *Keywords in Sound*, edited by David Novak and Matt Sakakeeny, 99–111. Durham, NC: Duke University Press.

Ricourt, Milagros, and Ruby Danta. 2003. *Hispanas de Queens: Latino Panethnicity in a New York City Neighborhood*. Ithaca: Cornell University Press.

Rios, Victor. 2011. *Punished: Policing the Lives of Black and Latino Boys*. New York: NYU Press, 2011.

Rivera, Eugene. 2011. "La Colonia de Lorain." In *The Puerto Rican Diaspora: Historical Perspectives*, edited by Carmen Whalen and Victor Vasquez, 151–73. Philadelphia: Temple University Press.

Rivera-Servera, Ramon. 2012. *Performing Queer Latinidad: Dance, Sexuality, Politics*. Ann Arbor: University of Michigan Press.

Robinson, Cedric J. 2000. *Black Marxism: The Making of the Black Radical Tradition*. Chapel Hill: University of North Carolina Press.

Rodriguez, Juana Maria. 2014. *Sexual Futures, Queer Gestures, and Other Latina Longings*. New York: New York University, 2014.

Rodriguez Soto, Isa. 2017. "Colonialism's Orchestrated Disasters in Puerto Rico," *Anthropology News.*

Rosa, Jonathan. 2018. "Community as a Campus: From 'Problems' to Possibilities in Latinx Communities." In *Civic Engagement in Diverse Latinx Communities: Learning from Social Justice Partnerships in Action*, edited by Mari Castañeda and Joseph Krupczynski, 111–23. New York: Peter Lang.

———. 2019. *Looking like a Language, Sounding like a Race: Raciolinguistic Ideologies and the Learning of Latinidad.* Oxford: Oxford University Press.

Rosa, Jonathan, and Vanessa Díaz. 2020. "Raciontologies: Rethinking Anthropological Accounts of Institutional Racism and Enactments of White Supremacy in the United States." *American Anthropologist* 122 (1): 120–32.

Rosa, Jonathan, and Yarimar Bonilla. 2017. "Deprovincializing Trump, Decolonizing Diversity, and Unsettling Anthropology." *American Ethnologist* 44 (2): 201–8.

Rosa, Vanessa. 2018. "Social Citizenship and Urban Revitalization in Canada." *Canadian Journal of Urban Research* 27 (2): 25–36.

Rosaldo, Renato. 1989. *Culture and Truth: The Remaking of Social Analysis.* Boston: Beacon.

———. 1994. "Cultural Citizenship and Educational Democracy." *Cultural Anthropology* 9 (3): 402–11.

———. 1997. "Cultural Citizenship, Inequality, and Multiculturalism." In *Latino Cultural Citizenship*, edited by William V. Flores and Rina Benmayor, 27–38. Boston, MA: Beacon Press.

Rosas, Gilberto. 2006. "The Thickening Borderlands: Diffused Exceptionality and 'Immigrant' Social Struggles during the 'War on Terror.'" *Cultural Dynamics* 18 (3): 335–49.

———. 2010. "Cholos, Chúntaros, and the 'Criminal' Abandonments of the New Frontier." *Identities: Global Studies in Culture and Power* 17 (6): 695–713.

———. 2012. *Barrio Libre: Criminalizing States and Delinquent Refusals of the New Frontier.* Durham, NC: Duke University Press.

Ross, Loretta J., and Rickie Solinger. 2017. *Reproductive Justice: An Introduction.* Berkeley: University of California Press.

Ruiz, Sandra. 2019. *Ricanness: Enduring Time in Anticolonial Performance.* New York: New York University Press.

Saldaña-Portillo, María Josefina. 2016. *Indian Given: Racial Geographies across Mexico and the United States.* Latin America Otherwise: Languages, Empire, Nations. Durham, NC: Duke University Press.

Samuels, David W., Louise Meintjes, Ana Maria Ochoa, and Thomas Porcello. 2010.

"Soundscapes: Toward a Sounded Anthropology." *Annual Review of Anthropology* 39:329–45.

Santa Ana, Otto. 2002. *Brown Tide Rising: Metaphors of Latinos in Contemporary American Public Discourse*. Austin: University of Texas Press.

Schafer, R. Murray. (1977) 1994. *The Soundscape: Our Sonic Environment and the Tuning of the World*. Rochester, VT: Destiny.

Schenker, Marc, Xóchitl Castañeda, and Alfonso Rodríguez Lainz, eds. 2014. *Migration and Health: Research Methods Handbook*. Berkeley: University of California Press.

Scheper-Hughes, Nancy. 1992. *Death without Weeping: The Violence of Everyday Life in Brazil*. Berkeley: University of California Press.

Sexton, Jared. 2008. *Amalgamation Schemes: Antiblackness and the Critique of Multiracialism*. Minneapolis: University of Minnesota Press.

Shange, Savannah. 2019. *Progressive Dystopia: Abolition, Antiblackness, and Schooling in San Francisco*. Durham, NC: Duke University Press.

Sharkey, Joseph R., Wesley R. Dean, and Cassandra M. Johnson. 2011. "Association of Household and Community Characteristics with Adult and Child Food Insecurity among Mexican-Origin Households in Colonias Along the Texas-Mexico Border." *International Journal for Equity in Health* 10 (19): 1–14.

Sharma, Nandita Rani. 2020. *Home Rule: National Sovereignty and the Separation of Natives and Migrants*. Durham, NC: Duke University Press.

Silliman, Jael, Marlene Gerber Fried, Loretta Ross, and Elena R. Gutiérrez, eds. 2004. *Undivided Rights: Women of Color Organize for Reproductive Justice*. Cambridge, MA: South End Press.

Sillitoe, Paul. 2015. *Indigenous Studies and Engaged Anthropology: The Collaborative Moment*. Farnham: Ashgate.

Simon, John K. 1991. "Michel Foucault on Attica: An Interview." *Social Justice* 18 (3): 26–34.

Simpson, Audra. 2007. "On Ethnographic Refusal: Indigeneity, 'Voice' and Colonial Citizenship." *Junctures: Journal for Thematic Dialogue* 9: 67–80.

———. 2008. "Subjects of Sovereignty: Indigeneity, the Revenue Rule, and Juridics of Failed Consent." *Law and Contemporary Problems* 71 (3): 191–215.

———. 2014. *Mohawk Interruptus: Political Life across the Borders of Settler States*. Durham, NC: Duke University Press.

Smith, Linda Tuhiwai. 1999. *Decolonizing Methodologies: Research and Indigenous Peoples*. London: Zed.

Smith, Neil, and Setha Low. 2006. *The Politics of Public Space*. New York: Routledge.

Snorton, C. Riley, and Jin Haritaworn. 2014. "Trans Necropolitics." In *Queer Necro-politics*, by Jin Haritaworn, Adi Kuntsman, and Silvia Posocco. New York: Routledge.

Soboroff, Jacob. 2020. *Separated: Inside an American Tragedy*. New York: Custom House.

Sommer, Doris. 2005. "Art and Accountability." *Review: Literature and Arts of the Americas* 38 (2): 261–76.

Speed, Shannon. 2006. "At the Crossroads of Human Rights and Anthropology: Toward a Critically Engaged Activist Research." *American Anthropologist* 108 (1): 66–76.

Stephen, Lynn. 2019. "Fleeing Rural Violence: Mam Women Seeking Gendered Justice in Guatemala and the US." *Journal of Peasant Studies* 46 (2): 229–57.

Stewart, Kathleen. 1996. *A Space on the Side of the Road: Cultural Poetics in an "Other" America*. Princeton, NJ: Princeton University Press, 1996.

Stryker, Susan, Paisley Currah, and Lisa Jean Moore. 2008. "Introduction: Trans-, Trans, or Transgender?" *Feminist Press* 36 (3): 11–22.

Tarasuk, Valerie, Joyce Chang, Claire de Oliveira, Naomi Dachner, Craig Gunderson, and Paul Kurdyak. 2015. "Association between Household Food Insecurity and Annual Health Care Costs." *Canadian Medical Association Journal* 187 (14): E429–E36.

Taussig, Benjamin. 2018. "Sound and Movement: Vernaculars of Sonic Dissent." *Social Text* 36 (3): 25–45.

Tomlinson, Barbara, and George Lipsitz. 2013. "American Studies as Accompaniment." *American Quarterly* 65 (1): 1–30.

———. 2019. *Insubordinate Spaces: Improvisation and Accompaniment for Social Justice*. Philadelphia: Temple University Press.

Torres, Andrés, ed. 2006. *Latinos in New England*. Philadelphia: Temple University Press.

Torres, Maria de Los Angeles, Irene Rizzini, and Norma Del Río. 2013. *Citizens in the Present: Youth Civic Engagement in the Americas*. Urbana: University of Illinois Press.

Triana, Sayak Valencia. 2011. "Capitalismo gore: Narcomáquina y performance de género." Hemispheric Institute. https://hemisphericinstitute.org/en/emisferica-82/triana.html.

Trouillot, Michel-Rolph. 1995. *Silencing the Past: Power and the Production of History*. Boston: Beacon.

———. 2003. "Anthropology and the Savage Slot: The Poetics and Politics of

Otherness." In *Global Transformations: Anthropology and the Modern World*, 7–28. New York: Palgrave Macmillan.

Trujillo, Patricia, and Tobe Bott-Lyons. 2020. "Geographies of Staying: Home and its Place in the Academy." Unpublished manuscript.

Trujillo-Pagán, Nicole. 2018. "Crossed Out by LatinX: Gender Neutrality and Gender-blind Sexism." *Latino Studies* 16 (3): 396–406.

Tuck, Eve, and K. Wayne Yang. 2012. "Decolonization Is Not a Metaphor." *Decolonization: Indigeneity, Education, and Society* 3 (1): 1–40.

United States Census Bureau. 2010. "SE: T56: Hispanic or Latino by Specific Origin." Washington, DC: US Census Bureau.

Valle, Victor, and Rodolfo D. Torres. 2012. "After Latino Metropolis: Cultural Political Economy and Alternative Futures." In *Latino Urbanism: The Politics of Planning, Policy, and Redevelopment*, edited by David R. Diaz and Rodolfo D. Torres, 181–201. New York: New York University Press.

Van Cleve, Nicole Gonzalez. 2016. *Crook County: Racism and Injustice in America's Largest Criminal Court*. Stanford, CA: Stanford University Press.

Vargas, Deborah R. 2014. "Ruminations on Lo Sucio as a Latino Queer Analytic." *American Quarterly* 66 (3): 715–26.

Vargas, Robert. 2016. *Wounded City: Violent Turf Wars in a Chicago Barrio*. New York: Oxford University Press.

Vega, Sujey. 2015. *Latino Heartland: Of Borders and Belonging in the Midwest*. New York: NYU Press.

Vélez-Vélez, Roberto, and Jacqueline Villarrubia-Mendoza. 2018. "Cambio desde abajo y desde adentro: Notes on Centros de Apoyo Mutuo in post-María Puerto Rico." *Latino Studies* 16 (4): 542–47.

Veracini, Lorenzo. 2010. *Settler Colonialism: A Theoretical Overview*. London: Palgrave Macmillan.

Vidal-Ortiz, Salvador. 2006. "Sexuality Discussions in Santería: A Case Study of Religion and Sexuality Negotiation." *Sexuality Research and Social Policy* 3 (3): 52–66.

Vidal-Ortiz, Salvador, and Juliana Martínez. 2018. "Latinx Thoughts: Latinidad with an X." *Latino Studies* 16 (3): 384–95.

Viego, Antonio. 2007. *Dead Subjects: Towards a Politics of Loss in Latino Studies*. Durham, NC: Duke University Press.

Villarreal, Aimee. 2019. "Sanctuaryscapes in the North American Southwest." *Radical History Review* 135:43–70.

Villarreal, Aimee, and David F. García. 2018. "Our Laboratory of Anthropolocura."

Anthropology News. https://anthrosource.onlinelibrary.wiley.com/doi /10.1111/AN.920.

Villareal Sosa, Leticia, Silvia Díaz, and Rosalba Hernández. 2019. "Accompaniment in a Mexican American Community: Conceptualization and Identification of Biopsycholsocial Outcomes." *Journal of Religion and Spirituality in Social Work: Social Thought* 38 (1): 21–42.

Visweswaran, Kamala. 1994. *Fictions of Feminist Ethnography*. Minneapolis: University of Minnesota Press.

———. 2010. *Un/common Cultures: Racism and the Rearticulation of Cultural Difference*. Durham, NC: Duke University Press.

Wacquant, Loic. 2008. *Urban Outcasts: A Comparative Sociology of Advanced Marginality*. Cambridge, UK: Polity Press.

Ward, T. W. 2012. *Gangsters without Borders: An Ethnography of a Salvadoran Street Gang*. New York: Oxford University Press.

Warner, Michael. 2002. "Public and Counterpublics." *Public Culture* 14 (1): 49–90.

West, Paige. 2016. *Dispossession and the Environment: Rhetoric and Inequality in Papua New Guinea*. New York: Columbia University Press.

Wheeler, William. 2020. *State of War: MS-13 and El Salvador's World of Violence*. New York: Columbia Global Report.

White, Kari, Joseph E. Potter, Amanda J. Stevenson, Liza Fuentes, Kristine Hopkins, and Daniel Grossman. 2016. "Women's Knowledge of and Support for Abortion Restrictions in Texas: Findings from a Statewide Representative Survey." *Perspectives on Sexual and Reproductive Health* 48 (4): 189–97.

Wilderson, Frank, III. 2003. "Gramsci's Black Marx: Whither the Slave in Civil Society?" *Social Identities* 9 (2): 225–40.

Wilkinson, Meredith T., and Karen D'Angelo. 2019. "Community-Based Accompaniment and Social Work–A Complimentary Approach to Social Action." *Journal of Community Practice* 27 (2): 151–67.

Wilkinson, Michelle. 2004. "Haciendo Patria: The Puerto Rican Flag in the Art of Juan Sánchez." *Small Axe* 8 (2): 61–83.

Wilson, Joshua C. 2016. *The New States of Abortion Politics*. Stanford: Stanford University Press.

Wolf, Diane, ed. 1996. *Feminist Dilemmas in Fieldwork*. New York: Routledge.

Wolfe, Patrick. 2006. "Settler Colonialism and the Elimination of the Native." *Journal of Genocide Research* 8 (4): 387–409.

Wright, Melissa W. 2017. "Epistemological Ignorances and Fighting for the Disappeared: Lessons from Mexico." *Antipode* 49 (1): 249–69.

Wynter, Sylvia. 2003. "Unsettling the Coloniality of Being/Power/Truth/Freedom: Towards the Human, after Man, Its Overrepresentation—An Argument." *CR: The New Centennial Review* 3 (3): 257–337.

Ybarra-Frausto, Tomás. 1991. "Rasquachismo: A Chicano Sensibility." In *Chicano Art: Resistance and Affirmation, 1965–1985*, edited by Richard Griswold del Castillo, Teresa Mckenna, and Yvonne Yarbro-Bejarano, 155–62. Los Angeles: Wight Art Gallery, University of California.

Zambrana, Ruth Enid. 2018. *Toxic Ivory Towers: The Consequences of Work Stress on Underrepresented Minority Faculty*. New Brunswick, NJ: Rutgers University Press.

Zavala, Oswaldo. 2018. Los cárteles no existen: Narcotráfico y cultura en México. Barcelona: Malpaso Ediciones SL.

Zavella, Patricia. 1996. "Feminist Insider Dilemmas: Constructing Ethnic Identity with 'Chicana' Informants." In *Feminist Dilemmas in Fieldwork*, edited by Diane Wolf, 138–69. Boulder: Westview.

———. 2011. *I'm Neither Here nor There: Mexicans' Quotidian Struggles with Migration and Poverty*. Durham, NC: Duke University Press.

———. 2017. "Intersectional Praxis in the Movement for Reproductive Justice: The Respect ABQ Women Campaign." *Signs: Journal of Women in Culture and Society* 42 (2): 509–33.

———. 2020. *The Movement for Reproductive Justice: Empowering Women of Color through Social Activism*. New York: New York University Press.

Participants in the School for Advanced Research Advanced Seminar "Ethnographies of Contestation and Resilience in Latinx America," co-chaired by Alex E. Chávez and Gina M. Pérez, April 7–11, 2019. *Left to right:* Aimee Villarreal, Jonathan Rosa, Alex E. Chávez, Ana Aparicio, Andrea Bolivar, Santiago Ivan Guerra, Patricia Zavella, Gilberto Rosas, Gina M. Pérez, and Sherina Feliciano-Santos. Photograph by Garret Vreeland. © School for Advanced Research.

ANA APARICIO
Department of Anthropology and Latina and Latino Studies Program,
Northwestern University

ANDREA BOLIVAR
Department of Women's and Gender Studies and Latina/o Studies Program,
University of Michigan

ALEX E. CHÁVEZ
Department of Anthropology and Institute for Latino
Studies, University of Notre Dame

ARLENE M. DÁVILA
Departments of Anthropology and American Studies, New York University

VANESSA DÍAZ
Chicana/o and Latina/o Studies, Loyola Marymount University

SHERINA FELICIANO-SANTOS
Department of Anthropology and Linguistic Program, University
of South Carolina, Columbia

DAVID FLORES
School of Architecture, University of Southern California

SANTIAGO IVAN GUERRA
Southwest Studies Program, Social Sciences, and Hulbert Center
for Southwest Studies, Colorado College

SERGIO LEMUS
Department of Anthropology, Texas A&M University

RYAN MANN-HAMILTON
LaGuardia Community College

GINA M. PÉREZ
Department of Comparative American Studies, Oberlin College

JONATHAN ROSA
Graduate School of Education, Center for Comparative Studies in Race and Ethnicity, and Departments of Anthropology and Linguistics, Stanford University

GILBERTO ROSAS
Departments of Anthropology and Latino/a Studies, University of Illinois, Urbana-Champaign

AIMEE VILLARREAL
Comparative Mexican American Studies, Our Lady of the Lake University

PATRICIA ZAVELLA
Emerita, Department of Latin American and Latino Studies, University of California, Santa Cruz

African American/Africana/Black: Afro-Latinx, xvii; and Blackness, xvii; communities, xi, xviii, 4, 26, 29, 31, 36, 37–38, 50, 128, 148–50, 156, 178, 187, 219, 222, 223; scholarship, vii, viii, xxv. *See also* Taíno/Afro-Taíno

anthropolocura, 195–217; defined, 196; anthropolocotes within, 213. *See also* Villarreal, Aimee

anthropology: and centering of whiteness, vii; and colonial doldrums, ix; and dominant value expectations, viii; and uncritical penchant for travel and discovery, vii–viii; continues to evade its settle colonial legacies, 199. *See also* Latinx anthropologists; politics of refusal

Anzaldúa, Gloria, xvii, 14, 23n48, 44n16, 199, 214n5, 215nn19–20, 215n40

Aparicio, Ana, xi–xxxiii, 93–114; dissent and trash talk, 109–12; environmental racism, 105–9; Latinx and trash talk, 99–105; trash disposal, 95–96; trash talk, 94; waste management, 96–97

Appadurai, Arjun, 67n39, 217n51

Asian Communities for Reproductive Justice, 10, 23n43

Asian/Pacific Islander: and Asianness, xviii; Asian American Movement, 219; communities, 4, 222

Behar, Ruth, xv, xxxiin23, 191n12

Berlant, Lauren, 191n7, 192n21

biopolitics, 175, 185, 186, 187. See also Foucault, Michel; Mbembe, Achille

BIPOC, vii, x, 224

Bolivar, Andrea, xi–xxxiii, 115–34

Bonilla. Yarimar, xiii, xxx–xxxin8, xxxinn11–12, 39, 45n26, 45n28, 88n4, 130, 133n27, 170, 172n23, 172n25

Border Patrol, 5, 140, 143, 176, 177; most agents are Latinos/Hispanic, 176

Butler, Judith, 132n5

capitalism: accumulation within, 184; crisis of, 196; culture, power, the state, and, 224; global ransacking by, 197; greed and, 200; links to settler colonialism, 29, 117; predatory, 190; racial, 117; in reproductive justice training, 14; White supremacist foundations of, 186. *See also* settler colonialism

Ceballos-Félix, Lucy, 7, 14, 15, 19

Center for Reproductive Rights (CRR), 5, 6, 7, 8, 19, 22n32, 22n34. *See also* National Latina Institute for Reproductive Health/ Justice

Chávez, Alex E., xi–xxxiii, 47–68, 133n26, 175, 191n1; aural ecologies, 55–57, 59, 60; aural public sphere, 56; sounding, 50, 51, 59, 60, 63; sound politics, 51–52; sound-scapes, 56, 57–61

Chavez, Leo, xii, 94, 122, 136, 189; and Latino Threat Narrative, xii

Chicana feminist scholarship, viii, 195, 199, 202, 208. *See also* Anzaldúa, Gloria; Chicana anthropologist; Chicanx; Moraga, Cherríe

Chicana anthropologists, 195, 208. *See also* Villarreal, Aimee

Chicanx, xv, 176, 199, 206, 208, 223. See *also* Chicana anthropologists; Chicana feminist scholarship

cisgenderism, 117, 121, 123, 126, 129, 130, 132n1

Collins, Patricia Hill, 21n13. *See also* intersectional analyses/approaches

Committee on Minorities in Anthropology (1973), x

communities of color, 83, 87, 148, 149, 150, 161, 198

Concilio Taíno Guatu-Ma-Cu a Boriken,
38, 39
Cotera, María Eugenia, 201, 202, 209,
215n23, 215n26, 216n41, 216n44
COVID-19, xi, 23n53, 60, 195, 219, 225
Crenshaw, Kimberlé, 21n13
critical perspectives on anthropology, power,
race, and society, vii, viii, xvi, xxvi, xxix,
48, 62, 120, 123, 189, 202, 209, 220, 221,
224; critical ethnographic work, xxvii;
critical politics, 111–12; interrogation of
home and homebuilding, xx. *See also*
Latinx studies; refusal
critical race theory, vii. *See also* Chicanx;
ethnic studies; Latinx studies
cultural advocacy and antiracism, viii

Dávila, Arlene M., vii–x, 44n21, 44n23,
64, 66n9, 67–68nn39–40, 89n23, 89n25,
90nn34–35, 90n41, 220, 226n7
decolonization, xxvii, 27, 31, 43, 70, 87,
192n23, 195, 196, 202, 207, 208, 213, 214;
decolonizing anthropology, xx, xxix,
198–99; demands rupture, restoration,
and reparation, 199
Deferred Action for Childhood Arrivals
(DACA), 8, 55, 158, 168, 173n35
De Genova, Nicholas, 66n9, 132n11, 171n8,
191n9
Del Castillo, Adelaida R., xxxiiin48, 67n27
Díaz, Vanessa, 219–26. See also Rosa,
Jonathan
Division Street riots (1966, Chicago), 50

ethnic studies, vii, viii, xv, xxvi, 136, 198,
200, 202, 214, 224; contentious relationship with anthropology, 200. *See also*
Chicanx; critical race theory; Latinx
studies
ethnography: and analysis of power and
white privilege, ix; and analysis of the
complexities and possibilities of Latinx
differences, xviii; and centering of
critical race studies, vii; and challenge

to ethnonationalist, anti-Mexican, and
anti-Muslim policies, xiv; and limits in
decolonizing anthropology, xx; and role
in social transformation, xvi; ethics in,
xxiii–xxvi; extraordinary possibilities
offered by, xiv; feminist, xv; of contestations and resilience, xiv; on aural
ecologies and public spheres, 47–68; on
Latina empowerment (*poderosas*), 1–24;
on Latina reproductive justice, 1–24; on
Latinx activism, 69–91; on Latinx asylum
seeking, 175–93; on Latinx production
of home/homeplace, xvi, xviii–xxi,
195–217; on marijuana legalization in
Colorado, 135–52; on the politics of
sanctuaries, 153–73; on Puerto Rican
place-making, 69–91; on suburban
dissent, 93–113; on Taino and Afro-Taino
performance and *resistencia*, 25–45; on
the war on drugs and reform, 135–52;
on the Texas Mexico border, 135–52; on
trans-Latinas, 115–33; refusal in, x, xv,
224. *See also* ethnic studies; fetishization;
Latinx studies; queer/queerness;
refusals

Fanon, Frantz, 179–80, 192n20
Farmer, Paul, xxiv, 192n33
Fassin, Didier, xxxiin25
Feliciano-Santos, Sherina, xi–xxxiii, 25–46
fetishization: of far-away places within
anthropology, xx; of research outside
Latinx communities, ix; of the Other by
anthropologists, vii–viii; of transgender
Latinas, 122, 124
Flores, David, xx, 69–92, 98, 111; and
thinking diaspora from below, 81. *See also*
Rosa, Jonathan
Foucault, Michel, 175, 185, 186, 187, 193n37,
193n39, 193n44. 193n48

Gálvez, Alyshia, xxxiiin48, 23n47, 67n27
Glenn, Evelyn Nakano, xxxiin30, xxxiin33
Gramsci, Antonio, 186

Grosfoguel, Ramón, 89
Guerra, Santiago Ivan, xi–xxxiii, 135–52

Harvey, David, 62, 64, 184–85; spatial fix, 62
Hinojosa, Jennifer, 88, 164. *See also* Meléndez, Edwin
Harrison, Faye Venetia, xxxin15, xxxin18, 226n13
home/homeplace, xvi, 57, 64; as a site of motion and a process of building and undoing, xix; as dialectical space, xix; as homeplace, xix; as homescape, xix; as space of historical memory and capitalist modernity, xix; conceptual space between movement and dwelling, xix; feminist critiques of, xix; homework and, xviii–xxi, xxix; the research field and, xix. *See also* Villarreal, Aimee
Hurricane Maria (2017), xiii, 27, 40, 41, 88n2, 153, 163, 167–68, 172n23, 172n28; and mobilization by Taínos, 39; as site of trauma and potential unification, 35; devastating aftereffects, 40, 164; economic crisis and, 34; highlighted deep-seated problems and limited autonomy, 39; mass population exodus, 163, 172n26. *See also* Taíno/Afro-Taíno; Villarreal, Aimee
Hurston, Zora Neal, xxvii, xxxiin20, 201, 209

Indigenous, vii, xvii, xviii, xx, xxv, 25, 26, 30, 31, 32, 33, 34, 36, 37, 38, 40, 43, 44n1, 74, 98, 104, 118, 179, 184, 189, 190, 195, 197, 203, 204, 209, 214, 217n48, 222, 225; afroindigenous culture, 32; and Indigeneities, xvii, xviii, 28, 36, 42, 220; Caribbean erasure of, 28; epistemologies, xix, 27, 41, 209; genocide of, 29, 36; *indigenismo*, xvii; informants, 201; in Puerto Rico and New Mexico, xxviii; pan-Indigenous uprising, 208; scholarship, vii, xv. *See also* Concilio Taíno Guatu-Ma-Cu a Boriken; settler colonialism; Smithsonian National Museum of the American Indian (NMAI);

Taíno/Afro-Taíno; United Confederation of Taíno People (UCTP)
Innis-Jiménez, Michael, 66n9
Institute for Puerto Rican Culture (ICP), 37
interdisciplinary scholarship, vii, viii, ix, xv, 170, 198, 214, 221. *See also* Chicana feminist scholarship; critical race theory; decolonization; ethnic studies
intersectional analyses/approaches, viii–ix, 3, 10, 19, 21n13, 158, 213, 219, 220, 224; defined, 21. *See also* Crenshaw, Kimberlé; Collins, Patricia Hill

Lamphere, Louise, xxxiin23
Latina Advocacy Network (LAN), 1–24; and discourse of being *poderosa(s)*, 1, 4, 6, 7, 12, 13, 15, 18; *poderosxs*, 15
Latinidad/Latinidades, xvi–xviii, xxix, 219, 220, 222, 223; obscure conditions of their own production, xvii. *See also* Latinx
Latino Threat Narrative, xii, 94, 98, 104, 136. *See also* Chavez, Leo
Latinx, vii, viii; as critique of White-Black binary, xvii; communities, ix; scholarship, vii; studies, vii, ix; "x" as reminder of refusal and exclusion, xvi. *See also* Latinx anthropologists
Latinx anthropologists: and challenge to stop appropriating other people's theories, words, histories, and experiences, vii; and modeling a revolutionary ethics, viii; and publicly engaged scholarship, viii; call for self-reflexive anthropology, viii; first study of, vii; marginalization, vii; minoritized, vii; promote equality- and justice-inducing social transformations, viii
Lefebvre, Henri, 105, 113n24
legal violence, 3, 4–6, 17, 18
Lemus, Sergio, 219–26
Lipsitz, George, xxiv, xxxiin22, xxxiiin44, 2, 21n6, 66n10, 66n12, 169, 170, 173nn39–40. *See also* Tomlinson, Barbara
López Rivera, Oscar, 70, 88n1

Maldonado, Korinta, 29, 44n3, 192n17. *See also* Nájera, Lourdes Gutiérrez
Mann-Hamilton, Ryan, 219–26
Marable, Manning, 31, 44n7
Martínez-Cano, Carlos, xii
Marx, Karl, 184, 193n36; *Das Kapital*, 184
Mbembe, Achille, 186, 191, 192nn24–25, 192n28, 193n41, 192n43, 193n46; critique of Foucauldian biopolitics, 186
Meléndez, Edwin, 88n2, 164, 172n23. *See also* Hinojosa, Jennifer
Middle Easterness, xvii, 222
migrant carceral complex, xii
Moraga, Cherríe, xiv, xvii, xxxin13, xxxiiin47, 44n16, 178, 214

Nájera, Lourdes Gutiérrez, 29, 44n3, 192n17
Nájera-Ramírez, Olga, 210
National Latina Institute for Reproductive Health/Justice, 1–24. *See also* Nuestro Texas Campaign; Zavella, Patricia
National Museum of Mexican Art (Chicago), 47, 48, 65, 65n1
nonbinary epistemologies, vii, xx
Nuestro Texas Campaign (2007), 7. *See also* National Latina Institute for Reproductive Health/Justice; Zavella, Patricia

Obama, Barack H. (President): Obamacare, 21n16; pardoning of López Rivera, Oscar, 88n1
Ong, Aihwa, 45n29
Operation Bootstrap (Puerto Rico), 36–37, 50, 223
Operation Intercept, 139; and the emergence of drug smuggling organizations, 139
Operation Serenity, 37
Ortiz, Alfonso, xxxii, 201, 202

Paik, A. Naomi, 162, 192n26; and abolitionist futures, 162
Pallares, Amalia, 61, 66n9, 67n28, 91n54, 112n4, 158, 159, 171n10, 171n13, 171n15; and family activism, 158

Paredes, Américo, xxvii, xxxinn16–17, 24n63, 191n4, 210
Pérez, Gina M., xi–xxxiii, 66n4, 66n9, 75, 88n3, 89n20, 90n36, 95, 112n7, 119, 153–74
Pérez, Laura Elisa, 208, 216nn39–40
politics of refusal, viii; refusal to work, theorize, and write, viii. *See also* refusals; Simpson, Audra
politics of representation, viii; and identity, viii; and performative spaces, viii; and sonic and aural realms, viii
predominately white institutions (PWI), 224, 226n18
Pueblo Revolt (1680), 205, 206, 207–8, 210, 212, 216n45, 217n50; as First American Revolution, 207
Puerto Rican Cultural Center (Chicago), 78
Puerto Rican cultural trauma, 164

queer/queerness, xxvii, xxviii, xxxiiin53, 116–17, 118, 122, 126, 127, 128, 129, 188, 189, 199, 208, 214; activism, 126; and Black Lives Matter Movement, 220; and inclusion, xxvii; and Latinidades, 219, 225; Black women, 220; defined, xxxiiin; genderqueer, vii, xvi, xx; Queer studies, xv, xxv; spaces of resistance, 120. *See also* Bolivar, Andrea; cisgenderism
Quijano, Aníbal, 180, 192n20; on race as the most efficient instrument of social domination, 179

Ramos-Zayas, 66n9, 90n30, 132n11, 217n52
refusals, vii, viii, xi, xiii, xv, xvi, xxi, xxiii, xxv, xxvi–xxvii, xxviii, xxix, 27, 61, 63, 64–65, 71, 96, 130, 132, 153–54, 162, 175, 187, 188, 190, 193n50, 194, 209, 221, 222, 223, 224; anthropology and ethnographic refusals, x, xv, 224. *See also* ethnography; Simpson, Audra
Remain in Mexico (Migration Protection Protocols), xii

Resurrection Project, 48. *See also* Solis, Danny

Rosa, Jonathan, xi–xxxiii, 66n9, 69–92, 98, 111, 130, 133n27, 170, 223, 226n11

Rosaldo, Renato, xiv, xxxin14, xxxiii48, 67n27, 86, 91n53, 224, 226n13, 226n16; critique of social anthropology research methods, xiv

Rosas, Gilberto, xi–xxxiii, 112n4, 175–93, 201; abolitionist anthropology, 179; as a brown witness, 178; *chuntaros*, 176; deportation terror, 177; Joaquín Dead, 189; killing deserts, 176, 177, 179, 188; necropolitical states, 183; necro-subjection, 175, 177, 178, 189, 191; political asylum, 177, 178, 179, 180, 181, 182, 185, 189, 190, 191; witnessing, 175, 176, 177, 178, 179, 180, 184, 187. *See also* zombification

sanctuary, 153–73, 196, 199; cities, 17, 24n57, 55, 101, 103, 210–14, 217n48; home as, xix; movement, xxviii; people, 153–73; spaces of, xxi. *See also* Trump, Donald J.; Pérez, Gina; Villarreal, Aimee

Santa Ana, Otto, 94, 112n3

selection of research sites, ix; in the service of antiracist scholarship, ix

settler colonialism, xvi, xvii, xix, 204, 211; defined, 29; desires and, xx; enslavement and, 29, 36; expropriation of Indigenous land and, 31; structures of violence and, xvii; narratives of genocide and, 36; tied to mestizaje, xvii, 38. *See also* Veracini, Lorenzo

Simpson, Audra, xxvi, xxxiii, 27, 44n6, 44n17, 45n29; and Mohawk refusal, xxvi. *See also* refusals

SisterSong Women of Color Reproductive Justice Collective, 10, 22n32, 23n43

Smith, Linda Tuhiwai, xxxin17

Smithsonian National Museum of the American Indian (NMAI), 27; criticism of Taíno exhibit, 27, 32–35

Solis, Danny (Chicago, 25th Ward Alderman). 48; and support for Resurrection Project

Solís, Diana, 48, 55, 66n14; artistic projects 53–54; on gentrification, 54; self-identified Mexicana-Chicana, 53

Speed, Shannon, xxxiin22, xxxiin25

Stephen, Lynn, xxxii, 183, 192n16, 192n29; gendered embodied structures of violence, 183

Taíno/Afro-Taíno, 25–45; and contention with Smithsonian National Museum of the American Indian (NMAI), 32–35; as Boricua, 28, 35; Indigenous activists, xxviii, 26; language changes, 36; performing Taínoness, 27–32; Puerto Rican Taíno, 36; refusal of nationalist Puerto Rican-ness, 26, 31; rejection of Spanishness, Americanness, and whiteness, 26; resistance, refusal, and struggle, xxviii–xxix, 25, 26, 27, 30–31, 32, 43; *resistencia*, 26–27, 38. *See also* African American/Africana/Black; Feliciano-Santos, Sherina

Tomlinson, Barbara, xxiv, xxxiin22, xxxii-in44, 2, 21n6, 169, 170, 173nn39–40. *See also* Lipsitz, George

trans Latinas, 115–33; activisms among, 129–32; creation and use of *fantasía*, 115–16; families and spiritualities, 126–29; fantasizing of, 123–26; *fatasía* as *suciedad*, 116–17; part of sexual labor economy, 119–23; violence against, 115

Trouillot, Michel-Rolph, 31, 44n7, 224

Trump, Donald J. (President), xii, xiii, xiv, 2, 3, 4, 5, 11, 12, 16, 17, 18, 19, 21n12, 22n25, 23n45, 24n59, 24n61, 27, 121, 130, 133n25, 136, 143, 162, 168, 190, 196, 211, 212

United Confederation of Taíno People (UCTP), 37

United States–Mexico border, xii, xxx, 1, 3, 4, 5, 7, 14, 18, 22n25, 55, 94, 103, 130, 131,

United States–Mexico border (*continued*)
137, 139, 140, 141, 144, 145, 177, 178, 179,
183, 184, 186–87, 191, 212; Ciudad Júarez–
El Paso border, xii, Texas-Mexico border,
xii, 5, 135–52

Veracini, Lorenzo, xxxiin32
Viego, Antonio, 191n7
Villarreal, Aimee, xi–xxxiii, 195–217. *See also*
anthropolocura; decolonization
Visweswaran, Kamala, 178, 191n11, 193n49,
199, 214, 214n1, 215n9, 215nn16–17, 217n54
Wacquant, 66n9, 66n16

Whole Woman's Health v. Hellersted, 579
U.S. 582(2016), 5

Zavella, Patricia, xi–xxxiii, 1–24, 132n10, 178,
191n11, 210
zombification/zombies, 179, 189; as brown
figures, 179; as not wholly living nor
wholly dead, 179; as variants of Fanon's
damnés, 179–80; as walkers, 189; asylum
petitioners as, 179; contrast to nonzombies, 189; fantasies and, 189; migrants
as, 179